THE HOUSE OF THE
RED DUKE

BEWARE THE LIZARD LURKING

Beware the Lizard Lurking is the second novel in *The House of the Red Duke* series. Rich in detail, it offers a sensual feast: a glimpse of life as we once lived it. Vivienne has a degree in medieval history, and a lifelong passion for the Tudors. For her research, she visited most of the places in the book, using it as an opportunity to step back in time….

Visit her website: www.viviennebrereton.com

VIVIENNE BRERETON

THE HOUSE OF THE RED DUKE

Love and War at the Candlelit Courts

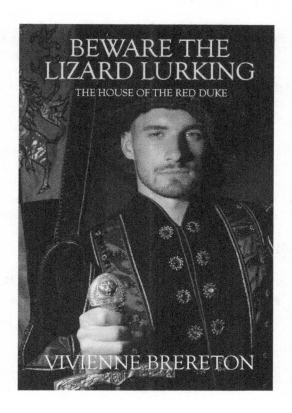

Book Two

BEWARE THE LIZARD LURKING

YULETIDE
PRESS

Published by Yuletide Press 2021

Paperback ISBN 978-2-9566531-2-7

A CIP catalogue record for this book is available from the British Library.

Cover design by Sasha Frost.

Photo Credits: Tony Marturano photography

Inside illustrations: Codex Manesse.

As a point of interest, a glossary of sixteenth century words and terms (as well as foreign expressions) may be found at the end of the novel.

For Sev

With love.

THE STORY SO FAR....

Set against the sumptuous backdrop of the Tudor, Stewart, and Valois courts, with imposing locations, from Zennor Castle, Cornwall; up to Holyrood Palace, Scotland; and across the Narrow Sea to Ardres Castle, Picardy; '*A Phoenix Rising*' traces the vicissitudes of several Howard family members, going back and forth between *1497...1520*. Central to the action and head of his House, stands the indomitable *Thomas*, approaching eighty, an outstanding soldier, able politician, valued courtier, and father of twelve. Thomas guards his secrets closely.

Zennor Castle. Twelfth Night, 1497.

Thomas's favourite son, *Edward*, secretly plights his troth to a young noblewoman, *Grace Tredavoe*. Two months later, we see her outside Ardres Castle in Picardy with her brother, *William*.

Hampton Court. May, 1520.

Thomas Howard, *Henry VIII* and *Thomas Wolsey* are discussing the forthcoming 'Field of Cloth of Gold': a magnificent festival to be held outside Calais. *Thomas Bullen* comes up with an original idea for the final day, and Thomas Howard presents it to the King: a symbolic marriage between two strangers, an Englishwoman and a Frenchman. We meet the suggested bridegroom, *Nicolas de La Barre*, but the proposed bride, William Tredavoe's beautiful daughter, *Cecily*, has not been told of the plan, and William has scant liking for it.

Holyrood Palace, Edinburgh. 1503.

Thomas Howard is drinking with the charismatic *James Stewart*, following the King's marriage to young *Margaret Tudor*. After a wee dram of the heady *usquebaugh*, secrets start to spill from careless lips. Both have a child from star-crossed love affairs. An old Scottish soothsayer appears, pointing at Thomas, calling him *"The Red Duke"* and predicting great misfortune for the House of Howard.

Ardres Castle. 1506.

Orphaned at thirteen, Nicolas de La Barre comes to live at the Castle, much to the chagrin of *Tristan d'Ardres*.
As a younger son, Tristan is destined for the Church; wanting none of it, he clashes with his father, *Guy d'Ardres*, Governor of Picardy. Meanwhile, a penniless Nicolas is betrothed to a sickly heiress.

London. 1509.

Eighteen-year-old Henry VIII, newly-crowned and hot-headed, is hellbent on war with France which puts him on a collision course with his Scottish brother-in-law, James, and older sister, Margaret.

La Colombe, Picardy. France.

Charles de Fleury is unaware that he's the product of a secret love affair between his mother and *King Louis XII of France*. Besides the spirited, inquisitive *Valentine*, Charles has four other daughters, but crucially, no male heir.

Twelfth Night, 1513.

Nicolas and Tristan find themselves in competition for the favours of the beautiful *Ysabeau de Sapincourt*, a seductive young woman married to the much older *Robert*.

'*A Phoenix Rising*' begins and ends with first love and talk of marriage on two separate Twelfth Nights. Thomas Howard's eldest son wants to marry the Duke of Buckingham's daughter, Lizzie Stafford. Already betrothed to her sweetheart, Ralph Neville, and horrified at the prospect of a match with the much older Sir Thomas, Lizzie is overjoyed when the two families hastily plan a secret wedding in Cornwall. Cecily Tredavoe is enjoying the exciting preparations taking place on Saint Michael's Mount - until the Howards turn up unannounced....

WHO'S WHO

(first names in alphabetical order. And age on January 1st, 1513)

TUDOR ENGLAND:

King Henry VIII (21)
Queen Katherine (27)
Princess Mary Henry's sister. (16)

A

Agnes Howard, née Tilney Thomas Howard's second wife. (35)
Alys Tredavoe, née Pendeen (39)
Anne Bullen/Boleyn (11)

C

Cecily Tredavoe (11)
Charles Brandon Henry VIII's best friend and Master of the Horse. (28)

E

Edmund Howard (34)
Edward Howard (35)
Edward Stafford Lizzie's father. 3rd Duke of Buckingham. (34)
Elizabeth Bullen/Boleyn, née Howard (32)
Elizabeth (Lizzie) Stafford (15)

G

Gabrielle Cecily's French nursemaid. (21)
George Bullen (9)
Gilbert Talbot (Sir) Deputy Governor of Calais. (60)

J

John Arscott The Archpriest of Saint Michael's Mount. (46)
John Skelton Poet Laureate. (52)
John Warner Wherryman on the Thames. (22)

M

Mary Bullen/Boleyn (13)
Matilda Pendeen, née Lacey Cecily's grandam. (died in 1508 aged 55)
Muriel Knyvett, née Howard (26)

R

Ralph Neville Ward of the Duke of Buckingham. (14)
Richard Fox Bishop of Winchester. (64)
Richard Pendeen Alys's younger brother. (36)

Robert Warner Wherryman on the Thames. (40)

S
Stephen Pendeen Alys's youngest brother. (34)

T
Thomas Bullen/Boleyn (35)
Thomas Bullen/Boleyn the Younger (14)
Thomas Darcy First Baron Darcy of Darcy (45)

Thomas Howard the Younger (39)

Thomas Howard the Elder (69)
Thomas Knyvett (died 10th August, 1512 aged 27)
Thomas More Lawyer and humanist. (34)
Thomas Wolsey Almoner. (39)

W
Will Compton Henry VIII's groom of the stool. (30)
William Tredavoe, of Zennor Castle. (37)
William Warham Archbishop of Canterbury. (62)

STEWART SCOTLAND:
King James IV (39)
Queen Margaret, née Tudor (23)
Janet Kennedy James's mistress. (32)

VALOIS FRANCE:
King Louis XII (50)
Queen Anne of Brittany (35)
Princess Claude (13)
Princess Renée (2)

A
Anne de Montmorency Nicolas's friend. (19)
Antoine Bohier Abbot of Fécamp. French Ambassador to England. (50)
Athénaïs de Fleury Baroness. (29)

B
Béatrice Housekeeper at La Colombe. (35)
Bonne Nursemaid at La Colombe. (15)

C
Charles de Fleury Baron. (29)
Charlotte de Fleury (8)

F

François d'Angoulême Count of Angoulême Duc de Valois (heir apparent). (18)

G

Gilles d'Ardres Son of the Comte's Italian first wife. (17)
Grace d'Ardres, née Tredavoe (31)
Guillaume Gouffier Best friend of François d'Angoulême. (24)
Guy d'Ardres Governor of Picardy. (37)

J

Jacqueline de Fleury (6)
Jean de Lorraine Tristan's best friend. (14)

L

Louise of Savoy Widow. Countess of Angoulême. (36)

M

Maître Jacques The cook at La Colombe. (35)
Margot de Fleury (11 months)

N

Nicolas de La Barre (21)

R

Robert de Sapincourt A wealthy local landowner. (43)
Robine de Croisic Nicolas's betrothed. (17)

S

Symonne de Fleury Charles's mother. (46)
Symonne de Fleury (4)

T

Tristan d'Ardres Younger son of Grace and Guy. (15)

V

Valentine de Fleury (9)

Y

Ysabeau de Sapincourt Robert's wife. (20)

HABSBURG EMPIRE:

Maximilian I Holy Roman Emperor. (53)
Archduchess Margaret of Austria, daughter. (32)

Prince Charles of Castile (12)

SPAIN AND CASTILE:

King Ferdinand II of Aragón King of Castile. Father of Queen Katherine
of England. (61)
Queen Isabella of Castile. Mother of Queen Katherine. Reigned over a
dynastically joined Spain, together with Ferdinand. (Died in 1504 aged
53)

OTHERS:

Desiderius Erasmus A humanist* from Rotterdam. (46)
Niccolò Machiavelli An Italian diplomat, writer and philosopher. (43)

* See glossary

'Why come ye not to court?
To which court?
To the king's court.
Or to Hampton Court?
Nay, to the king's court:
The king's court
Should have the excellence;
But Hampton Court
Hath the pre-eminence.'

John Skelton Regius Orator (1463-1529)

PROLOGUE

Twelfth Night, 1513. London.

Snow-laden clouds hung low in the evening sky, threatening to release their heavy burden at any moment. On Ludgate Hill, six chimes rang out from Old Saint Paul's, sending the gossips within scuttling back to their homes with the latest tidings from Henry Tudor's court. A man draped in a long dark gown with the tell-tale blue stripes of a barrister was hurrying from his chamber on the upper floor of Lincoln's Inn (nestled in the heart of Holborn), in the direction of Bucklersbury, on the edge of Cheapside. Pressing a letter and a manuscript to his chest with one hand, and swinging a lantern with the other, he was counting the chimes and willing himself home before the snow began to fall. His growling stomach spurred him on to greater effort thanks to his new wife, Alice, a most capable matron, excellent housekeeper, God's willing servant, stepmother to his four motherless children (and outstanding cook). She'd promised him a warming winter's eve supper of mutton broth with almonds, followed by her secret recipe for quince pie.

Let people sneer that he'd mourned the first wife he lost in childbed by appearing in a wedding garment with the second. Their children had needed a mother. And Alice was no sultry slip of a girl, wide of mouth and eye, but a slightly stout widow of forty-three, eight years his senior. Besides, her skills in the kitchen amply made up for any lack of lustful sport in the bedchamber. The anticipation of Alice's two dishes was so strong that Thomas More swore he could actually taste the tang of hyssop and marjoram in the pie, not to mention the subtle addition of cinnamon.

It had been a long, arduous day; an exceptionally chilly dawn had given him a disagreeable send-off for a meeting with the young King over at Greenwich. Responding to More's urgent message that he had something of great import to show their master, the royal summons had been issued by Thomas Wolsey who (to More's satisfaction) had made it clear in the past how much he valued More's legal brain. It was well-known in court circles that if you wished to secure a royal audience you had to partake in a game of leapfrog, or *sauté-mouton*, as it was known in France. Whether frog or sheep - and however much it stuck in the craw of some of the haughtier courtiers - in order to reach the King, it was first necessary to clamber over the increasingly powerful Wolsey. Glancing down at the manuscript, More recalled how Henry (whose every waking thought these days was focussed on a 'holy' war with France, on behalf of the Pope in Rome) had seized the spare copy with both hands, as if it were some priceless treasure from one of his grand warships sailing up the Thames.

"'*The Prince*'. '*Il Principe*', *by Niccolò Machiavelli. I'm curious to read it*," he'd said. "*In my experience, anything Desiderius Erasmus recommends is worth a few hours of my time.*"

More's good friend, Desiderius (like himself, a man of peace dedicated to God's work), had sent two copies of the manuscript as a New Year's gift. They'd arrived yesterday morning, accompanied by a letter stating his wishes:

'*Be sure to present one of them to King Henry at your earliest convenience. Better it comes from you or me: men of honour and great learning, than from another who does not truly understand its ability to change the world for good or evil.*'

ℒ

Unfortunately, Henry's sunny mood on receiving Machiavelli's work had quickly evaporated (leaving More with a slight megrim) when a servant returned with the seemingly calamitous news that none of the Howards could be found anywhere in the Palace. In particular, Edward, the Vice-Admiral of England, one of the King's favourites.

"How can we manage without Ned?" he stormed, his lower lip white and quivering in sulky protest. *"He's one of the six Lords of the Mount. It's too late to find a replacement."*

Wolsey had tried his best to placate his mercurial young master, even though it was well-known that there was no love lost between him and the Howards. No doubt the King's Almoner had no desire to be on the receiving end of an outpouring of wrath that had nothing to do with him: *"I'm sure there's a very good reason, Your Majesty. Perhaps the Earl's daughter, Muriel, has taken a turn for the worse.'*

Even this didn't appear to soften the King's heart: a Tudor thwarted was not a pretty sight to behold, More decided.

"They shouldn't have gone anywhere without my permission," he snapped back.

Wolsey's face became a perfect mirror of indignation, but also one tinged with the remnants of an appropriate morsel of sympathy for the ailing Howard girl. *'It's their loss if they don't make an appearance at what promises to be the best Twelfth Night at any court in Europe."*

More took note of Wolsey's ability to steer the royal vessel back to calmer waters. Distract and deflect. Two very important words to remember. Henry was at least looking slightly mollified.

"True, Tom."

"And what better start to a New Year that's going to end with you as the rightful King of England and France."

<<*Hold your bow steady*>> More thought to himself. <<*Take aim. And then straight through the heart! Learn from the master. No wonder hitting the heart of the popinjay is called "the King's shot"*>> He quickly made his polite excuses that he needed to catch a wherry back to London Bridge before the weather changed. And breathed a sigh of relief at the satisfying clang of the two heavy oak doors as they closed behind him.

He paused and peeled open Desiderius's letter again, peering to re-read the opening paragraph of the parchment by the light of the lantern:

' *What the Florentine, Machiavelli, writes here is most alarming. Let us hope his work does not become available to all and sundry for a very long time. Some of his ideas make me fearful for the order in the land. You and I both know it is far better to be a just man than an unjust prince.* '

Enormous changes were afoot in the world about them…especially in the courts of princes. Machiavelli's work reflected this. According to Desiderius, it was not only a labour of love, but had been born out of desperation after the fall of his beloved Florence…and thereby, his own personal predicament. The precious manuscript More had been clutching so tightly to his bosom was intended as a gift from Machiavelli to the ruling house of Medici: to ingratiate himself with them by setting out the best path for a prince to follow. More was about to roll up the parchment when his eyes alighted upon a part he must have skimmed over yesterday:

' *I'm sending this post-haste from Picardy where I've been spending New Year with the Governor and his English wife, Grace, in Ardres Castle. What a bedazzling family they are, Thoma. A perfect example of how the English and French can co-*

exist in perfect harmony. If only both Kings would allow it. The Count has two sons of his own, and a third who is his ward. Perhaps you recall how we once met Guy and Grace d'Ardres at Eltham Palace? This time I made the acquaintance of the younger son, Tristan. That boy has a fine mind, but no liking for a career in the Church. And no place in it, if truth be told. He's a born diplomat. Or a soldier. But I chose not to mention that to him, nor tell him that his name equally belongs to one of the Cornish Knights of the Round Table, or the great French warrior—'

To More's annoyance, just as he reached Candlewick Street, one of the pages of the manuscript beneath the letter came loose and - almost as if it had a will of its own - was instantly aided and abetted by a gust of January wind; vexed, he watched it quickly gather speed along the dusty cobblestones beneath his feet.

'God's Nightgown!' the lawyer muttered to himself. 'At this rate, it'll be over London Bridge before I can stop it.' Irked, he picked up the hem of his robes and scurried after it, wondering just which of the hundred pages of vellum had dared to commit such an act of rebellion. Puffing slightly, he finally managed to trap the corner of the page with the end of his brown leather shoe, before stooping down to retrieve it.

More stood up and looked around to check that no one was listening. Then he glanced down at the roguish runaway, squinting at the unknown translator's flowing black handwriting in the flickering light of the lantern. He began to read aloud some of the scholar's words in robust fashion, as if he were holding forth in one of the Inns of Chancery rather than on a deserted street lined with ghostly listeners (not the flesh and blood kind who were all safely nestled in their houses, save for the hapless beggars, hardy cutpurses, and desperate whores who were huddled in whatever shelter they could find):

'*I conclude therefore that, Dame Fortune being changeful and Mankind steadfast in its ways, so long as the two are in agreement, men are successful, but unsuccessful when they fall out.*'

Dame Fortune.

Shivering from the cold biting into his weary body, and still praying he made it home before the first snowflake fell, More tucked the manuscript and letter under one arm and set off again, determined not to stop until he stepped across his own threshold. His thoughts unwillingly turned back to war. Fresh from his meeting with Henry, a greenhorn hellbent on pursuing this costly (in terms of both lives and coinage) campaign across the Narrow Sea, More couldn't help wondering which of the two kings would be victorious and which would be left lying in the dust, humiliated in his defeat: the choleric English lion cub or the ageing, far more experienced Louis of France. The formidable Dame must be bored with kings, queens, cardinals and popes, ambitious knights and pampered damsels whose own greed invariably brought about their changing circumstances. Such as this folly-fallen war with France they were approaching with all the speed of a conquering knight charging down the lists, his very life at stake....

More pulled his long cloak around him, wondering what it would mean for all of them on either side of the Narrow Sea.

France and *England*...so close and yet so far.

Who knew how many lives were inextricably linked, and whose paths were yet to cross. As if in response to these musings, a flurry of snowflakes suddenly enveloped him from head to foot, blurring his vision. Quickly he thrust the valuable manuscript and Desiderius's letter beneath a fold of his cloak. Passing the shop of the apothecary where Alice bought spices with interesting names such as 'dragon-water' and 'grains of paradise', as well as treacle as an antidote for poison, through the material of his cloak pulled over his mouth for warmth, he managed a muffled greeting to the herbalist next door. It was a blessed relief when ahead of him, beyond a further row of shops, he caught sight of his own house at the very end of the wide paved street. There it was, 'The Old Barge': his pride and joy. He treasured the large stone building with its gardens stretching the length of the house at the back. Right at this minute, it looked both familiar and inviting as a thin wisp of smoke appeared from the brick chimneys and trailed up into the night sky. More convinced himself he could smell Alice's famous mutton broth within. His final image as he walked up to the front door with its impressive wrought-iron knocker, vigorously brushing snowflakes from his cloak as he did so, was of Dame Fortune giving a nod of satisfaction as (after the merest flick of her narrow wrist) she watched her wheel beginning to turn....

The same evening.
The Palace of Placentia, Greenwich, England.

John Skelton was uneasy.

In the role of poetic spokesman for his beloved King (and erstwhile pupil), he was sitting at his writing desk, swan's pinion feather quill in hand, hurriedly putting the finishing touches to a poem to be read aloud this evening, in both Latin and English. It was the latest in a volume entitled: '*Divers Ballads and Salacious Ditties*', of which he was particularly proud. He'd lit half a dozen more candles to guide him through to the end of his task. Outside the Palace window, he could hear six chimes of the clock so it was not a moment too soon. Narrowing his eyes against the darkness, he was able to make out soft snowflakes slowly starting to fall: a thousand goose feathers released from a gigantic pillow in the heavens above, billowing a soft trail down to earth.

However, judging by the bruised appearance of the evening sky, they would soon transform themselves into a spinning vortex of whiteness. Happily, he was secure in front of a blazing fire in the small room in the Palace: a veritable cocoon of comfort this evening. It gave him great satisfaction to know his words would be well-received later on. The Dutchman, Desiderius Erasmus, had once praised John for showing his royal pupil, "*the honour of England*", how to "*drink of the sugared well*", while acquainting him with "*the Muses nine*". John glanced down at the black letters scurrying across the parchment, aware that any humanist worth his salt would be wishing they had the ability to fly through the air and embed themselves in the brain of the King of England.

John knew that (as a scholar devoted to peace in the Catholic realms of Europe) Desiderius would be anxious about the storm clouds gathering over their heads. Against the good advice of wise old men such as Thomas Howard, Earl of Surrey (once John's mentor and his former gracious host at Sheriff Hutton Castle, near York - presently - someone had told him before, by his sick daughter's bedside in Hever), young Hal was intent on leading England into war against France, making the two countries bloody and ferocious enemies. John's former pupil was both stubborn and dangerously determined: a potentially fatal combination. Personally, John blamed Thomas Wolsey (or *Snake* as the old Earl chose to refer to him behind his back) for encouraging their new monarch in his folly, and adding fuel to the royal flames of war instead of dousing them with the candle-snuffer of good sense. Especially as Wolsey had once been dead set against the war - until he realized that such a viewpoint could cut short his fledgling political career.

Knowing Hal intimately from his time as royal tutor to the young prince, John was aware how mulish he could be once he set his mind upon something. He was still smarting from his humiliating dismissal by the old King, Hal's father, back in 1502. Like Wolsey, John had now decided to embark upon whichever course of action was required to regain full royal favour with this Tudor monarch. It was as well he didn't have the same scruples as men such as Desiderius, or another of his acquaintance, Tom More, a lawyer beginning to catch the eye of the King. As far as John was concerned, if a supposed man of God, such as the befrocked Wolsey, had decided his conscience could allow him to be a turncoat…then who was he to argue? Let war commence….

Dame Fortune was a fickle woman; all sensible men knew that. According to her whims, you could find yourself one day a rich man with a castle, family, and servants to cater for your every wish. And the very next, you could be flung into the gutter, diseased, dirty and penniless, without a friend in the world. Quite often, the cunning Dame would keep something back, ready to strike when you were at your most vulnerable.

Although he'd been bored to tears by his recent enforced sojourn as a rector in Norfolk, John couldn't help but be bothered by all the good cheer and excess of festive rejoicing in the Palace, on this Twelfth Night. He'd lived on this earth for just over fifty years and could not fathom why so many were unable to see both sides of a gold crown coin. True, the relationship between England and France was akin to a sore festering under the skin, waiting to burst through. But there were other far more peaceful, less costly ways to deal with such a problem.

To his regret, Hal seemed oblivious to the reality of the situation. At twenty-one, he was achingly young - and a royal orphan, to boot. John let out a sigh. He guessed that in the not too distant future he would be part of the English retinue, with his not particularly willing feet placed firmly on the soil of northern France. Still, better to be prepared for the worst (and publicly support it) than for it to happen and then be dashed to the ground with all the force of one tossed from a high tower: an image he'd once seen on a hand-painted Italian *Tarocchi* card.

Dame Fortune's disagreeable habit of springing a nasty surprise on some poor unsuspecting soul made John want to warn the world to beware a lizard hiding in the grass…waiting to strike when a man or woman was least prepared. Of course the warlike King and his closest companions such as Ned Howard, Will Compton, and Charles Brandon would think he was talking about France. And raise a goblet or two (or three) of hyppocras to that country's imminent (spectacular) downfall, as well as to the memory of their dear friend, Tom Knyvett (Ned Howard's brother-in-law), lost in the flames of the '*Marie la Cordelière*' off the coast of Brest, this past year. However, John knew only too well that such a lizard could appear in the everyday life of common folk too - with devastating consequences for any in its path. With this disturbing thought in mind, he reached for the small pounce pot next to him, containing a fine powder of dried cuttlefish bone to dry the ink. Then he swiftly re-read the words he'd just written before dipping his pen in the ink horn and signing his name with a flourish….

'Cuncta licet cecidesse putas discrimina rerum
Et prius incerta nunc tibi certa manent,
Consiliis usure meis tamen aspice caute,
Subdola non fallat te dea fraude sua:
Saepe solet placido mortales fallere vultu,
Et cute sub placida tabida saepe dolent;
Ut quando secura putas et cuncta serena,
Anguis sub viridi gramine saepe latet.'

'Though ye suppose all jeopardies* are past,

And all is done that ye looked for before,

Ware* yet, I rede* you, of Fortune's double cast*,

For one false point she is wont to keep in store,

And under the fell* oft festered* is the sore:

That when ye think all danger for to pass,

Ware* of the lizard lieth* lurking* in the grass.'

John Skelton, Regius Orator

{* See glossary}.

PART ONE

SECRETS OF THE MOUNT

'There are no secrets that time does not reveal.'

Jean Racine (1639-1699)

HOUSE OF HOWARD

Chapter One

The same evening. Saint Michael's Mount, Cornwall.

I've always believed in making a grand entrance. And I've made plenty of them in my time. On the battlefield, at court, in manor and at mass, at hearth and in harbour...in the bedchamber. Even the six chimes of the clock I can hear outside indicate wholehearted approval of our arrival. My time as a commander in battle has taught me that in order to defeat the enemy, a surprise attack is the best way to go about it. Catching someone unawares always gives you the advantage. Somewhere in the sea of faces in front of me is Edward Stafford, Duke of Buckingham, wealthy enough to turn the King of England's face pea-green with envy. Will he be in the mood to parley or to fight? As we reach one quarter of the length of the candlelit great hall, I make a small motion with my hand for my three sons to halt. I need time to put the almighty fear of God into my audience. Before bringing them to their knees>>

It gave me great satisfaction to witness the scene before me: a jumbled, sprawling tableau of utter dismay if ever I saw one. Every man, woman and child turned to stone, caught in some act or other. Not a word spoken - certainly not one of welcome. My white-faced granddaughter, Mary, still had her mouth agape, the sweet notes of her unfinished song left hanging in the air. I noted a lute that had tumbled to the floor, sliding through guilty fingers, a thin sheet of music resting atop to keep it company, like a woman shielding her lover from a jealous husband, or an archer clumsily dropping his last remaining arrow. One man had a cup of wine suspended in mid-air betwixt hand and lips, and was staring at us as if the ghosts of all his ancestors had just slipped through the door. He would discover soon enough that we were flesh and blood. More than

15

that, we were Howards. To my left, I could hear Thomas's breathing coming fast and heavy; no doubt he was scouring the room for his stolen prey, intent upon ensuring she hadn't been snatched from him forever by the Neville pup. On my immediate right, next to Edmund, Edward was very still, no sound coming from him at all. I guessed the place was bringing back memories of that girl who'd once lived over at the castle in Zennor.

It was certainly stirring memories for me. All of a sudden, I was twenty-nine again. Newly married and in love.

<<*Only not with my wife*>>

I'd bedded Lizzie Tilney with the due diligence of any bridegroom who wants to put a son and heir in his cradle as soon as possible. Now it was time for pleasure. The warmth of that summer of '72 came flooding back to me: the scent of Damask roses filling my nostrils, a pair of sapphire blue eyes fixed on me, tempting me and taunting me in equal measure, followed by full red lips teasingly joined to mine. I could almost hear the wild laughter of Matilda Pendeen (or de Lacey, as she'd been when I first met her, the name I gave her ever after). I could certainly hear her outrageous taunts, encouraging me to behave with reckless abandon, knowing full well she was a woman who now belonged to another. "*Little temptress*", I'd breathed when I pressed her up hard against a stone wall and lifted her velvet skirts to seek what she so willingly offered.

"*Little witch, you mean*", she replied, one delicate eyebrow raised in mockery as she ran her fingers through my hair. I had no doubt she came from a long line of beautiful witches, with the ability to rob a man of his very soul if they so wished.

<<*How could any woman ever compare to her?*>> It was akin to arguing that a cheap red wine burning your throat and producing a coughing fit, was equal to one of the King's finest Malmsey wines, shipped all the way from the Kingdom of Candia. She and I had certainly visited this place where I was now standing: a few lost August days when all the monks were absent - save a half-blind old brother, almost too frail to leave his chamber, let alone the Mount. I'd offered my services, assuring the Archpriest at the time that I'd willingly care for both the failing monk and the Mount in his absence. It was not such a bad idea. Only a year later, the Yorkist king, Edward, had to send an army to defeat John de Vere, the Lancastrian Earl of Oxford, who'd captured the Mount.

"*I'll take a few good men with me,*" I told the Archpriest.

But, of course, I only took one person.

Matilda.

I recalled running across the causeway with her, hand in hand, willing the waves to catch us out before we reached safety.

"*I dare you to drown us!*" the brazen-faced hussy called out in triumph, her red hair whipping around her face and tumbling down her back. With her creamy skin and lithe limbs, she resembled a mermaid who had emerged from the sea, destined to bewitch the first mortal to lay eyes upon her.

We carved our initials on the trunk of an ancient sycamore tree, on the way up the winding path to the Castle. We knelt down and traced the outline of the heart of Cormoran the Giant beneath our feet. Unable to wait a moment longer, we certainly took our pleasure of one other in the herb garden, inhaling the fragrance of wild thyme, mint and rosemary while sealing the deed with a thousand kisses, as if hoping they would bind us together forever. Bees, sated with nectar, hovered overhead, too drowsy to bother us. Succumbing to the magic of the place, seducing all the five senses at once, our young bodies came alive and responded in kind. Never in my life before - or since - had I felt such passion…or love. The need to entwine my body around hers was as desperate as a prisoner in a cell clutching the key to freedom in their hand, with only a few minutes to escape.

Standing in this hall of shades and shadows, facing my frozen audience still incapable of speech, my mind took off at dizzying speed to any number of untoward places where we'd torn off one another's clothes in a frenzy, overcome by a primitive urge to couple (as strong as any rutting deer) that would not be denied: near the well which afterwards provided us with water with which to slake our thirst; upon the rock known as Saint Michael's Chair, overhanging the battlements, set at a precarious angle and only visited by foolhardy pilgrims willing to risk their necks for redemption. In the dairy; in each corner of the Castle; at every window overlooking the Narrow Sea; almost inside the chapel, beneath the high altar, until I managed to persuade Matilda (at the last moment) that the entrance would suffice.

"*We have no need of God to bless our love,*" I pointed out.

Little wonder she told me she believed our daughter was conceived somewhere in this place. <<*Perhaps in this very chamber*>>

This thought made me look harder at the shocked faces, realizing that amongst the guests were surely my long-lost daughter and granddaughter. A few discreet enquires when I sent my yearly Damask roses to Matilda, right up to her death a few years ago, had given me some of the answers I needed. Respecting her wishes, I'd never tried to contact her again after our boy died and she rejected me. Ten years younger than me, unkind old age had nevertheless come to whiten that glorious red hair and dim for eternity the high spirits and zest for life that had so enchanted me. Sometimes I wondered whether I'd made a pact with the Devil without knowing for here was I still standing, vigorous in my seventieth year, able to plant my seed in a woman's womb and see it bring forth fruit—

'Lizzie Stafford,' Thomas next to me suddenly said, his gruff voice rudely startling me out of my reverie. He was sucking in the words under his breath as though uttering a curse. For some reason, this set my teeth on edge; after all, he could have had one of the other Stafford girls and avoided us riding like the clappers of a bell to spoil everyone's fun. I could have remained where I belonged, at Greenwich with the King, and within easy riding distance of Thomas's gravely ill sister, my Muriel, at Hever. Long ago, I'd stamped on his younger brother's love affair with the girl in Zennor Castle, not far from here - a candle burning bright and true - snuffing it out long before Edward had chance to reach a church door with her. *<<And aren't I doing the same again?>>* Well, not quite. By arranging for a secret wedding, the Staffords had openly challenged we Howards. Unfortunately for young Lizzie Stafford and Ralph Neville, my family could never be seen to be weak, beaten, or - worst of all - foolish in the eyes of the world. Thank goodness Tom Bullen had the wit to warn me what was afoot. It seemed that as revenge for excluding him from their games, my young grandson, George, had run telling tales on his sisters about plans he'd overheard for a forthcoming wedding.

<<With his ear to the door of a church, no less. Clever little Howard mumble-news!>>

By now I'd picked out the bride's white-faced parents, Edward Stafford and his wife, Alianore, in the crowd near their tearful daughter: a virginal vision in pale silver. Next to her must be the quaking groom, dressed in crimson and gold: the boy with the fallen lute. I pitied both the lad and the lass; he was about to lose what I guessed he held very dear. As for pretty little Lizzie, if I knew Thomas, he'd give her a wedding night to remember. He'd show her that no one dares cross a Howard. It worried me that he'd probably charge into the marital bedchamber with the same ferocity he showed in battle - or hunting down a defenceless doe in the forest near our castle at Framlingham. As a man who'd never experienced love, only ambition fuelled by personal pride, I feared he'd treat his new wife like a bawd in a stew, expecting her to satisfy his needs as if he were a marauding soldier in a vanquished city. And she a helpless female at his mercy…deprived of the respect due to the first-born, virgin daughter of the foremost peer in England. I shuddered to think that my son might find her tears a balm for his cruelty. I took a deep breath; I might not approve of such behaviour but I wasn't about to dwell on matters that didn't concern me, I could not change, or touched upon my conscience. It was time to bring this sorry matter to a swift end—

My eyes travelled around the room again, trying to see if I could put names to the faces of those who had dared plot against the Howards.

And then I saw her….

<<*God's Heart!*>> I felt as if I'd received a body blow as my knees seemed to give way beneath me. Reaching out blindly, I grabbed Edward's arm. My heart was thudding so hard in my chest I feared it was about to stop completely….

CECILY

Chapter Two

Look at my Grandsire, Cecy,' whispered Nan, breaking the awful silence which seemed to go on forever. 'He's staring at you as if he's seen a ghost.'

Nan and I were still holding hands as if somehow it would give us strength. I had to admit she was right about Thomas Howard. He *was* giving me a very strange look. It didn't make sense as I'd never been introduced to him, only seen him from afar at Hever. The four men draped in cloaks, standing so still, made a formidable sight: I knew the Earl of Surrey was a very old man but he somehow looked and acted like a young one, seemingly at least as powerful as his three sons. With his ermine-lined cloak now swept back across his shoulders, exposing an expensive black doublet with silver damask sleeves beneath, and a dark hose tapered to his frame, I could see he wasn't carrying any spare weight. I'd met plenty of other red-faced old men who spent their final years over-indulging themselves at the table, eating and drinking to their fill (the worst ones belching afterwards) and then twiddling their thumbs over their large bellies. By contrast, the Earl was pale-skinned, quite tall and very straight-backed, with flattering grey streaks shot through still thick black hair, and dark piercing eyes that I'd watched darting around the room until they settled on me. For such a grand old age, I had to admit he was surprisingly pleasing to look at, much more so than his rather forbidding portrait at Hever. His face gave the impression of a man of high intelligence: one firm but fair, one who would know how to act amongst kings and commoners. And have many a tale to tell. At any other time, I wouldn't have felt terrified of him. But this evening was different.

He and his sons were clearly not here to celebrate a wedding, at least not that of Lizzie Stafford and Ralph Neville. I gave a shudder as I looked at the dark-haired man next to his father; from a former introduction at Hever Castle, I knew this was the Earl's son and heir: the man intent upon marrying Lizzie. His thin face with its gaunt cheeks and colourless lips was completely different to that of his father; it was that of a man who had been disappointed by life and drank freely from the cup of bitterness. The way he was staring at Lizzie reminded me of Clotilde, my nursemaid's cat, when she was about to pounce on some poor defenceless bird on the Castle battlements, or a shrew in the undergrowth. It turned my insides to water, and made me fear for our poor friend if ever he managed to get his hands on her.

All the Howard men were dark but one of the Earl's sons was far more handsome than his brothers. I guessed immediately this must be Tristan's famous 'Edward Howard'. I'd heard the Vice-Admiral's name so many times I'd grown heartily sick of it, teasing my cousin mercilessly for his excessive admiration of a man he'd never even met.

<<How envious he'll be when I tell him about today>>

All of a sudden, the Earl stepped forward several paces and put out his hand to Lizzie's father, the Duke of Buckingham.

'Good evening, Edward,' he said, his voice strong and brisk, his words echoing around the great hall, slicing through the silence in the manner of a dagger through a sleeve. This was a man who was used to taking command of a situation, I thought.

'I believe my sons and I have some pressing business to discuss with you. In private. You, Tom Darcy, the Archpriest, and William Tredavoe.'

'Indeed, we do.' The Duke's set expression and sombre tones were more suited to a man at a funeral than a wedding. He turned to the Archpriest. 'John, I am sure you can lead us to somewhere quieter.'

As John Arscott bowed his head in acquiescence, I wondered what was going through his mind. A tall dignified man in his late forties, with greying hair and kindly blue eyes, one moment he'd been laughing with the parents of the bride and groom, the next he was being led away in the manner of a prisoner in his own home.

The Earl turned to the third man, one who had neither inherited the family looks nor their brooding presence. To me, there was something slightly insipid about him. 'Edmund, you can stay here…to keep Lady Elizabeth company.'

I put one hand to my throat.

<< *"Keep her company"? He means…guard her so she doesn't escape! And why on earth does he wish to speak to Father? He's done nothing wrong*>>

Watching John Arscott turn on his heels, followed by three monks bearing flaming torches, Lizzie's father, my own, Ralph's step-father, Nan's grandsire and two of his sons, I had a great sense of foreboding.

The moment they'd left the great hall, Lizzie burst into noisy sobs that quickly turned into a long anguished wail. Hardly knowing what she was doing, she ran to the middle of the hall. Ralph, his face turned to quivering whey, rushed over to comfort her. In the manner of bees hovering over a fragrant crushed flower, Lizzie's sister, Kat; my cousin, Margery; Mary, Nan and I formed a protective circle around the two lovers. Daring Lord Edmund Howard to break the circle.

'He can't make me m-marry him!' wept Lizzie. 'I hate him. I want to be *your* wife, Ralph.'

I could tell that all this was almost too much for a fourteen-year-old boy to bear. He was staring at Lizzie wide-eyed, as if he knew his cause was hopeless and so should she.

'There there, it'll be all right,' he murmured, patting her shoulder but without any real conviction.

Deep down, everyone in the great hall knew he couldn't win. The odds were overwhelmingly stacked against him; facing a strong wilful man like Sir Thomas Howard, determined to wed Ralph's betrothed to bear him sons as quickly as possible, was like pitting David against Goliath, only with the predicted outcome. Not the one wrought by a miracle. How could a boy of fourteen take on a man of forty who (according to Nan) had the ear of the King. Thinking of David's giant again, and Ralph challenging Nan's uncle, I decided it was like a youth turning up to his first tournament with a hobby horse as a means of transport, and a clothes pole for a lance.

My Pendeen uncles, Richard and Stephen, were deep in conversation with Lord Edmund Howard, perhaps trying to persuade him to let Lizzie's wedding continue. I suddenly felt a hand slip around my waist, and a loving kiss on my right cheek. 'Father will do what he can,' murmured Mother, coming to stand next to me. But when I turned and looked up into her cornflower blue eyes, all I could see there was despair.

And no hope at all.

Chapter Three

As William followed the others through the small arched door into John Arscott's private study, he was thinking of that other time he'd been given an audience with the old Earl. He had no difficulty working out how long ago it was; all he had to do was add a few months onto Tristan's age. Next month it would be sixteen years since that fateful conversation that had changed the course of Grace's life…and that of Edward Howard. William still experienced moments of terrible guilt, especially knowing that Tristan's relationship with Guy d'Ardres (thankfully, a loving husband to Grace) was troubled, to say the least. He couldn't help feeling as though he and Thomas Howard the Elder had ventured into territory that rightly belonged to God, not mere mortals. His only comfort was that Grace had never discovered his secret, and as far as the rest of the world was concerned, she'd given birth to a healthy baby boy slightly earlier than expected. It helped that she lived in France, not so far that she couldn't come home to visit, but far enough to keep her away from such an explosive revelation. So God mend him, a fleeting meeting with Edward at a tournament in London (with Guy, of all people, next to her) hadn't managed to unravel affairs.

It pleased William that this was one secret the all-powerful Earl of Surrey had never managed to uncover. It was best that way. He could still remember how his heart had been in his mouth last May during a meal at Zennor. Alys's two brothers had come back fresh from London, bearing news of the Howards. He could also picture the look of anguish on Grace's face when their names were banded about so freely, even after nearly two decades had elapsed. To make matters worse, Tristan had shown an unexpected interest in Edward, almost as if Dame Fortune were mocking them all. Then, to his horror, Cecy produced the very posy ring that Edward had given Grace as proof of his honourable intentions towards her. Grace turned so pale William thought she might faint. Thanks to him and Thomas Howard, she still believed her lover had cruelly deserted her, as Edward must in reverse. All those years ago, it had seemed auspicious that the wretched ring vanished, probably stolen, soon after Edward returned to his family home. William felt shame when he recalled his petty behaviour during a quarrel with Grace over Edward after the meal at Zennor. Cecy and Tristan had been caught out the previous day by the incoming tide, and he placed all the blame on Tristan for having a Howard for a father.

With these thoughts going around in his head, William was startled when Edward came to stand next to him, giving him a brief nod, as if in recognition of a past shared. Grace's first love had prospered in the intervening years. Entering the room (well-lit thanks to the wrought-iron candelabra hanging from the ceiling above) with the same boundless energy as William remembered, he was dressed in the latest Italian fashion, in a costume of blue and gold brocade, with gold lozenges around the neck and adorning the border of very wide sleeves. He was easily the best-dressed man in the room, and perhaps even more handsome now in his mid-thirties than before. He exuded the confidence of a man who'd risen high at court and was adored by all and sundry, not least the King himself. A pang of guilt tugged at William's innards again when he remembered that after Grace, Tristan's father had settled for two marriages with much older women: cold-blooded business arrangements, a sure sign for William that his heart had been well and truly broken. The women paid for a charming young bridegroom, fêted at court, and in return, he got his hands on their purses.

He had no idea what the Earl of Surrey had said to Tristan's father to extinguish all hope of a future with Grace (nor did he wish to know); it was bad enough that Tristan had been denied the pleasure of taking part in everyday pastimes with his true father: archery, chess, Shrovetide football, the list was endless. And that Edward had been denied the chance to be a proud father to his son. It seemed monstrous to William that he'd been able to indulge his own daughter and watch her blossom into a delightful young girl while depriving Edward of the same opportunity. Thanks to William's interference, Edward's son had been forced to learn life's lessons from someone else. Another man had lifted Tristan onto his pony for the first time (perhaps not even Guy d'Ardres), a child's lance in his hand in readiness for running at the ring. Another man had—

'Now, gentlemen,' said Thomas Howard the Elder, pulling closer an ornate silver candlestick holding tall tapers, and settling himself into a high-backed oak chair at the far end of the table: the top (of course). William knew the chair well; engraved with a scene from the Book of Daniel, it had been gifted to the Mount by the Mayor of Marazion.

'If the Archpriest will permit me to take charge for a while,' the old Earl continued, 'I think this matter can be presently resolved. And then we can all get back to enjoying ourselves. Is this to your liking, Reverend Father?'

'A peaceful resolution that is swift is always welcome in a house of God,' muttered John Arscott.

John should be the one sitting in the Earl's chair, thought William. The carving suddenly took on a new significance; what could be more apt than the ornate depiction of the beautiful Suzanna defending her honour to the elders, championed and rescued by Daniel. But sadly, hapless Lizzie Stafford was no Suzanna, and the Archpriest...no Daniel. Even though their host's disapproving expression belied his mild words, William knew he had no choice when faced

27

with three of the best-connected and most powerful men in the whole of England. Realizing that the Earl had adroitly snatched the leadership in the manner of a deputy countermanding his general in battle, they all (reluctantly or otherwise) took their seats at the long table beneath the impressive timbers in a roof that formed an archway of perfect symmetry.

Glancing up, in a flight of fantasy, William imagined it instead as a dozen two-handed longswords held high above the heads of a youthful bride and groom at the church door of a wedding. Dismissing this image of what might have been, he returned to the present: to John's study, normally a haven of peace and quiet. It had been lovingly tended to by the island monks, right down to the smallest detail: a wallflower of a cheery yellow hue had been placed in a clay pot on the table whose surface shone and smelled of beeswax. These men on the Mount embraced peace and love in a manner that seemed alien to the Howards: going about their daily tasks of praying to their God, tending to their plants and vegetables, looking after their bees. And offering succour to those in need beyond the Mount. William doubted whether the indomitable old man in front of him had ever known true love with a woman - unlike his second son. His disagreeable first-born definitely didn't look as though he even knew what love was. All this family seemed to care about were titles, high standing with the King and financial gain….

For a moment, William felt a surge of hope; perhaps this second time around, the old Earl intended to do the right thing and let young love thrive, not crush it underfoot. After all, it was quite possible to come to a financial settlement beneficial to the Howards. As the Third Duke of Buckingham, and a man whose lands were to be found in twenty-four counties, including the Marches of Wales, Edward Stafford had coffers galore to be flung open in an eventuality such as this. There was certainly enough to replace the two thousand marks Thomas Howard's son would have gained from young Lizzie's dowry. William caught the eye of Edward Stafford and could tell he was having similar thoughts.

Thomas Howard gave a thin smile and held up a parchment, perhaps the document to be signed by the Duke, handing over an eye-watering amount to a rival for his daughter's hand.

'As I said, this should only take a short while. What I have here is a signed letter from His Majesty, agreeing to the marriage between my eldest son, Sir Thomas Howard, and Lady Elizabeth Stafford.'

There was a sharp intake of breath around the table, and William could hear a rushing sound in his ears. Tom Darcy, Ralph's step-father, was the first to speak; a man around ten years older than William, he was obviously not going to go down without a fight. 'Thomas,' he said, clearing his throat several times, 'I understand your wish to see your son marry Edward's daughter. But I'm afraid your suit has come too late. Everything is prepared for Lizzie's marriage to Ralph. Approved by the King. It is all complete, except for the ceremony. The King will see the sense of that.'

Not a muscle moved in Thomas Howard's pale face and the room went deathly quiet. Was that amusement in the old man's piercing dark eyes when he finally spoke? 'Oh, he will, will he? Even if he knew of the match before, I would have thought our collective absence from his Twelfth Night celebrations would bother him very much indeed. Not to mention news of a secret marriage at the far end of his kingdom, involving the daughter of his richest subject.' He waited just long enough to let his words sink in. 'Especially as this letter proves he's given permission for Edward's daughter to marry elsewhere. To a man of his choice…not of yours, Tom. A man who was knighted on the battlefield while on the King's business, created Knight of the Garter, and given lodgings at court.'

It was as if he'd lobbed a cannonball into the middle of the room, and was calmly waiting for the dust to clear. Baron Darcy opened his mouth (undoubtedly to object) but then closed it again. After all, what was there left for him to say? Indeed, for any of them to say. Even so, William knew he had to at least try, for the sake of Cecy and her little friend. How would he feel if it were his daughter about to be handed over to a man like Sir Thomas, with his cold face and a reputation for brutality? He looked at the old Earl and started to speak, choosing his words with care:

'Your Excellency, let's not forget that Tom Darcy has also served the King faithfully. He was part of a commission down here in Cornwall to fine those who supported Perkin Warbeck. He fought against the Scottish King in Northumberland with you and your sons, if I recollect rightly. Nay, isn't he the second most powerful man in the North of England? Surely all this cannot be dismissed without an appeal to the King.'

Tom Darcy laid his hand on William's shoulder. 'Thank you for your kind words, Will. But we must be sensible. The Earl has a signed letter from the King. As far as I am concerned, that is enough to accept that Ralph has lost his bid. Regretful as it is.'

The Earl smiled at him. 'I am glad to see your judgement is as good as it ever was, Tom. All is not lost for young Ralph. Fortunately for him, Lady Elizabeth is not the only Stafford daughter needing a husband. Am I right, Edward?' he said, turning to the Duke.

'You are,' said Edward Stafford. His face wore the same expression of defeat as Ralph's stepfather, mixed with apprehension at turning his daughter over to a man (older than himself) he knew she heartily detested.

'Now that the matter is settled,' Thomas Howard the Elder continued (with a certain amount of glee, William thought, transporting him straight back to that long-ago meeting at Ashwellthorpe Manor in Norfolk), 'I'm going to hand over arrangements to Thomas here. As the lucky groom, it's only fitting.'

"*Lucky groom*!" Everyone, including William, knew that Sir Thomas Howard was a nasty piece of work…as far removed from good-natured Ralph Neville as the moon was from the earth. William pitied Lizzie Stafford for this last minute swap. It only proved that nothing was ever certain until Dame Fortune turned her wheel one last time.

❧

John Arscott stood up, his face unusually serious. 'Gentlemen, I have to admit that although I agree to marry the couple, I am most perturbed by this outcome. But the King's word is the King's word and must be obeyed.'

'To the letter,' said the new bridegroom, unsurprisingly less than pleased at such criticism, his lips curling in what resembled less of a smile and more of a snarl.

'I suggest, t-therefore,' said the Archpriest, slightly losing the composure that came from a life-long devotion to God, stumbling on his words as if Sir Thomas had drawn a sharp-bladed sword, 'that we toast the health of the new couple.'

'That can wait,' snapped Sir Thomas, 'until after we are wed.'

Although John Arscott looked as though he'd been struck across the face, his tone remained mild. William guessed he was heartily tired of the interlopers who'd brought such chaos into God's House. 'In that case, I propose we all retire early in readiness for the ceremony tomorrow.'

Sir Thomas gave a harsh laugh. 'What do you take me for, man? A complete fool. I intend to marry Lizzie Stafford before the hour is out. And what's more I'll have Ralph Neville as my ring bearer.'

Tristan's father turned to stare at his brother, a look of outrage on his striking features. 'Tom,' he said, 'please have more respect for our gracious host. And remember where you are. Surely you can spare the lad the humiliation. I'll happily step in for you.'

Fury blazed on the face of the Howard heir. 'No need, Ned. I wouldn't want to risk giving offence to Edmund by choosing you. Ralph is a fitting choice and he's the one I'll have.' He suddenly plucked something out of his pocket and held it high up in the air: a gleaming, golden posy ring. The gesture was one of triumph, mingled with a certain amount of delight in the havoc he was wreaking. 'One that I had made especially for today.' He pretended to read its inscription, although of course he must have known it by heart: '"*A true Howard wife*". And now you must all excuse me. I need to prepare myself to wed my bride.'

Getting up, he strode towards the door, pulling it open so hard that he left it swinging on its hinges as he marched out - a villain's victory hot on his heels. Thoroughly relieved that the inauspicious meeting was finally at an end, William stood up and made as if to follow everyone else. However, just as he reached the door, the Earl's voice (still imperious after all these years) rang out:

'William, I would be obliged if you'd stay behind. I have one or two matters I'd like to discuss with you.'

Edward Howard turned to stare at William; clearly this was news to him. He patted William on the back. 'Good luck,' he whispered companionably, as if the years had slipped away and they were twenty and twenty-one all over again....

HOUSE OF TREDAVOE

Chapter Four

Willi"illiam returned to his chair around the table, taking care to create a distance between himself and Thomas Howard. The air in the chamber was slightly oppressive from the scent of the numerous beeswax candles on the table, and around the room. The wax was pooling at the base of many of them, and one or two were already flickering in readiness for the moment they would fizz into nothingness, as surely as the union between Lizzie Stafford and Ralph Neville. The other men must have reached the great hall by now, bearing the sad tidings. He half-expected to hear heartrending cries of anguish coming from young Lizzie; he prayed she was going to be brave enough to face what lay ahead.

'You wished to speak to me, Your Excellency,' he said, unable to keep the coldness from his voice.

'I did, William, I did.' The Earl pointed over at a jug on the intricately carved sideboard (portraying a grapevine from the days of Ancient Rome, on either side): one of John Arscott's most valuable possessions. 'Pour us both a goblet of wine, will you. My throat is quite parched from so much talking.'

Hearing this, William felt incensed at the old man's heartlessness that bordered on gloating; if only he were back in the great hall with his Alys and Cecily. But when England's Lord High Treasurer snaps his fingers at you, you have no choice but to obey. He got up to pour the wine.

'Your health, William,' said Thomas, raising his goblet. 'And that of the bride and groom. Though I think I'm right in assuming that your heart is not in such a toast. And that your loyalties lie elsewhere.'

'I cannot pretend I am not perturbed. I came to celebrate the marriage of a young boy and a young girl. And now she is to be wed to a man older than myself.'

'Ah, the voice of reason. I am sure you would have thoroughly disapproved of my second marriage to a girl more than thirty years younger.'

Although it pained him, William knew he couldn't voice his true opinion; the last hour had proved beyond any doubt that the Howards were far too powerful a family to cross. If both Edward Stafford *and* Tom Darcy, both very high-ranking subjects, had seen fit to acquiesce to the Earl's demands so easily, then William was not about to risk his livelihood or the safety of his wife and daughter in an attempt to rescue a cause that was well and truly lost. 'I am sure you have found happiness with the Countess,' he said evenly.

'Verily, I have. And, it seems you have found it too. The last time we met, you were but a boy. Not yet wed.'

'I was the same age as our King now, your Excellency.'

The Earl laughed. 'So no boy, then. I like your spirit, William. You are still the same brave young man who took it upon himself to come and warn me what was going on between my son and your sister. For the sake of our two families.'

Before he could stop himself, William blurted out, 'I've regretted it many times since. It's been a difficult secret to keep.'

'Yet your sister wed well?'

'Yes. She did. But I don't think it was my place to play the part of God in heaven.'

'Nor mine either is what you mean?'

'Your Excellency, I cannot speak for you. We each have our own burden of conscience to bear.'

'True. But if I could peel back the years, I would do the same thing again. With the Cornish rebellion brewing down here, and my all too recent disgrace on the battlefield at Bosworth, Henry Tudor would never have agreed to such a match. And suspicion would have fallen on our two families forever more.'

Although William wanted to ask if Edward Howard knew what they'd done (he guessed not), he was eager to change the subject. And escape from this room; Thomas Howard must never find out that Grace had borne his son a child. Such knowledge would give the old man terrifying power. 'Your family has risen high since such troubled times,' he said, hoping to put an end to such dangerous talk.

'As has yours, William. Let's drink to family.'

Feeling relieved that they had negotiated rocks as treacherous as any on the Cornish coastline, and were safely back on very welcome firm sand, William raised his goblet. It was obvious that it was only for the sake of old times that the Earl had asked him to stay. Deep down he knew Thomas Howard spoke the truth and they'd taken the only path open to them. The present King's father would never have countenanced a match that could threaten his throne in any way. Although the Tredavoes had remained loyal to the crown during the Cornish rebellion, and been richly rewarded afterwards, they still lived in a part of England that produced men willing to march to London in defiance of the King.

'Now, you're probably wondering why I wanted to speak to you.'

'To talk about old times?'

'Yes. Exactly. And to talk about the future.'

'The future, Your Excellency?'

'Oh, I think with our family connections, you can call me Thomas.'

For some reason that he couldn't quite put his finger on, William was beginning to feel uneasy. He glanced over at an interrupted game of backgammon on a table in the corner, wondering what kind of game he himself was playing. 'If you wish, Your Ex…I mean…Thomas.'

'I do. After all, men with secrets need to stick together.'

Uncomfortable with the false tone of camaraderie creeping into the conversation, reminding him of the stealth of a hungry cat who's spied a sparrow, William decided a brisk approach was best; Thomas Howard was a soldier with a soldier's mind. Any kind of feeble-mindedness would be anathema to him. 'As far as I am concerned, that's all in the past. Both my sister and your son are married to other people. And have no knowledge of our part in what happened. My sister has her own family to consider now.'

'Ah, all this would be well and good. Apart from the fact that your sister's family is also mine.'

There was a long pause that seemed to last an eternity. William found himself strangely transfixed by the frieze behind Thomas Howard's head, illustrating a variety of beasts being pursued.

'You look discomfited, William.'

'Your Ex…Thomas?'

'Why don't we talk about your nephew.'

'My nephew?'

'Yes.'

The room seemed to shift on its axis. He couldn't possibly mean—

'Tristan.'

All of a sudden, the Earl's words seemed to be coming from a long way away. William felt an unexpected affinity with the model of an ostrich above the south-west window, a horseshoe stuffed into its mouth. God's Blessed Mother! How did he know Tristan's name?

'Or perhaps I should say…my *grandson*.'

❧

For a few long moments, the only sound was the screeching of gulls outside the window, probably squabbling over food, and the loud ticking of a particularly fine old clock in the corner. God's Bones! Why was he even thinking about how the cunning object (a gift from William's father, Hugh, to the Mount) showed the times of high water?

In the end, he could bear the tension no longer. 'How did you find out?' To his ears, his own voice sounded strange and hoarse.

Thomas Howard leant back and let out a long whistle. By now the candlelight was casting distorted shadows on his face, giving him an almost satanic appearance, decided William.

'We Howards always find one another,' he said. 'Your friend, and my son-in-law, Tom Bullen, thinks he's the master of an upcoming dynasty. But he's not. He's merely tethered an inferior banner to a far superior one: to a name that will still be famous five hundred years from now. Mark my words, we Howards will still be playing a part in running the country...while the name "*Bullen*" will be a mere whisper from the past. So you see, Tom Bullen's children will always be Howards. To answer your question, I was fortunate enough to make the acquaintance of your sister and her French husband at a tournament a few years ago. Grace and I had a few words, not all of them as agreeable as I would have liked. And when Tristan arrived on the scene, I immediately recognized him as one of our own. He's a Howard as much as any of the rest of us.'

"*As one of our own*". "*A Howard.*" Much as he wanted to protest until his voice disappeared that Tristan wasn't a Howard, William knew there was no point. His biggest worry was what the Earl was going to do with the knowledge. He remembered Grace telling him about meeting Thomas Howard at the tournament (and how distressed she'd felt to see Edward again). He'd meant to attend with his own family, but Cecy came down with a bout of quinsy and they remained at Zennor.

'I can see you're troubled by this, William. But there is no need. After all, you and I are family now.'

Becoming Thomas Howard's kin was the last thing William wanted but he couldn't drop the semblance of deference. 'That's very kind of you, Your...Thomas.'

Thomas Howard raised his goblet again. 'To family.'

William made a feeble effort at repeating the words, having great difficulty getting them out of his throat. It was as if a thick layer of dust had settled there. 'To family,' he finally croaked.

The Earl looked thoughtful as he drew his hands together and linked his long fingers together. 'I am not sure what degree of family you and I are, sharing a nephew and grandson. Perhaps we should ask John Arscott. Oh, don't look so alarmed. Just think of me as a father. After all, I think of you as a son.'

This was too much. Thomas Howard was never going to be anything to William...let alone a father.

'Verily, in the eyes of the law, you are my son.'

William had no idea what the old man was talking about. After the last few minutes, it came as a relief to discover that the Earl's wits had deserted him. In truth, he must be almost seventy. William had heard about Muriel Howard's illness, so *that*, coupled with a long journey down here, would explain why his words were making no sense. William's eyes slid to two roundels in the stained glass windows on the north side of the room. They were representing heaven and hell, with Saint Peter dutifully greeting the fortunate on one side, and Satan's gatekeeper greeting the damned on the other. Up until now, Thomas Howard had been doing a very fair imitation of the gatekeeper from hell, thought William. Now he hoped the Earl's memory, obfuscated by his nigh on eight decades, would conveniently erase Tristan from its many layers.

'By marriage. You are my son by marriage. In the same way as your friend, Tom Bullen.'

William stared at him blankly. 'What? I don't understand.'

'Tom Bullen married my daughter, Lizzie. And you married my daughter, Al—'

A red mist seemed to descend on William's mind. Although he could hear the words of this nightmarish conversation, he couldn't make head nor tail of them. What was the Earl implying? How could he be Alys's father?

…Unless….

All the business with Lizzie and Ralph belonged to a night of imagined terrors. So did this. He so hoped he was about to awaken and go down to break his fast in the great hall in Zennor. Except he knew he wasn't and what Thomas Howard was telling him was the truth. In a moment of piercing clarity, he saw himself ensnared in that second roundel…with no chance of escape.

'You and Matilda Pendee—'

'De Lacey, as she was then. That was her name when we met and that's what she'll always be to me.'

Nothing Alys's mother had ever done could surprise William; he recalled how she'd wanted to shelter Perkin Warbeck at the Castle, believing him to be one of the princes in the Tower who managed to escape. Still, this latest claim was almost too fanciful. 'With all due respect, Your Excellency, do you have any proof?'

'William...please, spare me this insult. Proof of my love for your late mother-in-law? Plenty. But none I could show you. Even the Damask roses I used to send her have long since wilted.'

William felt chilled to the bone. '*The roses*!' he managed to gasp. 'That was you?' How ironic that Cecily still had some petals in a book of hours. Given to her grandam, not by...a pirate...or a lecherous neighbour...but by Thomas Howard. Her *grandsire*.

૭

'How blessed I am to have discovered two lost grandchildren,' the Earl was musing, 'both connected to the wild land down here.' Doesn't this make Tristan and Cecily first cousins twice over? Firstly through my son and your sister. And secondly through Matilda and me.'

William's head was spinning as fast as one of the brightly-coloured tops Cecily used to play with when she was little. Dame Fortune must be out there somewhere cackling wildly at the spectacular unravelling of this sorry tale. 'I have no idea.'

'You're probably wondering why I'm telling you all this now. Well, it's because if anything should happen to me, I want you to know that Cecily and Tristan are Howard born. And I always look after my own—'

'Tristan already has a father.'

'But not his true one. And from where I was sitting at that tournament, relations between the two of them seemed strained. Put a Howard into the Church?' The Earl gave a dismissive laugh.

'And my wife and daughter already have a father and a grandsire respectively whom they think is dead.'

'And yet he's not, is he?'

William felt as though his world was crumbling about his ears. 'Grace must never find out what I did. I take it Edward has no idea either.'

'No. I thought it for the best then and I do today. What good could come of telling them what we did? You and I once shared a secret and today we share another. Whether or not you choose to tell my daughter is up to you. You have a husband's knowledge of her. To my regret, I know her not at all.'

William couldn't bear the thought of giving anyone such appalling tidings; they were best consigned to some place in his head, buried away, shrouded in the gloom of deceit. He also doubted whether Thomas Howard, Earl of Surrey, had ever regretted anything in his entire life.

His new father-in-law stood up. 'I'll tell you this, William, from now on, I'll be keeping a very close eye on your daughter and my grandson. Dame Fortune has already seen fit to join your Cecily together with her cousins, the Bullens, making us a true family. And after today, we are complete. So let's go back to the others. And prepare for a Twelfth Night Howard wedding that none of us will ever forget.'

CECILY

Chapter Five

Finally. The door at the end of the corridor opened and Father appeared alongside Nan's grandsire, both of them carrying a torch that illuminated their faces, throwing peculiar shadows on their features. My greatest fear was that Father would be blamed for what had so nearly happened between Ralph and Lizzie. However, the Earl was smiling and had one arm around Father's shoulder so the meeting must have gone well…even if, as they drew closer, I could see Father had a very strange look on his face. It must be because of his distress at the change of wedding plans. After her initial outburst, Lizzie had become remarkably calm, in the manner of a prisoner being led to the block on Tower Green, knowing there was no hope of a reprieve. I wasn't even sure she could hear what we were saying to her as we stood around petting her, combing her long yellow hair, and arranging the folds of her silver satin gown.

"Will he hurt me?" were the only whispered words that passed her lips, as white as the rest of her face. None of us knew the answer to that…although Mary Bullen tried to reassure her: *"I'm certain he won't. What kind of man would want to hurt his wife?"*

As Father reached me, I was tempted to fling myself into his arms but didn't quite dare in front of Thomas Howard. However, I gave him my most loving smile as I dropped a little curtsey to the pair of them.

'Charming,' said Nan's grandsire. 'The perfect image of her grandam.'

'Do you mean Grandam Matilda?' I asked, momentarily forgetting that this was one of the men who'd stolen Lizzie's chance of happiness.

'I certainly do, my child. For a moment, I thought you were her when I first laid eyes on you.'

<<*So that's why he couldn't stop staring at me in such an odd manner*>>

'But of course she had eyes of blue sapphire…not the green of a lagoon like yours.'

I smiled at this unusual description. 'You must have known her very well, Your Excellency, to remember something like that.' I glanced at Father to make sure I wasn't being too familiar and was surprised to see a look of pain on his face; perhaps he had toothache back again, like before Christmas.

The Earl gave a deep throaty laugh that was surprisingly pleasing. 'I did know her well but I also have a singular memory for people. I won't forget you in a hurry, little maid. Now why don't you go and find your friends. And tell them we're ready for the ceremony to begin. With so many guests and such inclement weather conditions, my son and I agree that the wedding should take place inside the chapel as arranged, and not at the door as is the custom.'

As soon as I entered the chapel blazing with candles, I knew there was something wrong with the scene in front of me; it looked the same as when we'd decorated it yesterday…but it also looked completely different. The air was fragrant with the scent of beeswax, as well as the sweet aroma of plants and flowers, with not a single one out of place. Sprigs of holly, ivy, and mistletoe were tied to the end of every available pew with ribbons of red and green, as well as to the wooden rafters above. Delicate white camellias adorned the altar on either side, a fitting companion for the magnificent central piece: an abundance of Christmas roses, their snow-peaked pink and white petals and dark green leaves surrounding what resembled a crown of gleaming gold within. This crown, with its plentiful delicate yellow stems shooting upwards, was so pretty that any queen in Christendom would be proud to place it upon her head. My Tredavoe grandsire, Hugh, used to say that the first Christmas roses came from the tears of a poor shepherd, distressed that he had no gift for the Baby Jesus. To the man's delight, his tears were transformed into roses, making him swell with pride and declare that he had the best gift of all. When she heard this, Grandam Matilda had made a tutting noise.

"Nonsense! Everyone knows witches use Christmas roses for their curses while wizards use them to make themselves invisible."

Even though the chapel today (filled to the brim with guests wearing morose expressions) was no place for rejoicing, I couldn't help but suppress a little smile at this memory.

<<I wonder what Grandam would say if she were here now>>

She'd probably say witchcraft was afoot, I thought. It was as if an evil fairy had entered the place with her wand and cast a spell, reversing everything in her sight. Although she hadn't touched our decorations, she'd changed everything else: she'd replaced the smooth-cheeked young groom with one long since past the first flush of youth: an old one with lines of bitterness etched onto his brow. She'd exchanged the joyful congregation of a wedding with the glum-faced guests of a funeral (apart from the three Howards in the opposite pew to me, at the front of the chapel, who were looking remarkably pleased with themselves). There was only the odd murmur here and there. The evil fairy might as well have turned our clothes to the shade of the black starless night outside. I gave a little shudder.

Nan took her place next to me. 'Mary's worried that Lizzie won't make it to the end of the aisle without fainting. Especially knowing that Ralph is right behind her, being forced to bear Uncle Thomas's ring.'

Hearing this, I frowned. 'I can't believe your uncle can be so cruel,' I whispered back.

'Oh, I can. I'm convinced his heart is black...not red.'

With this disturbing thought in mind, we both turned at the sound of voices at the entrance. There was the black-hearted bridegroom standing next to Lizzie clad in her beautiful silver gown, gripping her arm tightly, as if he, too, could see she needed to be helped to the altar. In fact, to my mind, he looked like a man so eager to be wed he would have raced her up the aisle if he could. Then dragged her down both it and the Castle steps, before pulling her with him across the causeway onto dry land…and out of our lives forever.

I didn't know whose face looked more like driven snow: Lizzie's or Ralph's (although his was tinged with green).

<<*I can hardly bear to look at them. Poor things*>>

The new bridegroom's face was set like granite as he marched up the aisle, clasping poor Lizzie's hand; she, on the other hand, seemed to be floating as if in a trance. She put me in mind of a ghostly wraith from the spirit world, not truly here…or there either. When Ralph passed us, his shoulders hunched, bearing a gold band resting on a length of crimson velvet, I could hear his ragged breath. He was the very picture of heartbreak. John Arscott was waiting by the altar, an expression of disapproval on his face mixed with something resembling distaste. We all watched Sir Thomas pulling his future wife down hard onto the step next to him, not giving a fig if her exquisite dress got crumpled. He didn't loosen his grip on her arm, almost as if he feared she might flee the scene of the crime.

The Archpriest cleared his throat. 'As all of us gathered here today know,' he began (the Latin words he used giving the occasion a grandeur it did not, in my opinion, deserve), 'marriage is one of the seven Holy Sacraments. Marriage between a man and a woman is no different than that between God and the Church. And the two of them can never be torn apart.'

I gave a little shake of my head. <<*Surely the Archpriest must see the irony of his words. "Torn apart" is exactly what's happened to Lizzie and Ralph*>>

'Get on with it, man,' I heard Sir Thomas say in a low voice filled with impatience. I had a sudden vision of him snatching the Holy Book out of the Archpriest's hands in order to conduct the service himself. There were a couple of gasps of surprise from guests near the altar; no one spoke to a man of God in such a way.

<<*These Howards seem to be a law unto themselves*>>

I glanced over at the old Earl who was scowling; either he agreed with his boorish son, or he, too, disapproved of such disrespectful behaviour. It was hard to tell.

The tips of John Arscott's ears turned pink but he didn't grace Sir Thomas's rudeness with a reply. Instead, he made the sign of the cross. 'Repeat after me. "I, Thomas, take thee to be my wedded wife, to have and to hold, from this day forward. For better for worse, for richer for poorer. In sickness and in health. Till death do us part. And thereto I plight thee my troth."'

The Earl's son reminded me of a particularly ill-favoured wild boar the way he grunted his way through his vows, rushing through them as if he'd spied something tasty to eat on the other side of the altar.

Lizzie.

The Archpriest turned to our friend whose whole body was as still as an ice maiden atop a subtlety. 'And now you, my child,' he said in a gentle voice, glaring at Sir Thomas (who responded in kind), while placing deliberate emphasis on the word: "*child*". 'I take thee, Thomas, to my wedded husband....'

I could hardly bear to listen to Lizzie's response that was barely above a whisper, her abject misery evident in every syllable until the very last one had left her lips: 'I promise to be bonny and buxom in bed and board.'

<<*Can it really only be a couple of hours since I heard these last words causing such mirth to Lizzie and Mary?*>>'

'And now the ring, if you please, Ralph,' said John Arscott in a voice that sounded more sorrowful than congratulatory.

I looked over at Ralph who seemed to be rooted to the spot in the manner of one of the statues I'd seen in a book on Ancient Greece. For an infinitesimal moment, it seemed to me as if the statue was starting to sway. But then Lizzie's rightful betrothed steadied himself, turned his back on the altar and fled down the aisle, flinging the length of crimson velvet (containing what looked like a posy ring) into Nan's lap as he went. A collective gasp of dismay rippled around the chapel. As quick as a flash, a smiling Sir Edward Howard leapt up and held out his hand. 'I'll take that for you, little Nan.'

If Lizzie had noticed what was happening behind her, she made no show of it; instead she stared straight ahead while waiting for John Arscott to bless the ring and then place it on the fourth finger of her left hand: evidence that she was no longer a Stafford...but a Howard.

I watched her hold up a small hand that visibly shook.

<<*Now three of my best friends are Howards, by kinship or marriage. And I'm the odd one out*>>

CECILY

Chapter Six

Nan and I huddled together for warmth as we followed the other guests out of the chapel.

'I c-can't believe Lizzie h-has wed my uncle,' she said, her teeth chattering like those of a monkey at a fair.

'Nor can I. Poor Ralph. I wonder where he is now.'

'If I were him, I would have r-run away.'

I sighed. 'He can't. The causeway is closed until nearly midnight. And there's no light of a full moon to guide him over the rocks in the early hours. Besides, he'd freeze to death. He'll have to wait until morning and leave with everyone else in the boats. The tide will be out again by noon so I suppose he could stay behind and walk across.'

We'd only made our way half-way along the path leading back to the great hall when we were greeted by the sound of angry voices.

'Quick,' said Nan, dragging me behind a stone pillar, 'it's my grandsire and uncles.'

—'Stay out of my affairs, Ned! It's nought to do with you how I treat the girl.'

I peered around the corner of the pillar so I could see them better. The four Howard men were standing in a little group, pulling their cloaks around them to shield themselves from the biting wind that had whipped up in the last hour. I could see flecks of sleet settling around their collars.

The most comely of Nan's three uncles, Tristan's Vice-Admiral, was holding a lantern in one hand and jabbing a finger at Lizzie's new husband with the other. 'It is if you besmirch the family's honour with dog-hearted behaviour.'

'I agree,' said the third brother.

Sir Thomas reached out and shoved that one roughly. 'Still your mammering, you blockhead! Who are you to lecture me, Edmund, when you've had about as much luck with women as a blind man trying to win an archery contest.'

'Be reasonable, Tom,' said the pleasing uncle. 'Everyone knows that in order for a woman to conceive, a man has to ensure she has pleasure.'

The bridegroom…as black-hearted as Nan had described, I was sure of it, had a sneering expression on his face as he swung a lantern to and fro. 'And what would you know about pleasing a woman with those two hideous old crones you've taken to wife?' He gave an unpleasant laugh. 'If you even share a bedchamber, that is. I imagine you close your eyes at night not knowing if you're going to awaken to a corpse lying next to you.'

Tristan's Vice-Admiral gave a shrug of his shoulders. 'Rather marry a woman of maturity than a child still needing a nursemaid. Which of us is the craven one now?'

'Enough! All of you, enough.' Nan's grandsire held up his hands as if he knew a fist fight was about to break out. 'Thomas, you will show Lizzie Staff—Howard some care this night, or you'll have me to answer to in the morning. None of us have any place meddling in your marital affairs but Edward is right. Both a man and a woman need to produce seed for a child to be conceived. Lizzie is but a child herself who, thanks to your infernal pride, has today lost the boy she loved. So I trust you to be the man she needs. Now let's away to your wedding feast.'

Although Lizzie's husband made some grumbling noises, I could see that his father's words had chastened him for the moment. Or perhaps it was the freezing conditions that had made him acquiesce. I only hoped for Lizzie's sake, he'd taken his father's words to heart.

～

Again, it seemed wrong - as if we were sitting down to a candlelit feast that had been prepared for somebody else: a daytime celebration taking place in the gloom, as dark as the thoughts of the discomfited guests. The expression *'waiting to fill dead men's shoes'* came to mind. Ralph Neville wasn't dead, but as far as Lizzie was concerned, he might as well have been. Nan, Mary, Lizzie's sister, Kitty, all the other children and I were seated right below the top table, beneath the newly wedded couple in the middle. All the important adults were seated on either side. The mood was no lighter than it had been in the chapel; a funeral couldn't be worse than this. At Grandam Matilda's there had been laughter as the guests recalled some of her more outrageous antics. But then she was an old lady who'd had flowers on her coffin when everybody else had sprigs of rosemary for remembrance - not just any old flowers either, but pink Damask roses.

Lost in thought, I traced my forefinger over the pattern of flowers and herbs on the tablecloth in front of me. The monks had excelled themselves, bringing out the very best plate and silver cutlery, and a salt-cellar in the shape of a ship, with the names of Tristan and Iseult engraved on its side. Somehow their star-crossed love story seemed to be more than appropriate at this particular nuptial feast. I watched a line of monks bringing in the food, their black cowls pulled back to reveal their gentle faces. For the first course, there were baked teals, hen boiled with leeks, chicken pottage in white wine, salted beef and crayfish. Unfortunately for the hard-working monks, none of us had much appetite to eat. Or talk either. Conversation was lack-lustre at best, non-existent at worst.

'Lizzie hasn't eaten or drunk a thing,' said Nan after the third course.

'She looks like a doll made of clay,' sighed Mary.

'Yes. One that could crumble at any moment,' I agreed.

<<Into a thousand pieces>>

Not surprisingly at such an ill-omened wedding, talk at the top table had turned to war. Or at least that's what I could tell from snatches of conversations here or there.

'Yes, it's true,' Nan's grandsire was saying, 'His Majesty and we, the Council, have approached Luis Caroz—'

'The Spanish Ambassador,' explained his third son, looking about him.

He was rewarded by a glare from the Earl. 'By the Rood, Edmund! I think everyone here knows who he is. As I was saying, the Spaniards will attack Aquitaine, aided by English money, and then turn it over to us. Meanwhile, the King plans to take Picardy or Normandy.'

<<Picardy. Isn't that where Tristan and Aunt Grace live?>>

'It helps that we now have the support of the Emperor,' said my father, somewhat reluctantly entering into the conversation. 'So we'll probably land at Calais which is right next to the Burgundian Netherlands. Maximilian's daughter, Margaret, is definitely on our side.' He turned to Lizzie's father. 'Tom Bullen told me that.'

'Well, he should know,' replied Edward Stafford, 'having been an ambassador at her court.'

'Parliament has granted us money for supplies,' said Sir Edward Howard—

Mary Bullen leant across the table, her face tight with the same anxiety we all felt. 'I've just heard one monk saying to another that no one knows what to do about the subtlety they made especially for Lizzie and Ralph.'

We'd all seen it yesterday: a sugary replica of Saint Michael's Mount, with tiny figures dressed as Benedictine monks encircling the happy bride and groom. I'd been amazed at the detail; there were even dolphins leaping in the blue water surrounding the island. The cook had explained how he managed to reproduce the colour of the sea:

"By using cornflower petals. And spinach juice for the grass near the shore."

Nan wrinkled her brow. 'You mean the monks don't know what to do because it's too late to change Ralph with Uncle Thomas.'

'Exactly,' said Mary.

'Don't forget the motto,' I said. Carefully carved in letters around the sides had been the words: '*Marriages are made in heaven*'.

I looked over at Sir Thomas nibbling on a custard tart. <<*In hell more like*>>

'Oh yes, the motto!' cried Mary. 'I'd completely forgotten about that. Whatever happens, they mustn't serve the subtlety.'

Nan put a finger to her lips. 'Sh!'

I glanced back at the girls' Uncle Thomas and, to my horror, found him staring straight at us as if he'd heard every word Mary said. I held my breath, hoping he hadn't been paying much attention and wishing that every last candle in the great hall would suddenly burn down to the wick, plunging us all into welcome darkness.

<<*Who knows, perhaps Lizzie and Ralph could even escape across the causeway like Tristan and I did last May Day*>>

But no…no such reprieve was to be forthcoming When the bridegroom beckoned to one of the monks standing at the edge of the top table, I knew he'd been paying the greatest of attention. 'Bring out the wedding subtlety,' he commanded in ringing tones. 'My bride and I wish to taste it.'

I watched the monk cast a horrified look in the direction of the Archpriest who turned to Sir Thomas. 'I fear that it didn't turn out quite as our cook would have lik—'

Lizzie's new husband rose to his feet, his dark eyes blazing in his white face. 'I said bring it out. Now!'

John Arscott gave the merest nod to the server who went racing out of the great hall. By this time, conversation at the top table had ground to a halt, followed by the rest of the room. Almost everyone realized what was happening; as a matter of fact, many of us had seen the monks' wonderful creation. And not one of us thought that bringing it out would bode well for poor Lizzie.

After what seemed like ages but probably wasn't, four very red-faced servers (including - I guessed - the one Mary had overheard) came in through a side door, bearing the offending subtlety aloft.

'I'm so sorry,' whispered Mary. 'I had no idea he'd hear me.'

Sir Thomas watched the nervous procession making its way up the centre of the hall, his lips pressed together in grim satisfaction. He reminded me of a stern schoolmaster waiting to administer the cane to disobedient pupils. As the subtlety was placed in front of him, I noticed his eyes narrow at the sight of the small figure of the bridegroom, clearly intended to depict Ralph Neville, not him. For some reason, the absurd thought came to me that the monks had had no choice but to leave it there. There had been no time to create another subtlety replacing Ralph with the new bridegroom. To remove Ralph would have left Lizzie alone on the subtlety, and to take away both Ralph and Lizzie would have left the miniature monks, dressed all in black with a cross around their necks, standing in a circle around thin air. For some reason, the idea suddenly seemed so knotty-pated that before I could stop myself I let out an inadvertent giggle.

Clapping my hand to my mouth, I felt a dozen pairs or more of disapproving eyes looking down at me from the top table. Nan tutted and gave me a hard nudge. Appalled, I looked up and met the eyes of her grandsire. But instead of disapproval, I was surprised to find mirth there.

<<*He's obviously thinking the same thing as me*>>

I almost felt grateful when he motioned to a monk seated behind a harp at the other end of the table. 'Come, brother, I think it is time you played for us. And gathered your fellow brothers to sing.'

There was a collective sigh of relief as the opening notes of '*The First Nowell*', a traditional Cornish carol, echoed around the room:

'*The First Nowell, the Angels did say*

Was to certain poor shepherds in fields as they lay...'

I loved to hear the monks sing, their voices as rich and warm as the mead from the monastery over at Saint Buryan which they served to guests:

'*On a cold winter's night that was so deep.*

Nowell, Nowell, Nowell, Nowell.'

Unfortunately, Sir Thomas was in no mood to be entertained, or set aside his foul mood.

<<*Not until the wicked deed is done!*>>

Not waiting to hear the rest of the verse, he leapt to his feet while jerking Lizzie up by her arm. I heard Mary gasp as he reached out and plucked the tiny figure of Ralph Neville from the surface of the subtlety. Such an innocent gesture...but one laden with ominous intent.

᪣

Popping his vanquished rival into his mouth, he looked at Lizzie. 'Come, wife,' he said, chewing on the little figure with relish, 'you and I have no need of others to distract us. We have each other for that.' He reached down and seized the figure of the bride from the surface. I watched in frozen horror as he held the replica of his new wife to his lips for a moment before biting down hard and swallowing it. An animal devouring its prey could not have outdone such a performance. Bending down, he whispered something in Lizzie's ear which made her turn a dozen shades of crimson. Seeing this, I shuddered. I had no idea what he'd said but whatever it was, she was now shaking like a leaf.

'And now,' Sir Thomas said, 'I intend to take my bride and show her that marriages are indeed made in heaven.'

The old Earl stood with all the grace of one far younger, raised a goblet in the air and fixed a gimlet eye on the rows of dejected faces around the great hall. He was wearing a forced smile of his own, making it hard to tell what he was feeling beneath his nobleman's mask. 'Very well spoken, my son!' he said. 'I laud that sentiment entirely. And now, one and all, raise your glasses to toast the happy couple and wish them health, prosperity and fecundity.'

As he spoke these last three words, the candle burning brightly directly in front of him, hissed, spluttered, and suddenly went out. It wasn't a good omen. I glanced around me but I could tell I was the only one who'd noticed. The way Lizzie's new father-in-law uttered the words made it quite clear that he expected them to be obeyed forthwith. There were some coughs and clearing of throats, and some less than enthusiastic murmurs of approval around the hall. But every glass was dutifully raised.

Still holding onto his bride's arm…in the manner of a gaoler, I couldn't help thinking…the Earl's son started off down the great hall (in the opposite direction of the servers who'd delivered the ill-fated subtlety) at such a pace that it was almost unseemly. At least there was to be no public bedding as there would have been with Ralph and Lizzie: with family and friends giving the happy couple (modestly dressed in night attire) a suitably ribald send off. The Archpriest would have blessed the bridal sheets beforehand and all of us been offered warm spiced wine to sip upon, and fennel or aniseed comfits to nibble upon to sweeten our breath. Perhaps a few of us would have lingered to see the first shy embrace or two before returning to the great hall to join in further merrymaking. I only hoped Sir Thomas Howard would not insist on presenting a bloodied sheet tomorrow to prove Lizzie's virginity.

'It's finally over,' said Mary.

As they disappeared through the main door, the wedding day of Lizzie Stafford, so nearly Neville, but now completely Howard, came to an abrupt end.

<<*But her wedding night is only just beginning*>>

CECILY

Chapter Seven

I found it almost impossible to sleep that night, tossing and turning in the tester bed I was sharing with the Bullen sisters. At some point, I'd heard two chimes of the chapel bell to call the monks to Matins. Once, I awoke from a nightmare in which an enormous sea-monster was in pursuit of a terrified mermaid, reaching out its tentacles to entrap her by her long yellow hair. My heart was thumping as I sat upright, reliving the moment when the sea-monster took on the human shape of Sir Thomas Howard looming over Lizzie Stafford in the bridal bed.

<<*Lady Lizzie Stafford. No longer. But Lady Lizzie Howard*>>

I pushed aside the embroidered velvet curtains (its design of dolphins and other creatures of the sea, perhaps the culprit responsible for such disturbed dreams) and crept from the bed. On tiptoe, I felt my way over to the window seat overlooking the Narrow Sea. The room was extremely chilly now the fire had burnt down to the embers, and outside I could hear the soft patter of sleet against the window pane. Grabbing my woollen cloak which I'd carelessly tossed onto the lid of a trunk on the floor, I pulled it tightly around myself. I glanced back at the bed to check I hadn't awoken Nan or Mary, smiling at the sight of them snuggled up to each other, fast asleep. Seeing them there so innocent and peaceful brought me some comfort. Part of me was alert, fretting in case I suddenly heard screams from another part of the Castle. The three of us hadn't spoken much when we got into bed; our thoughts were dark and filled with Lizzie and her Howard husband.

It seemed there was no escaping the Howards; even Nan and Mary were more Howard than Bullen, at least that's what Lizzie's new husband, their uncle, had once said. I was glad to be a Tredavoe, not part of such a family, even if I didn't have any brothers or sisters. How could I complain when I had my Pendeen cousins...and Tristan. He was more a Tredavoe than a member of the Ardres family. Yet even he was enthralled by these Howards he'd never met - or at least by stories of Edward Howard. I recalled how the hero of Tristan's imaginings had taken his older brother to task outside the chapel over his treatment of Lizzie. Nan and Mary always spoke of their Uncle Ned with great affection, telling stories of his kindness and humour. And he was a clear favourite of King Henry. I was sorry Tristan couldn't have met the middle Howard. Like the Howard brothers, Tristan lived in a household with three boys, growing up alongside his half-brother, Gilles, and another boy called Nicolas, the one taken in by my Aunt Grace and Uncle Guy. Tristan never had a good word to say about that one.

<<*Perhaps he's another Sir Thomas Howard in the making, the eldest boy who strays from the path of decency and humanity*>>

I had the impression that the Earl's eldest son was the one who'd forced through the marriage yesterday, and that the Earl had gone along with it for the sake of family honour. Although it was unbearable for Lizzie, I could understand why the Howard family set such store by appearance; after all, Nan occasionally spoke of her grandsire's time in the Tower of London. According to her, the battle where old King Henry had won his throne spelt out disaster for families who'd fought on the other side, such as the Howards. I suddenly remembered the Earl saying he'd once known Grandam Matilda—

'Move up, Cecy, and make room for me.'

Nan climbed onto the window seat, wrapping my cloak around the two of us. 'I can't sleep either. Are you thinking about Lizzie?' she whispered.

'No. I was thinking about your grandsire. It seems he knew my grandam.'

Nan gave a soft laugh. 'Sometimes I think my grandsire knows the whole world. Just so that he can control it.'

'Grandam Matilda would never have allowed anyone to control her.'

'Poor Lizzie. If only she were more like your grandam.'

'She had no need to be anything more than herself…until yesterday.'

'Seeing what's happened to Lizzie makes me think of the husbands we predicted for ourselves, Cecy.'

I gazed out at the whiteness beyond the window. 'This New Year brings me closer to the time I'm supposed to wed mine. Only seven years left.'

'Don't I still have another score left to wait for mine?'

I reached out and took hold of her cold hand. 'They were only cherry stones and an apple, Nan. Nothing more than that. You're so beautiful you'll be wed before me.'

'Tom says no man will want a woman with a witch's finger on her hand.'

Knowing how she fretted over a tiny extra nail on her right hand, it made me cross that her older brother would make fun of it. I gave her a reassuring hug and gently squeezed her poor little hand. 'Don't be motley-minded. We both know that Tom plays the fool. Come on, they'll be ringing the bell for Lauds soon. Let's go back to bed before we freeze to death. And then we'll have no husbands at all.'

When I next awoke, the cold grey light of dawn was filling the chamber: a fittingly gloomy greeting for the first day of married life for the second Lady

(Thomas) Howard. Mary and Nan were already up, breaking the ice in the jug of water placed at the foot of the bed for us to wash our faces.

'I don't know how you managed to sleep through the bells for Prime,' said Mary. 'Make haste. Or we'll be late to break our fast.'

Nan nodded her head in agreement. 'Yes, make haste. So we be can off this island as soon as possible.'

'I want to know Lizzie is all right,' I said. I wanted to say 'survived the night' but thought it would sound too shocking.

Dressing quickly, I followed the sisters down two flights of steps and into the great hall. The top table was already almost full…but there was no sign of Lizzie, only the bridegroom. Conversation was livelier today, probably because people were relieved to be going home soon. My parents hadn't noticed our arrival because they were talking to the Duke and Duchess of Buckingham and Ralph's parents. Not surprisingly, Ralph was nowhere to be seen. I noticed Sir Thomas Howard cutting a slice of my favourite creamy hard cheese (wrapped in nettles), fresh from the Mount's dairy, as we took our places on the bench below. He began to devour it with as much gusto as he'd used to do away with the little figure of Ralph Neville.

'A good swiving does wonders for a man's appetite!' I heard him exclaim. He turned to his youngest brother and dug him in the ribs. 'You should try it sometime, Edmund.'

He suddenly caught sight of the three of us and flushed angrily. Such crude talk had no place in the presence of ladies, even for one who seemed to take great pleasure in flouting the rules. I knew that "*swiving*" was what some called what took place between a man and a woman in the bedchamber, but I'd never heard it used by anyone. He lifted a finger and pointed it at his nieces. 'Go and find my bride. Your new aunt. Tell her it's not a day to linger abed. I want to be gone from here forthwith if we are to reach Truro by nightfall.'

We didn't need to be told twice. Instantly losing any appetite we'd had, we raced from the great hall in search of our Lizzie.

≈

<<How strange that Lizzie is now to be called 'Aunt' by Nan, Mary, and their two brothers. Especially as Tom is a mere one year younger>>

Such were the ways of the world, especially when someone such as Sir Thomas came along to turn it on its head. I followed Nan and Mary up the stairs which led to the grandest bedchamber in the Castle. Normally for such an occasion, Mary would have refused to let the two of us come with her, but I could tell she was as afraid as we were of what we might find behind the heavy oak door. Pushing it open gently, we ventured inside.

Lizzie was lying on the rumpled bed, very white and still, dark rings beneath her eyes; for one terrible moment I imagined she was dead…until she turned her head to look at us. Her long fair hair was tangled in knots and her crumpled night shift of white linen, trimmed with lace, was open at the neck revealing a couple of livid bruises. I tried to compare the dazed young girl with the one who'd been laughing and joking on the eve of her wedding to Ralph Neville. But I could find no similarities there. There were no tears for her lost love; undoubtedly she'd shed them all yesterday.

'Are you all right, Lizzie?' asked Mary, reaching for her hand.

Nan sat down on the bed. 'Was our uncle gentle with you?'

If it had been Ralph breaking his fast below instead of Sir Thomas, I knew Lizzie would have been full of coy giggles and secret smiles. Teasing us with her superior knowledge, letting slip little nuggets of knowledge. As it was, she stared down at the slender gold band firmly placed on the fourth finger of her left hand. It might as well have been a noose around her neck, I thought. 'I have no one to compare him with,' she said at length. 'It hurt a lot to begin with but then he told me I must have pleasure.'

61

'And did he give you it?' I asked.

'Yes.' Her voice was very small, almost as if she didn't want to admit it to herself.

I remembered the bridegroom eating her sugary replica and then whispering something in her ear that made her blush. Perhaps he'd kept his promise to his father not to mistreat her. That was all that mattered.

'But he must have hurt you,' said Nan. 'Look at your neck.'

'Don't be clay-brained,' scoffed Mary. 'Those are marks born of passion not pain. Do you think you could grow to like it, Lizzie?'

'I don't think your uncle is going to give her much choice,' I said, gazing around the disorderly chamber. It looked as though two children had been playing a frenetic game of hide and seek...except that, in this instance, there had been nowhere for the bride to hide. Lizzie's beautiful silver dress was flung unceremoniously across an upturned chair on the floor, and her petticoats and undergarments were strewn around the room. I noticed the hem of the dress was shredded. It made me think that the bridegroom must have scarcely waited until the door was closed before staking a frenzied claim on her.

Lizzie pulled back the bedclothes, wincing a little as she stood up. 'He told me I'd be saddle sore for a few days until I got used to it.'

<<*What an odd way for a bride to describe her wedding night*>>

There was no emotion in Lizzie's voice, just an acceptance that these nightly visits would be part of her life now, whether she wanted them or not. I could tell she didn't want to discuss Ralph Neville; he belonged to the past now, just as surely as Sir Thomas belonged to her future.

HOUSE OF HOWARD

Chapter Eight

S o, Father, are you going to let me see Hal's letter?'

I glanced at the boatman nearest to us to see if he was listening, but he was no Robert Warner dissecting vital matters of state under a watery microscope, and then giving an opinion as valuable as any member of the Privy Council. Thankfully for our privacy, he was engrossed in his own conversation with his fellow boatman, possibly his brother from the looks of him. They were a couple of brawny Cornish churls with gnarled hands, and weather-beaten faces long exposed to an excess of salt spray and sun beating down on them. I wouldn't have been surprised to see a length of seaweed protruding from their shirts, or an eel around their necks for warmth. I hoped they could make no more sense of our words than I could their Cornish.

No, these men rowing Edward and me back to the shore at Marazion were simple Cornishmen as far removed from my Robert as the moon from the earth (but canny enough, with a good eye for making money), probably thinking about how many sardines…or cups of ale they'd be able to buy with our two-penneth fare. The one next to us, with more missing teeth than his brother, had also doubled up as a stable boy yesterday, offering to take our four horses overnight to the Mount Bay Arms while promising us he'd be able to find another steed on the morrow for Thomas's new bride.

Edward cleared his throat. 'Hal's letter, Father?'

'I'm afraid I can't let you see it.'

Edward looked surprised. 'For any particular reason?'

'Yes. A very good one. Because there isn't one.'

'There isn't what?'

'A letter.'

'I don't understand. I'm talking about the one you had in John Arscott's study.'

'That was no letter but a list of expenses for the royal household. It happened to have the King's seal on it because I only showed it to him last week.'

'You mean, the let—'

'Yes, the letter approving your brother's marriage was no more than an account for various parts of the King's new armour he intends to take to France. The breastplates, gauntlets, pouldrons and corselets…if I remember correctly.'

Edward stared at me for a full minute as if he was trying to take in what he'd just heard. Then he threw his head back and let out a roar of laughter. 'You crafty old—'

'*Genius*? I had no intention of coming all this way for nothing. Not when I should have been with your sister or the King.'

'But what will Hal say when he finds out? Won't we be in the same position as the Staffords?'

'Edward, do you take me for a fool? When I mentioned it to Henry during our meeting last week, he was not against the match. In fact, he said that with your brother being his uncle by marriage the last time around, and my having served the Tudors so faithfully for so long now, a match between Lizzie and Thomas seemed appropriate. I didn't mention the Neville boy and nor did he. You know how much he dislikes the Duke of Buckingham's staggering wealth. And Edward Stafford does little enough to hide it—'

'Hal still hasn't forgiven him for wearing a gold gown at the royal wedding that outdid his own. Or interfering in Will Compton's supposed dalliance with Anne Stafford, his younger sister.'

'George Hastings' wife? All of us knew Will Compton was acting as a go-between for Henry. That was where the real interest lay.'

'Did I ever tell you what happened after Anne's older sister, Elizabeth, went running to her brother?'

'No.'

'Edward Stafford burst into Anne's rooms to find Compton comfortably settled in a chair?'

I was intrigued. 'God's Blood! What on earth did Buckingham say to the pair of them?'

Edward took a moment to reflect. 'That *women of the Stafford family are no game for Comptons. Nor for Tudors either.*'

'Didn't Buckingham give Anne back to his brother-in-law who put her in a convent? Henry must have been furious at having his plaything snatched away.'

'He was. We could hear him yelling at Buckingham from one end of Greenwich to the other.'

'Did Stafford apologize?'

'No. He galloped off to nurse his wounded pride as if he had all the hounds of hell in pursuit.'

'Well, maybe your older brother will bring some reason into the Stafford household.'

'I doubt it. Hal bristles at every tale of wealth that comes out of Thornbury Manor, now a grand castle from the sounds of it—'

'We'll find out soon enough once the dust has settled and the Staffords invite us there.' I allowed myself the glimmer of a smile. 'Hopefully for the christening of Lizzie and Thomas's first-born son.'

'In that case, we're in for a treat. Last year, nearly three hundred sat down to dine at Christmas. And near enough five hundred at Epiphany. Will calls Buckingham: *"the thorn in Hal's side".*' He stretched his arms above his head. 'Tell me, Father, how do you intend to keep Hal's favour? And my brother's posy ring on Lizzie Stafford's finger.'

'Lizzie Howard, you mean. Easy. By now the King will have received a completely different letter…one from an apologetic old man, explaining that with your sister, Muriel, so sick but wanting to be present at the marriage of her brother, we had no choice but to bring the marriage forward. And to beg his forgiveness for doing it in such haste, and without his prior knowledge.'

'But we did it down here, not at Hever.'

'Which of the wedding party is going to place a pair of iron fetters around their ankles by admitting to that?'

My son let out a low whistle, an unmistakable look of admiration on his face. 'None.' He reached out to pat my shoulder. 'Still living up to that name I gave you, I see. *"Phoenix"* you were. *"Phoenix"* you remain.'

'The King still relies on the Howards a great deal, son.'

'True. Upon you in the north for many months this past year. Defending our northern frontier against the Stewart King. Holding high the banner of Saint George and the red dragon.'

'And upon you and poor Lizzie's Tom defending the Narrow Sea while your older brother, Thomas, crept home from Spain in disgrace with Thomas Grey and all the King's men.'

'Hal abhors failure.'

'That I know. It was as well that the Marquis of Dorset was in charge of the fiasco in Fuenterrabia, and not Thomas. A king's cousin can expect more leniency.'

❧

The rowing boat ahead of us, bobbing up and down like a cork over the choppy sea, contained the newly weds and Edmund. As we'd waited at the small landing stage, I could see from the dark rings under my brand-new daughter-in-law's eyes, and her pale face (not to mention the swollen lips), that my son had given her no peace all night. If truth be told, from the way he sauntered into the great hall to break his fast, Thomas seemed to have gained a new spring in his step, one that had been missing since the death of Anne of York the year before last. Whichever demons that had been pursuing him on the ride down here, he clearly managed to exorcise them during the one last night. I was quite certain that - in spite of my warning - he'd ridden Lizzie Stafford as hard as he could to punish her for choosing another over him.

<<*But a lass of fifteen has her whole life in front of her to forget such a harsh beginning. She'll soon learn how to please my son. I think he's chosen well*>>

'I was just thinking that your brother has got himself a worthy bride.'

Edward rolled his eyes. 'Stolen her, you mean. Knowing Tom, the challenge was part of her appeal. He's always wanted whatever he couldn't have.'

'What about you, Edward. Seeing your brother's tasty little morsel, doesn't it make you want one of your own?'

Edward bit his lip. 'To be truthful, if you'd asked me on the way over to the Mount, I might have given you a different answer. But being in Cornwall again has brought back memories best left forgotten. Memories of another Twelfth Night. When I was perfectly happy.'

I pretended not to know what he was talking about. 'I don't understand.'

'You've probably forgotten. It was a long time ago. I met a beautiful girl down here and fell in love with her.'

<<As did I, my son. As did I. I might have met my girl elsewhere but we celebrated our love in Cornwall>>

I waited. 'Did you? Oh, you mean that girl…I've forgotten her name—'

<<May my tongue tumble from my lips>>

'Grace. Grace Tredavoe.'

<<Thank God's Blessed Mother you're looking at the shore, my boy, and not at me>>

'I remember now. Didn't she go off to France?'

<<Thanks to my cunning and her brother's desperation>>

'Yes, she did. So no, I wouldn't want to marry a young girl. They only bring heartache and unhappiness.'

<<No, they don't. I'm sorry I stole your chance to discover that. I will love Matilda until the day I depart this earth>>

'They can also provide you with a proper heir, Edward. Unlike your Alice. A woman of fifty is supposed to hold her grandchildren to her breast, not a suckling babe.'

<<Matilda barely made it to fifty>>

'You didn't say anything when we wed.'

<<No. And that was very wrong of me>>

'I don't like interfering in affairs of the heart. Even if I knew yours wasn't in the match.'

<<My tongue deserves to shrivel like a fallen leaf in the sun>>

'You know, Father, I sometimes think about what would have happened if Grace hadn't left me. If she'd given me a child. A son.'

℘

<<Now I know Dame Fortune is toying with me>>

I couldn't help myself. A wicked goblin had seized my guilty tongue to punish me further. 'But you already have two sons…even if they weren't born in wedlock.'

<<You wouldn't have strayed from your great love any more than I>>

'They weren't born out of love. Only lust.'

<<None of you were born out of love either…only duty. Except the half-sister you don't know about. The one you politely said goodbye to on the shore of the Mount. I could see you were siblings, even if no one else could. Except William Tredavoe whose pain was written all over his face as he watched the two of you together>>

The goblin began to speak of its own accord, intent upon bringing me distress and shame:

'What kind of son do you think your Grace would have given you?'

<<God forgive me for such a cruel question>>

Edward turned to look at me, his dark brown eyes shining. 'He'd be brave, clever, witty. Kind like his mother. You've met her, you know.'

<<Of course I know. And you're describing your son as only a father could. From what I've seen, he's all those things and more>>

'I have?'

I glared at the boatmen. *<<Hurry, you pair of wastrels! The Warners would have rowed me back and forth twice in 'The Thames Rose' in the time it's taking you to make any headway in this fen-sucked bucket. Pull those hell-hated oars until you rip your arms from their sockets, or else you'll not get so much as a farthing from me at the other end>>*

'Yes. Do you remember that joust when the French Ambassador made a terrible scene?'

'The Abbot of Fécamp?'

'Yes.'

'Was your Grace at the joust?'

<<How much more of this can a man take?>>

'She was. Except she was no longer "my Grace". She and her French husband suddenly appeared right in front of me. At first I thought she was an apparition…until she spoke. I thought I was going to collapse. All I could think to do was send her over to you.'

<<The very man who'd brought about your sorrow. She had an inkling…even if you didn't>>

'I do remember now. A very pretty blonde girl. But I don't think we exchanged many words.'

<<Tell him about his son. Tell him about Tristan. Even if he hates you to his dying breath>>

'Let's not talk about it any more, Father. It's finished. It's over. It's in the past.'

<<My soul will be damned forever. I've deprived my favourite son of the love of his life…his son…his sister…his niece. How can I not be punished for my wickedness?>>

To my great relief, the boatmen were pulling the oars for one last time. Feeling the stones grating against the bottom of the boat was the best sound I'd heard in months. Edward jumped out to help the men heave the boat out of the water. He turned to offer me his hand.

'I've enjoyed our conversation, Father.'

<<If only you knew>>

'It felt good to discuss it again after all this time. Hal is the only other person I've told about her. This New Year's Day.'

<<What! The King knows? God's Wounds! This could be disastrous…for all of us>>

A large wave sprayed my face with icy water as I stooped to gather the folds of my cloak, the salt stinging my chapped cheeks. I hardly dared ask. 'So Hal knows who she is?'

<<What am I going to do? He'll find out about Tristan and never forgive me. I couldn't endure it, even though I know I should confess>>

'He didn't ask her name. And I didn't tell him. I didn't see the point.'

<<Sweet blessed relief!>>

'You're right. All that is in the past now. And we have to think of the future. The first thing we need to do is get back to your sister.'

<<As we leave your other one behind>>

'Have no fear, Father. We'll be gone within the hour.'

<<Not a moment too soon for me, my boy. I would fly from this place if I could>>

I followed him up the beach, my boots sinking into the damp sand as soft as marchpane. I didn't dare turn my eyes back to the Mount for I knew what I would find there: a young woman with long red hair and blue eyes, pointing a finger at me. Blowing me a careless kiss while mocking me for my deceit. And what it had brought me to.

<<No daughter, no granddaughter. No grandson!>>

Desperately, I shut my mind to her taunts.

'Come, Edward. Once we've seen that Muriel is on the road to recovery, we must make haste to court. The King is waiting to take us all across the Narrow Sea.

To France....'

PART TWO

IF THE KING WILLS IT....

*'Be very, very careful what you put inside that head
because you will never pull it out again.'*

Thomas Wolsey to Sir Thomas Howard, Earl of Surrey.

NICOLAS

Chapter Nine

January 7th, 1513. The great hall, Ardres Castle.

As the only occupant at the high table so far, Nicolas was relishing the opportunity to break his fast in pleasant solitude. As he reached over for some more anchovies, he felt a pang of disappointment when the brass handle of the heavy oak door, at the far end of the hall, slowly started to turn. Disappointment swiftly gave way to disgust when he saw who it was bursting through the doorway jostling and jesting as usual, like a pair of eight-year-olds: Tristan and that earth-vexing friend of his, Jean de Lorraine. Still licking his wounds from last night's humiliating *débâcle* of his planned wooing of Ysabeau de Sapincourt, not to mention his very public defeat to Tristan, Nicolas glared at them as they approached with all the swagger of a couple of street ruffians seeking out a brawl. Thinly disguised hostility towards himself was evident in every insufferably nonchalant step. His only consolation was that they weren't accompanied by Guillaume Gouffier; *that* one had left the great hall last night with a pert young woman hanging onto his arm who definitely wasn't his wife, Bonaventure. With his expression of a cat that's got the cream, *Gascon* (as he knew him better) had put Nicolas in an even worse mood than before.

The pain of losing Ysabeau to Tristan hurt as much as salt being rubbed into an open wound. The realization that the scurvy-valiant, younger son of Monsieur Guy might prove a very real threat to him in the joust of love, had hit Nicolas with all the force of a thunderbolt from the heavens. Gone was his erstwhile notion of Tristan as a mewling jolthead, snivelling in protest all the way to the door of Anderne Abbey.

Destined for a wretched existence…devoid of the pleasures of the flesh.

❧

Nicolas couldn't even bring himself to entertain the thought that the future devil-monk might well succeed in luring Nicolas's precious prize to his bedchamber.

As the two of them reached Nicolas, the cullionly Jean put one hand to his mouth in mock horror, his eyes - a pair of ridiculously radiant forget-me-nots - wide with *faux* concern. 'What ails you this morning, Nicolas? I think the frozen plains of Siberia would offer us a warmer welcome.'

'Perhaps he had unpleasant dreams,' smirked Tristan. 'The kind where you're pursued by a bear, or find yourself in the Castle courtyard as naked as the day you were born. Without even a horse in the stables upon which you're able to flee. Or a fair maid nearby to kiss your cares away. Just a pot of linseed oil to keep you company while you polish the mud-crusted saddles.'

Although Nicolas wanted nothing more than to put out a boot to send his toad-spotted rival flying back from whence he'd come, he knew he couldn't simply ignore this insult. 'I can see you're trying to make hay while the sun shines, Tristan. After all, the Church will soon be your only mistress.'

There was a momentary flash of anger on his adversary's face that disappeared as quickly as it had come, in the manner of a cloud passing in front of the sun. Even so, Nicolas was gratified to see it. Served Tristan right for daring to steal Ysabeau right from under his nose.

'Don't be so sure of that!' was the only weak parry of the sword Tristan managed.

Unable to resist going in for the kill, Nicolas shrugged, feigning indifference. 'Wars and women. Who in their right mind would desire either? But if we're forced to become involved, we should take heed of the old saying: *"All's fair in love and war"*.'

꽃

Jean threw himself into a chair right next to Nicolas and rudely leaned across him to spear a sliver of Maroilles cheese, thereby releasing its pungent smell. Biting into it, he put his head to one side. 'Mm, *délicieux*! I was just wondering what Dame de Sapincourt's doing at this very moment. Whether she's—'

'Preparing a potion to relieve her husband's megrim?' suggested a female voice from behind them.

Nicolas's chair made a loud scraping noise as he rose to his feet to greet Grace d'Ardres who'd arrived through a side door, accompanied by Gilles. A waft of violets assailed Nicolas's nostrils, sweet and warm.

'I think he'll need several potions to relieve it,' smiled Gilles.

Pleased he was no longer alone with the two errant Jack-a-napes, Nicolas shot Gilles a grateful look. Taking after his father in appearance, Tristan's older brother possessed an Italian gaiety he'd obviously inherited from his mother, punctuating many of his sentences with a ready laugh. Turning back to Tristan and his friend, Nicolas was glad to see a satisfying stain of scarlet on each of Jean's cheeks. Making unseemly remarks about one of your hostess's other guests was not the wisest course of action. Even though Nicolas knew Dame Grace to be exceptionally amiable, he couldn't help wishing she wouldn't accept the kiss the wastrel quickly planted on her hand, with quite such equanimity.

꽃

As if she could sense Nicolas's disapproval, Dame Grace turned her gaze on him. 'I plan to use the saddle you gave me today, *mon chéri*. I've heard that heavy snow is on its way and I want to take advantage of the weather while I can.'

Basking in the Countess's favour and the gentle smile she gave him, Nicolas felt all the tension from his run-in with Tristan and Jean miraculously melting away. 'I will gladly come to the stables to help you. Perhaps I could accompany you on Minuit.'

<<*The horse Monsieur Guy gave me as a mark of favour, not his second-born*>>

'With the greatest of pleasure,' Tristan's mother replied, noticeably not extending the invitation to her son. Was it possible she hadn't approved of his outrageous flirting from the evening before either, even though she appeared to be enjoying herself.

Nicolas nearly burst out laughing at the black scowl that suddenly appeared on Tristan's face at the mention of Monsieur Guy's New Year's gift. If they'd been engaged in a game of archery, Nicolas had just hit the heart.

Tristan leant back in his chair while feigning great interest in the sleeve of his doublet. '*Quelle dommage*! I don't think Nicolas will be able to accompany you, Maman. Père has set him tasks in the stables.'

'And you in the kitchens, surely,' Dame Grace said, without missing a beat, coaxing a tendril of blonde hair back beneath her headdress. 'As it happens, you're both in luck. I argued on your behalf yesterday and, as it was my birthday, your father agreed that you and Nicolas can begin your punishments again once Jean has left.'

Although Nicolas was relieved to hear of a temporary reprieve from his stable cleaning duties, he regretted mentioning a ride for pleasure when he knew Monsieur Guy wouldn't approve. It made him seem as much as a varlet as the wayward Tristan.

'Now, *mon coeur*,' Dame Grace said, reaching out to stroke Gilles's cheek, 'your father tells me you brought back a manuscript for him: one that will cause an uproar if it ever sees the light of day.'

'You must mean the one by the Florentine, Niccolò Machiavelli,' said Jean, irking Nicolas that he hadn't heard of it before.

'Monsieur Erasmus read it while he was here,' said Tristan. He shot Nicolas a taunting grin. 'He mentioned it when we talked for an hour outside his room. He was excited, yet cautious, and told me he'd already sent a copy to his great friend, Thomas More, in England.' He turned to Jean. 'Their friendship reminded me of yours and mine.'

Even though Dame Grace was there, Nicolas couldn't resist a well-aimed taunt. 'How admirable. I take it this means the two of you intend to spend this coming week poring over dusty manuscripts in the Castle library. But then I suppose you are "brothers-in-books" rather than "brothers-in-arms". Monks...not men of action.'

'Nicolas,' said Dame Grace, frowning, 'I understand, as a young man, you're eager to experience war. But as I've told you several times, please don't wish it on us too quickly. Ours is a household where England, France, and Italy manage to live together in harmony.'

'Well said, Maman,' said Tristan.

'*Bravo!*' put in Jean.

Nicolas bit his lip, hating to be wrong-footed where Dame Grace was concerned.

Dame Grace looked first at Nicolas and then over at Tristan, shaking her head. 'That is, we manage it for the most part. And long may it continue.' Beckoning to a servant to bring her more butter, she turned back to Gilles and gave him a fond smile. 'Now, why don't you entertain us all with tales of your Yuletide in Venice....'

Later that afternoon, Nicolas and Gilles were walking in the direction of Monsieur Guy's study where Gilles had promised to show him the famous manuscript. Nicolas's thoughts were firmly on the increasing hostility between England and France (in spite of Dame Grace's recent rebuke). With the exciting news of the impending war, Nicolas was about to experience it himself. It was as if he'd waited all his twenty-one years for such an event.

One he hoped would change his destiny.

<<*If Dame Fortune is looking favourably upon me* >>

He'd been forced to miss last year's military excursion into Italy to take up arms against Papal-Spanish forces, which culminated in the Battle of Ravenna in April. Monsieur Guy had insisted Nicolas stay behind to help Bernard Guillart watch over the Castle.

"*And my wife and son, of course,*" he'd said, meaning the younger one, not Gilles who was accompanying him.

Nicolas had managed to put on a brave face, solely because of his devotion to the Countess. Certainly not because he'd wanted to act as a nursemaid to the spoilt brat that was the Count's younger son.

Once inside Monsieur Guy's study, Nicolas stared at the pages spread across the oak table.

'Père always takes great delight in adding to his already extensive collection of books,' said Gilles, reaching out to brush a finger over the front page. 'I knew this would be the perfect present for him.'

'Tell me more about it,' Nicolas said companionably, easily slipping into the Italian tongue they tended to use when alone.

'It's called *"Il Principe'*, or *"Le Prince"* in French. My cousin, Giovanni, found a Frenchman living in Venice to translate it from the Italian for my father. When I was visiting Florence with Giovanni, we dined with an Italian scholar one evening...the author of the manuscript. This Italian - like you, another "Niccolò" - has been setting the world around him alight with his ideas.'

Nicolas couldn't help notice the way Gilles used the familiar first name address and envied him for his closeness to such a brilliant mind. That was another grievance against Tristan. He'd somehow managed to defy belief by impressing that visiting Dutch scholar, not at all the result for which Nicolas had been hoping. 'Find me a part you enjoyed,' he said to Gilles.

The Governor's elder son turned to a page he'd marked with a piece of red thread and began reading:

"'Not to extinguish our free will, I hold it to be true that Fortune is the arbiter of one half of our actions, but that she still leaves us to direct the other half, or perhaps a little less.'"

Listening to this, Nicolas was struck by how this tenet could equally apply to his own life as to that of Monsieur Guy's two sons. He knew how deeply Gilles minded that he'd never known his mother at all, unlike his half-brother who had only known stability and constant love from both parents. In Nicolas's opinion, thus far, neither son - even the extremely likeable Gilles - had proved worthy of their father. On the other hand, he himself had experienced major obstacles in his life, but was determined to overcome them and make his own fortune. It seemed most auspicious that he shared the same first name as the clever Italian scholar; he resolved right there and then to change the name of his beloved black stallion, Minuit, as a tribute.

Next to him, Gilles was rapidly turning the pages of the manuscript, obviously excited by what he found there. 'Here, Nicò, listen to this,' he said.

"'*For my part, I consider that it is better to be adventurous than cautious because Fortune is a woman, and if you wish to keep her under, it is necessary to beat and ill-use her. It is seen that she allows herself to be mastered by the adventurous rather than by those who go to work more coldly....*'"

Although Nicolas recoiled at the very idea of using force on a woman, he had no problem with being adventurous....

య

He noticed a jug of what was probably Ardres perry (distilled from the pears in the Castle orchards) on a nearby shelf, and walked over to pour them both a drink. While Tristan and that dissolute friend of his were up to no good around the Castle, he and Gilles had far worthier matters to occupy them. Nicolas held out a goblet to Gilles and lifted his own in the air.

'Here's to whatever God and Dame Fortune decide to bring us in 1513. And may Signor Machiavelli help us prepare for it.'

Nicolas had lost count of the number of times he and Gilles, aware of the very real possibility of a war with England, had sat up long into the night debating the dual topics of war and destiny. Both of them knew that within a short space of time, their very lives might be in jeopardy: a sobering thought for two young men who'd hardly begun to sample all that life had to offer. Even though Gilles had experienced his first brush with war in Ravenna, Nicolas knew Monsieur Guy had ensured that his son stayed back from any real fighting. As for the younger son of the House of Ardres, Tristan was never invited to take part in these conversations; to Nicolas's great satisfaction, the destiny of the younger son of the House of Ardres lay somewhere else entirely.

HOUSE OF HOWARD

Chapter Ten

February 2ⁿᵈ, 1513. Feast of Candlemas. London.

I watched Robert fussing over the fur wrap covering my knees, tucking it in with meticulous care: a loyal steward aiding his ageing charge, too feeble to take care of himself. Where was the fearsome warrior of yesteryear? The one who used to emerge from every skirmish (mostly victorious) bloodied, covered from head to foot in livid bruises and coated in battlefield dust. The one with both his pride and courage (of the lions on his coat-of-arms) intact. The one still capable of lively action in the bedchamber at an age when most people had long taken their leave of this world.

'You need some of my Mabel's barley and leek pottage to fatten you up,' my wherryman friend scolded, grabbing one of my bony knees and giving it a little shake. 'I'll ask her to make you some. A battle-scarred old soldier like you needs fuel to restore his strength. To remind the world that here is the man who once held the sword of state upright for the King of England.'

'The *wrong* King of England,' I snarled, unnerved by his extraordinary prescience where my innermost thoughts were concerned. I was also jolted into the memory of the procession from the Tower of London to Westminster that warm July day, long ago. Richard of York had recently made me a councillor and a Knight of the Order of the Garter. Truly, the sun had been shining down on the House of Howard.

'*This* King of England saw fit to create you Earl Marshal at his coronation, making you head of the College of Arms and in charge of state occasions. What better indication of his trust in you than that?'

'He's rewarded others equally, if not better.'

'You are a difficult man, Thomas Howard.'

'I've agreed to come on this folly-fallen outing, haven't I?' I growled, not caring how ungrateful I sounded. 'You know quite well I have no appetite for anything. Stop pecking at me like a scold. Or I'll be forced to put a bridle on you.'

Robert let out a good-natured guffaw. 'We are both aware you only agreed to come because you knew I would have dragged you kicking and protesting from your bed in Lambeth down to the Horse Ferry landing stage, if you'd refused. I wouldn't have hesitated even if - as a common man laying his hands upon an earl - it meant I'd be destined to meet my maker dangling at the end of a rope.'

<<Damn the man for being so plain-speaking. And being such a true friend. For all the time I've known him>>

I was aware I was acting as badly as one of my four small children (or numerous grandchildren) having a full-blown tantrum. All I wanted to do after the mass held in Saint Stephen's Chapel at the Palace of Westminster was slope off and take straight to my bed again. Even the sea of blazing candles, blessed in the name of the Virgin Mary, hadn't been able to move me. At this moment, I was stubbornly refusing to be affected by what I saw around me. In spite of my many protests, here I was (harried by the fearless, undaunted Robert) in the strangest of places: part of an improbable winter's morn scene upon a frozen Thames, where the entire world around me was whiter than the whitest rose of the now nearly defunct House of York. The imposing building behind, and all its neighbouring dwellings, had been transformed into an enormous palace of ice (such as to be found in one of the lands of the Far North), its wondrous beauty quite startling at first glance.

On the river, gone was the pride and joy of the Warner wherrymen: '*The Thames Rose*', and instead I found myself seated upon a long wooden sled, painted red and gold. In front of us, several grooms and some young pages had tight hold of several slightly skittish draught horses that clearly had even less desire to be upon the ice than me. Beyond us were three more sleds, similarly tethered, the furthest one empty but the two immediately in front occupied by young members of the Howard family.

'Fine sleds, Robert,' I murmured, feeling I had to at least be civil.

'My nephew, Nathaniel, is an excellent carpenter and made all four for me.'

Gazing around, I had to admit that the long expanse of ice was extraordinarily beautiful: its virgin whiteness and eerie silence, fitting companions for my present gloominess. There was something ethereal about the glistening surface of the ice packed several feet deep, and even though I hardly cared whether I lived or died, I knew we were totally safe.

'My Grandsire Robert used to tell my father tales of how the river froze over for fourteen weeks when he was twenty-five,' I said.

'I've only known it freeze over like this once in recent times.'

'The year of the water?'

Robert nodded. 'Yes. 1506. Seven years ago. The Thames certainly held us captive that year, didn't she?'

His words made me think of a memorable (unexpected) visit to our shores that year. I didn't know where it came from, but somewhere deep within myself I managed to rejoin his comment with a wry retort - not a dozen leagues removed from my normal self. 'She held more than the country captive.'

Robert frowned but then (like the self-educated man he'd become) gave a knowing smile. 'Forsooth, you're speaking of Philip of Burgundy. The one they called "The Fair".'

To my surprise, my retort turned into something that could have passed for an attempt at humour in different circumstances. 'Yes. Also the short-lived King of Castile. Let's not forget his mad Queen, Joanna, our own Queen's sister. Or how the pair of them were shipwrecked that January off the South Coast *en route* for Spain and—'

'Taken to meet *Goose* who greeted them with open arms and told them—'

'He couldn't find a single royal ship to take them back to Burgundy until—'

'He forced Philip to sign the most underhand treaty of all time,' I finished, my voice beginning to crack a little as I thought of the best-treated prisoners in the history of Christendom. Young Prince Henry - as he was then - became an avid admirer of the foreign Duke; I recalled Edward telling me of his distress when Philip perished that same year in September.

Mirth was bubbling up in Robert now at the memory of Philip's visit: big raucous gales of laughter, sweeping over me like unexpected gusts of fresh air. 'And then a ship was suddenly found as if plucked from thin air. What was *Goose's* hell-hated treaty called again?'

My throat was tight from trying to prevent a laugh escaping - and my voice hoarse from the effort. '*Maius Intercursus,*' I finally spluttered, no longer able to keep my emotions in check.

'"The Evil Treaty"!' Robert boomed, wiping tears from his eyes. 'Forcing Philip to hand over the Pretender—'

'Edmund de la Pole. The Yorkist "White Rose".' I jerked my head in the direction of the Tower downriver.

'A name that's been a curse not a blessing for him.'

I sucked in some icy air through my teeth, wincing from the discomfort. 'I've lately thought a curse sits upon my own House. Just like that old Scottish witch predicted up in the court of King James.'

Perhaps fearing my thoughts were beginning to plunge into darker waters, I guessed from the look of concern on his face that Robert would swiftly try to draw them back upwards into safer, more sunlit ones.

'Don't forget the trade agreement, Thomas. The one that allowed our merchants to import cloth into Burgundy free of tax. We had those hapless Burgundians by the ballocks, that's for sure. One of *Goose's* greatest achievements.'

I smiled at Robert. '*Goose* certainly had his moments.'

'He did.' Robert cleared his throat several times and I could see tears in his eyes. But this time…not of mirth. 'And he would have known what to say to you now. Far better than a clumsy old wherryman with hardly a day's schooling in his life. Look at you. He's got you smiling.'

'Not every scholar emerges from a schoolroom,' I told my friend. 'Some are born on water.'

Dragged kicking and screaming to the truth, I had to admit Robert was right. <<*How surprising that Goose is the one person in the world capable of cheering me*>> I cracked another smile at my companion as a mark of gratitude to him for his infinite patience, while raising an imaginary goblet in the direction of heaven.

'She would have loved this,' I muttered, a pang of loss gripping my insides, so powerful that I almost cried out in pain.

I felt a reassuring hand on my arm. 'Then you must force yourself to enjoy it for her.'

My moment's peace shattered, I found myself outraged by such a profane suggestion. I deliberately twisted my body to the left to loosen Robert's grip. 'You don't know what you ask of me. Give me one good reason why I should do that.'

'I'll give you more than that. Look ahead of you. What do you see?'

I groaned and clutched my head in my hands. 'A brood of yelping brats determined to snatch away my tranquillity.'

'No, Thomas. Look again and you'll see the future of the great House of Howard. Three beautiful girls and two handsome lads. Four of them here by dint of your daughter and her husband. And the fifth by dint of you and the woman you loved above all others. Lift your head. Now!'

Begrudgingly, I did as he commanded; sure enough there were Tom Bullen's two boys in the second sled, red-cheeked from the cold, and right in front of us: Tom's two girls. My gaze came to rest on their playmate - the one they had no idea was their first cousin - my beloved Matilda's (and my) flame-haired granddaughter.

Cecily.

The name pleased me: a clever tribute to the young King's aunt, Cecily of York. With her looks, so near to the King's favourite sister, and her winning personality, she was an asset to the Howards. It pleased me to see the five cousins delighting in each other's company. What a shame William Tredavoe couldn't be here to witness the natural order of things.

'The red-headed girl will hold the heart of many a man in her hands when she is old enough,' said Robert, once more displaying the uncanny ability of being able to read my thoughts: a product of our long years of friendship. 'What about your other boy across the Narrow Sea. Would he enjoy this too?'

'Oh yes,' I smiled. 'From what I've seen of him, Tristan would leap onto the ice at the thinnest part just to appease the hothead in him.'

'Very like his father then? Not to mention his grandsire once upon a time, I imagine.'

Instead of taking the companionable road to humour, I scowled at my friend. 'I know what you're doing, Robert. You're trying to make me forget that it's not even a full month since I buried my precious girl beneath the freezing sod.'

Robert glared straight back at me. 'What kind of unfeeling wretch do you take me for? Your Muriel was a nymph from the heavens above, never to be forgotten. She's in my mind and will stay there forever. Just as surely as my Mabel will shed tears for her, and continue to lay flowers on her grave in the churchyard at Greenwich, til the end of her days.'

Somewhat chastened, I acknowledged I wasn't the only one feeling pain. 'It is not for us to question God's decision to take her early. A young mother who had barely enjoyed twenty-six summers on earth. No masses said for her soul can make up for the loss. Or bring comfort to those poor orphans.'

'But you buried her with pomp befitting her rank. And with love. We did her proud, Thomas, didn't we?'

Although the memory of the large gathering of our clan who came to honour Muriel at the Palace of Placentia, still cut through my innards like a hunting knife slashing through raw flesh, I knew he was right. 'We did, Robert. We did.'

'Now where's that second son of yours? I don't know how much longer the little ones can wait.'

'Edward told me he was going to have a word with the King and then would come.'

As I uttered these words, the younger of Tom Bullen's daughters, a fetching enough black-haired maid, not with the rosebud looks of her older sister, Mary, but perhaps more arresting for that, jumped to her feet and began waving at someone behind me whom I guessed must be Edward. Turning, I could see my son at the far end of the pier, just beyond the gatehouse entrance, returning her wave. At the sight of him approaching us with typical alacrity, something inside me finally relaxed and I found I could breathe more easily.

<<If my golden boy can ease his way through tragedy then so can I>>

As the head of the House of Howard, it was up to me to lead the way, not take to my bed in imitation of my lost child. Typically, Edward wasn't alone but had brought a friend along; I marvelled at the way he drew men and women to him with such ease. As they drew nearer, I heard a quick intake of breath from Robert.

'God's Nigs! Surely that's—'

CECILY

Chapter Eleven

'T*he King*!' cried Tom Bullen, his face alight with excitement. 'Look George, Uncle Ned has brought the King!'

Mary, who was sitting between Nan and me, nearly knocked me off the sled in her eagerness to turn around. I had to duck to avoid being hit by the long veil of crimson velvet attached to her gable hood.

'Yes, it really is him,' she breathed, a thin stream of vapour escaping from her pursed lips, flowing outwards in the direction of the approaching King. It almost resembled a finger beckoning, I thought.

Even from the end of the long pier, I was able to recognize the girls' beloved Uncle Ned from the ill-starred wedding feast at Saint Michael's Mount. My thoughts briefly flew across the Narrow Sea to Tristan, wishing he could be here to share this adventure.

<<*The King. And Sir Edward Howard. I can't wait to tell him.*>>

'Of course it's him!' cried a scornful Tom, straightening his black lambskin fur hat as though the King of England was on his way to see him alone.

The two men were slipping and sliding along the pier, their cloaks flapping around them in the manner of excitable twin bats. They seemed to be exchanging jocular comments that were too indistinct to hear. It was obvious they'd made some kind of wager with each other about who would be the first to reach us. Luckily, they looked very different so it was easy to tell them apart. Dark-haired Edward Howard was smaller and wirier than his red-headed companion which at times seemed to give him the advantage. But then the King, several years younger and taller, would suddenly fling himself in front. I let out a gasp when the girls' Howard uncle lost his footing and looked certain to fall until the King quickly hauled him up again.

'Isn't it exciting?' gasped Nan, hugging her arms around her body as the two of them drew nearer to the top of the steps, still neck and neck. At the very last minute, I could have sworn that Edward Howard suddenly slowed his pace because it was the King who reached the top step first. Catching hold of the railings, he expertly navigated the steps and leapt onto the sled occupied by the old Earl. Red-faced from his exertions, he panted out a greeting to Thomas Howard. By this time, out of respect, all of us were on our feet. I had butterflies in the pit of my stomach as I dipped a slightly wobbly curtsey. <<*After all, what are you supposed to do when the King of England appears in front of you when you're seated on a sled?*>>

To me he was a fairie knight from tales of old, as unreal as the snowy scene and the river encased in ice upon which we found ourselves. Except that he was all too real; up-close, he was a living, breathing, vigorous young man with blue eyes that seemed forever darting here and there. He had even features, delicate not coarse: a straight nose and a mouth shaped in the fashion of Tudor rose petals, I decided. For some reason, when I looked at him I felt a mixture of admiration and pity; even though his actions were boisterous and his voice loud, there was a gentleness I sensed beneath the surface. I knew that as a boy, he'd mourned his beautiful Yorkist mother deeply when she died in childbed. I'd heard he was not only outstanding at all sports but devoted to God; cultured and clever; a poet and a musician. You could tell he had musical talent from his long slender fingers, and poetry in his soul from his watchful eyes, the exact shade of where the sky meets the sea. Perhaps that's where Henry of England lived: in a secret place where his heart could never be broken again. People said he loved his Queen, a few years older than himself: a Spanish princess equally educated and sharp in wits.

I suddenly had one of those strange moments of mine when the world about me seemed to shake and shimmer.

<<*But she's not the one who will one day capture his heart in its entirety, turning it upside down and inside out. Storming that secret place of his with all the force of an army besieging a fortress and watching it crumble to the ground. Playing on his sentiments like a bow sweeping across the strings of a viola da gamba. That honour belongs to someone else entirely*>>

It was fortunate that the King was oblivious to any of my thoughts, especially this last one that had come from goodness knows where. He was smiling at the Bullens' grandsire: 'Your son certainly gave me good chase, didn't he? Be seated, Thomas. I pray you.'

'He did indeed, Your Majesty,' said the Earl, giving a little bow of his head and sinking slowly back down onto the bench. Gratefully, I thought. 'But not quite fast enough to beat you.'

Following the King's example, a moment later, a breathless Edward Howard leapt onto his father's sled shaking off a flurry of snowflakes as he did so. He smiled as the King turned to him and clapped him on the back. I took note of the royal gloves of buff leather (no expense spared there) and the cuffs of colourfully embroidered satin. 'Better luck next time, Ned. Now, where's this sled ride you promised me?'

The moment King Henry uttered these words, the entire assembly jumped into action; even the waiting horses seemed to know they'd been given a royal command because they immediately straightened up, pawing at the ice with their forelegs as they did so, their ears pointed backwards, tails swishing with impatience, poised for take off.

<<*So this is what it must feel like to be the King of England*>>

Both men reached their sled at the front by gracefully leaping over ours, whooping with laughter in the process. As he landed on the boys' sled, Edward Howard turned around and winked at us - as if he knew our three hearts were fluttering at the sight of what must surely be the comeliest ruler in Christendom.

'No match for your rich old king, eh?' I murmured to Nan, giving her an affectionate nudge.

'"*Rich old king*"?' repeated Mary, never one to miss a snippet of gossip. 'Who's that?'

'Merely a figment of Cecy's equally rich imagination,' retorted Nan, pulling a goggle-eyed expression at me behind her sister's back. The two of us knew from old that once Mary had seized upon something with which to tease us, she'd never let it go again. I pulled a face of apology back.

Mercifully, for the moment, Mary was far too taken up with the King. 'I think he was smiling at *me*,' she murmured, placing one black velvet mitten upon her heart. A shadow suddenly fell over her face. 'I miss Lizzie. If only she were here now. Instead of with our loathsome unc—'

'Giddup!' cried the lead boatmen (presently…sled driver), a member of the same family as the others, it seemed. I felt guilty that his cry had interrupted Mary's remark, but for once there was no time to dwell on the fate of our lost friend (so cruelly snatched away on Saint Michael's Mount) because we were off….

꧂

It was my first sled ride, made even more exhilarating by the presence of the King, just a few feet ahead. As soon as our horses took off, slipping and sliding across the ice as they found their footing, it was clear that there was going to be a race to the death between the Palaces of Westminster and Placentia at Greenwich.

'Hold tight, my three young maids!' called out our driver who'd just told us his name was John Warner.

Nan and Mary were shrieking with delight as we clung onto each other, their cheeks bitten red by the freezing cold. I was glad of the warmth of their bodies as well as the linen coif tucked snugly over my ears, my velvet cloak lined with fur, and my favourite grey mittens. Even so, the wind chafed the skin on my face and made my eyes sting as we flew along the ice, slightly bumpy in places, gaining ground on the royal sled. Very wisely, the old Earl's sled was not in the race but travelling at a much more sedate pace, in keeping with his advanced years; the girls had told me he was into his seventieth year. But "*still producing babes*", they said, snickering behind their hands. Even so, I pitied his old bones being roughly shaken on this icy journey, giving him discomfort in a way that younger ones couldn't even imagine. I thought of Grandam Matilda who'd been dead these past four years.

<<Even she wasn't that old. Perhaps he'll live forever. Like one of the fairy folk on the Mount >>

As we hurtled on, the landmarks so familiar to Londoners appeared in a blur through my eyes watering from the cold wind. All of a sudden, a myriad of tiny snowflakes began whirling about us, leaving diamonds encrusted on our eyelashes. There was the majestic Cathedral of Saint Paul's jutting into the skyline: a place I'd heard my parents mention with awe in their voices. Father had also spoken about how exciting it was to navigate the rapids at London Bridge, something I was sure our wherryman had done a thousand times before. But there was no need for John to show such skill today as our sled glided easily beneath the bridge with its nineteen arches; above, in between the shops and houses of wealthy merchants, hoards of excited children raced from one side of the bridge to the other, frantically waving and shouting, trying to get our attention.

'I wonder what they'd say if they knew their king was on the front sled,' I said.

Nan turned to me and cocked her head on one side. 'More's the pity that they don't have that privilege.'

Mary clutched her hands together and gave a beaming smile. 'So we must give thanks that we do.'

Hearing this, John, the wherryman, turned around. 'You three young maids will be able to boast about this to your grandchildren many winters from now.'

'I'm never going to be a grandam!' cried Nan. 'That's only for really old women. I never intend to grow old.'

For some reason, such cheerless words, coupled with another gust of chilly wind, turned the blood in my veins to ice. I noticed the wherryman cross himself, obviously agreeing with me that it was unlucky to jest about such matters.

'Oh, don't be so knotty-pated, Nan!' scolded Mary. 'If you never grow old, that means you'll die young, you silly goose.'

'I'm sure Nan has no intention of doing that,' I protested.

Mary gave a small shrug. 'Perhaps her thoughts have grown dark because she can see the Tower looming up before us.'

That was true; the most forbidding landmark of them all was coming up on our left. Nan pointed a finger at it and then back in the direction of her grandsire. 'Three years,' she mouthed at me in dramatic fashion, referring to the time I knew Thomas Howard had been imprisoned within the thick stone walls.

<<*Well, it doesn't seem to have affected him too much*>>

'I would hate to be cooped up in there,' said Mary in a loud voice, typically not caring who overheard her.

'Well, you'd better make sure you never disobey the King,' replied Nan tartly.

'Why ever would I disobey him?' laughed Mary, never one to take offence easily. 'I'd be as sweet as honeyed candy to him. You're the one who can be a crosspatch, not me.'

'Sh! Both of you,' I scolded, 'today is not a day to squabble.'

<<*It makes me glad I have no brothers or sisters. Like the four Bullens. I only have Tristan and we hardly ever have a cross word. Even when I nearly drown him!*>>

John cracked his whip to make us go faster. I didn't know why but he seemed to want to leave the Tower behind us as much as I did. The very sight of it shifted the mood in the sled from one of frivolity to one where a darker note had been struck. I, for one, didn't want to dwell on what had taken place within its walls over the years for a moment longer than I had to. I remembered the two golden princes who'd disappeared without trace, leaving an accusatory finger pointing at their Uncle Richard: the Yorkist who made himself king in the stead of Edward, the older brother. Aunt Grace once told all of us King Richard had never showed any signs of the monster he was going to become. Rather, he'd always been a loyal, trusted brother.

The final part of the journey passed very quickly as it was taken up with the race between our four sleds…although there was never any doubt who was going to win. As we drew nearer, I was captivated by the beauty of the frozen Palace of Placentia, sprawling along the banks of the Thames - a wondrous ice statue on this perfect day.

'They say King Henry is going to make it his personal residence after the fire at Westminster last year,' said Mary.

'I can see why,' murmured Nan, clearly as overawed as I was.

'Father said he's going to build an enormous tiltyard and move his German armourers into the Palace,' said Mary. 'I'll make sure I come to one of the first jousts. And let him have a length of ribbon in the Tudor colours of green and white for his breastplate.'

'As if he'd ever ask you,' scoffed Nan.

'Why wouldn't he?' I asked, seeing an expression of fleeting hurt on Mary's face. 'Mary's so pretty.' I gave her a little smile, glad to see the expression of familiar bravado back again. I loved Mary but she did have a habit of drawing every conversation back to herself, and what she was going to do. Typically, Nan was far more thoughtful and, most of the time, I had no idea what was going on in her head. Unless she chose to tell me. I'd always thought I was the missing middle sister as I seemed to have character traits of both of them. Not that I ever wanted to be a Bullen.

<<*Being a Tredavoe is all I ever want for myself*>>

As Edward Howard and the King drew level with the pier at Greenwich, the girls' uncle threw the horse's reins to one of the grooms who'd already hopped off the sled. Then he strode over to help us. Standing right next to me, his good looks were apparent: warm brown eyes in a slender face with a long straight nose, and a smile that would melt even the iciest of hearts. I thought he was even more well-favoured than I remembered from Saint Michael's Mount. He had an extraordinary presence and a winning smile that had probably enthralled many a woman on his travels.

<<*No wonder Tristan likes the sound of him so much. The way he talks about Edward Howard sometimes makes me think he'd prefer him to be his father rather than Guy d'Ardres. Perhaps it's because Edward Howard is English and Tristan is half-English*>>

CECILY

Chapter Twelve

I've never been very nearly transported to the door of my house before, young mistresses,' laughed John the wherryman as we stopped outside a tall wooden building. 'Number Ten, Turnpin Lane,' he said. 'Well, it's Number Ten, *and* Number Eleven, thanks to the Earl here. He told us he wanted us to be comfortable. And we are,' he went on as he ushered us up the path with all the gallantry of one of the King's courtiers.

Looking at the two black and white timber-framed buildings, I could easily see why they were the wherryman's pride and joy. He stood there grinning at us: the very picture of the lord of a manor. I smiled back at him.

<<*No wonder they like Thomas Howard so much if he's gifted them such an enviable home*>>

'Come and meet my family,' John said to us.

'Thank you,' I replied as the oak door in front of us opened. A plump woman in her forties, with rosy cheeks and a smile that reached from ear to ear, stepped forward to greet us.

'Thomas, husband, son,' she said to the three men in front of her. Thomas Howard stepped forward and grabbed her around the waist, planting two kisses on her cheeks which seemed to greatly please her.

'Mabel, as alluring as ever, I see.'

'Oh, get away with your words of flattery, Thomas,' she laughed, shooing him away. 'Save them for those far younger and prettier than me.'

Mistress Warner glanced at the rest of us. 'Welcome all of you. Come in, come in.' She wiped her hands on a crisp white apron. From the kitchen somewhere behind her, I could smell an inviting aroma of freshly baked bread that was making my mouth water. I could also hear a great commotion: no doubt an excited household waiting to greet the old Earl and his grandchildren.

All of a sudden, I saw her gaze alight upon the King who was standing next to Edward Howard, with whom she'd just exchanged a friendly greeting. A whole range of emotions appeared on her face (curiosity, admiration, pleasure, swiftly followed by incredulousness, and a rapid dawning of the truth) as she ran an experienced eye over the prohibitively expensive cloth of gold doublet on this red-headed giant, beneath his cloak of ermine. I watched her glance askance at her husband (clearly demanding an explanation for this apparition at her door), but before he could say anything Thomas Howard took her hand in his. 'Mabel, today we have an extra guest. A special one.'

At this confirmation of her suspicions, the colour faded from Mabel Warner's cheeks and she half-knelt in an awkward curtsey. 'Y-Your Maj—'

'Now, now,' soothed the King in a rather high voice that I nevertheless found agreeable. 'If Thomas here can be "Uncle Thomas", then I can be "Henry" for the day.' He turned to face the rest of us, looking very pleased with himself, I thought. 'That goes for the rest of you too.'

As he stared at the five of us, his eyes rested on me and opened wide in surprise. 'By my troth! You are the very image of my sister, Mary. Exactly the same hair of spun gold. Only the dimples are different and your eyes...the colour of a cat's.'

Unlike Mary, who would have basked in the King's attention, I suddenly felt shy. I was about to reply when the Bullens' Uncle Edward glanced at me and took over. 'Hal, she won't look like anything except a block of ice unless we go indoors right away.'

The King gave a laugh and rubbed his gloved hands together. 'Of course, of course. How remiss of me.' He lifted his right hand and gave a dramatic flourish. '*Avanti*, my frozen friends!'

❧

Once inside, Mabel lost all her initial reserve and regained her good spirits; it was quite clear that we were now in her domain which was (blissfully warm and) every bit as much a kingdom as England, Wales, and the Pales around Dublin and Calais were to the King. I was quite certain you could count on the fingers of one hand the number of times this lady of the house had been at a loss for words. 'Please let Peter take your cloaks and wet mittens,' she said, nodding at a skinny youth in the entrance hall. He was no more than sixteen and was blushing furiously; I was sure I could see his knees knocking together.

The house was much bigger inside than I'd anticipated; I could tell where the adjoining wall to the second house had been knocked down to create more room for the family. Ornate cloth hangings and wood panelling (both worthy of a far grander home) covered the brickwork, and a pleasant smell of beeswax suggested hours of polishing by the lady of the house and her servants. Mabel and Robert clearly had a huge family who seemed to be descending on us from every direction: of all ages and sizes. Certainly, none seemed timid about greeting the Bullens' grandsire, although they held back from the King who was standing alone in a corner, a satisfied smile on his face. He was clearly enjoying himself a great deal.

'Now, Your Maj...I mean, Henry,' Mabel said, 'let me show you into the dining-room where I've prepared some refreshments for your pleasure.'

At this, King Henry jumped forward and linked his arm through that of his hostess. 'Gladly. Please lead and we shall follow.'

I decided that the King was playing a part as if he were the lead actor in one of the court disguises I'd heard the Bullens talk about. At this moment, he had taken on the role of guest of a family of humble wherrymen. Later on, he would take his rightful place on a throne in a palace, and this would seem but a distant dream. As would his presence back here at Number Ten, Turnpin Lane.

102

<<What will Tristan say when I tell him? Being led into a dining chamber several paces behind the King of England. Tristan will never believe me. Any more than he'll believe that Edward Howard has just winked at me again>>

Perhaps it was as well that it was only the King, Thomas Howard and his son, the four Bullens, the two senior Warners and me who were ushered in by Mabel to sit in high-backed chairs, almost as stately as the ones in our great hall in Zennor Castle. Outside the door, I could hear laughter and whispering that grew fainter and fainter as the various small children we'd seen obeyed an obvious order from the lady of the house to make themselves scarce. I watched Mabel bustling around the chamber, helped by a nervous looking Peter who brought to mind one of the more skittish horses at Zennor, showing only the whites of his eyes. Two far less uncertain young maids hovered in the background. I was in no doubt that all three still had their mistress's strict instructions ringing in their ears. I wondered what these were. Mayhap: *"Keep your eyes lowered at all times. Do not look directly at the King. And certainly do not address him. Or the Earl and his son. Unless you are spoken to."*

When I caught sight of Peter's shaking hands, a mirror image of his bony knees, I feared he might drop a plate. I so wished I could leap up to help him.

<<But forgetting my manners in royal company would bring down shame on Mother and Father>>

I glanced over at Mary and Nan and almost burst out laughing; it was as just as well those two brazen minxes weren't employed by Mistress Warner. The former was openly staring at the King as if he were a tasty sweetmeat she'd love to devour. Nan, on the other hand, had a fervour about her I'd never seen before. Her eyes were dark fathomless pools, the shade of crystallized sugar, while her lips were crimson from where she'd been nervously chewing them. I wished I could read her thoughts but alas, they belonged in a Nan Bullen book that was kept firmly closed. Except when she chose to open it. It suddenly came to me that she and the King had that in common. Growing up in a family where she was expected to further the Bullen interests from a very early age, must have taken its toll.

At all times, Thomas Bullen's questioning gaze was on his children as if he could control them with a look. I knew King Henry had grown up in the shadow of his brother, Arthur. He'd been the second son: the spare, not the heir. Nan was the second daughter, not expected to make as grand a marriage as Mary— I gave myself a little shake, leaving the past behind and bringing myself back into the present.

Mistress Warner was a very efficient housekeeper and had lost all nerves, even in the presence of the most important man in the kingdom. This was her kingdom. And here she was queen.

She waved a hand at a ruddy-cheeked girl idling in the corner. 'Marion, go and fetch some white gingerbread and quince jam.'

'Aggie. Bring the butter and one jar of apricot marmalade, and another of orange.' She clapped her hands and glared at the pair of them when they didn't spring into action immediately. '*Now*, you two! No dawdling by the fire either. Oh, and don't forget the honey,' she called after them.

<<*Definitely a queen in her court*>>

'Mistress Warner, I think you need to come and help me with my courtiers,' smiled the King, obviously in agreement with me. 'Or take charge of my army.'

Mabel blushed bright red and bobbed him a little curtsey. 'Thank you, Your Maj— Henry.'

I held my breath as Peter entered the chamber clutching an earthenware pitcher. Catching sight of him, the mistress of the house beckoned to him.

104

'Come, boy, serve our honoured guests some hyppocras. They all look as if they could do with some warming food and drink in their bellies.' She looked straight at the King. 'Forgive me, Henry. But 'pon my honour! A king on a sled. And then in my dining-room, no less. As long as my bones rest on this earth, I don't think I'll ever see such a sight again.'

Thomas Howard laughed. 'Nor I, Mabel. And I've seen a lot of sights in my lifetime.'

'A king sits very well upon a sled,' smiled Henry. 'Especially when he has a feast waiting for him.' He raised his goblet and we all followed his lead.

As I ate a slice of Mistress Warner's delicious white gingerbread and felt the smoothness of the apricot marmalade on the back of my throat, I began to enjoy the conversation around me.

'Imagine using a sled in battle,' said Henry, changing the topic from the weather to war.

'You'd have to add wooden sides for safety,' said Edward Howard, reaching out for the pot of honey. 'Without holes to keep the arrows out.' He turned to look at his two nephews. 'What say you to that, lads?'

Tom's eyes were shining. 'It sounds like an excellent idea, Uncle Ned!'

Behind the esteemed guests at the table, Peter (not so scared witless looking now he'd completed his task of pouring out the hyppocras) was adding more logs to the fire, the occasional dampness of the ones brought in from the cold cellar sending shooting sparks into the fireplace. I wonder what he thought about war.

'Enough of building weapons for battle, Edward!' growled the old Earl, sounding tetchy and disapproving. (His thoughts on war were as plain as the scowl on his face). 'Enjoy this day while you may.'

<<I remember Nan telling me the violence of his feelings about the possibility of a war with France>>

I saw the King and the Earl's son exchange a glance and Henry suppress a smile. He turned to Thomas Howard.

'Thomas, I must congratulate you on the beauty of your granddaughters. All three of them are true Tudor roses.'

'Except that two of them are Bullens, and one a Tredavoe,' said Edward. 'And they're not all my father's granddaughters. Only two of them are.'

<<Praise be to God. I pity the Bullens having Thomas Howard as a grandsire>>

'Well, all three of them are still very fair,' said Henry.

The Earl looked over at Nan and Mary. 'A Bullen is every inch a Howard.'

Mary cleared her throat. 'Forgive me, Grandsire, but I'm not sure Father thinks of us as Howards.'

I watched Tom turn bright red, and next to me, Nan let out a little gasp. Meanwhile, Mary was pulling a face of innocence, fully aware of what she'd just said. I wondered how Thomas Howard would reply.

'Come now, Thomas,' said Henry, not giving the Earl the chance, 'your expression is as sour as a bowl of curds and whey when it should be joyful that you have such quick-witted offspring. What's your name again, my bold maid?'

'Mary, Your Maj— I mean, Henry.'

'And your sister?'

'I'm Anne, but everyone calls me Nan.'

'Nan. A pretty name. Like its owner.'

Henry turned his gaze on me. 'And you? The living image of my own fair sister, Mary. Cecily, wasn't it?'

'That's right.'

'An excellent name. My mother had a sister named Cecily.'

106

He raised his goblet into the air again. 'May I propose a toast on this day of frozen beauty outside. To all the beauty inside.' He pulled a face of mock sorrow. 'And now, ladies and gentlemen, I fear that my court beckons and our sleds await.' He turned back to us. 'Cecily, Mary, Anne. Howard grandsons. Your King thanks you for brightening up this snowy day.'

VALENTINE

Chapter Thirteen

Saint Valentine's Day, 1513. La Colombe.

Valentine was bored. She'd sought out Béatrice but now she was being shooed into the garden, and told to go and find Bonne and her little sisters.

'I need to go the kitchens and ask Maître Jacques for some soft-boiled eggs for your mother,' said the housekeeper. 'Her food was too salty yesterday. Everyone knows that an excess of salt in a woman's diet results in a babe born without nails.' She gave Valentine a gentle push. '*Vas-y, ma petite.* And don't take your mittens off. You'll catch a *rheum.*'

Valentine shuddered at the thought of this latest little baby brother being born without nails. Poor Maman. Preparing for a babe seemed very tiresome, especially as you spent your days sore ailing. And all that for a babe who was born sickly and ended up in the churchyard of Notre-Dame de Grâce. *<<I'm quite sure I never want to be with child>>*

Wandering down to the herb garden, from the steps above, Valentine could see two of her sisters but they were with Barbe, the pastry cook's young daughter, not Bonne. Knowing there would be little likelihood of Barbe wondering where she was, Valentine decided to seize the opportunity to go off on an adventure.

<<I'll go to the Castle to see what Tristan's up to. It'll vex him and give me some sport. Everyone here's been far too busy to remember it's Saint Valentine's Day, as well as my name day>>

Even though it was still early in the morning, Valentine had convinced herself there'd be no gifts for anyone this year. She was quite certain she'd have more luck chasing a moonbeam in May than waiting around at La Colombe.

All of a sudden, she brightened at the thought of going over to the Castle. *<<Who knows, they might be giving each other gifts and I might get some marchpane from their cook>>*

Deciding to take a short cut, she hurried across several frost-gilded fields, and up a very long winding path to reach the Castle. She could feel her spirits lifting the moment she set eyes upon Tristan's magnificent family home, nestled comfortably on a hill high above the banks of a lake. She and her father often passed it on one of their many walks so she knew that it was several hundred years old, and each successive member of the Ardres family had inherited it from his own father.

<<Unlike our home. And poor Papa who might have to suffer a distant cousin coming to live at La Colombe, just because all of his children are girls>>

Although this thought made her chest feel very tight, Valentine allowed the scene before her to soothe away such unwelcome thoughts. She turned to look back down at the lake. Pretty blue turrets, sunlight playing on the walls, various trees and, in particular, a nearby overhanging weeping willow, were all reflected quite spectacularly in the water lapping against the sides.

She knew all about the Castle's history from her father who delighted in teaching her facts from far-off times. Tristan's family home dated back five hundred years: to when the first Comte d'Ardres, commanded by Duke William of Normandy to visit the Abbot of Saint Michael's Mount in Cornwall, England, with the Abbot of the Mont Saint-Michel (who lived near the original family seat, not far from Saint-Malo) had taken a fancy to the green, fertile countryside, and decided to build his principal dwelling there. Ever since that time, the black and golden eagle of the Ardres coat-of-arms - with its outstretched wings signifying protection - had been proudly displayed above the entrance to the Castle.

"*And,*" her father had told her, "*every single lord and master who's ever lived there has tried his best to live up to the family motto: 'Verum animi et robore mentis'.*"

❧

Skipping across the drawbridge as she'd done so many times before, Valentine walked under the arch, past the heavy studded gates and entered the large courtyard. Half-expecting to find Tristan there, she was slightly crestfallen when she came across his brother, Gilles, and the Count's ward, Nicolas, engaged in a noisy sword fight. Nicolas was obviously much more accomplished than the Ardres heir (a worthy claimant to the family fortune, like the one her father was longing to appear at La Colombe), and as light on his feet as one of the acrobats who'd performed at her home on Twelfth Night.

Both young men were comely but Nicolas was by far the more eye-catching, she decided. With his dark eyes, curls as black as a pail of tar, and a well-shaped mouth, now pressed tight in concentration, she could see why all the maids at La Colombe admired him. They were both so engrossed in their game that she stood there for several long minutes before they noticed her. Holding up his sword straight in front of him to signal to Gilles that he was taking a break, Nicolas gave her a sweeping bow.

'*Bonjour, ma petite* Valentine. Have you come to watch two knights in training?'

'*Ou—*'

'*Non!*' interrupted Gilles, mopping his brow with a large white handkerchief. 'She's come to smile prettily at our cook, knowing he can't resist her charms. He'll probably make her some tasty titbit, such as a necklace of dried fruit and almonds that's been caramelized using the heat of the fire. *C'est vrai, n'est-ce pas*, Valentine?'

Nicolas smiled at her. 'And why shouldn't the cook give her something? As it's your name day today, it's only fitting that you should have a gift.'

'*Merci*, Nicolas!' exclaimed Valentine, jumping up and down in the air, clapping her hands together. 'Everyone at La Colombe is far too *triste* to bother with any of that.'

'Then we must make amends right away,' he replied. 'Come, let's go to the kitchens.'

'What about your fight?'

'Oh, don't trouble yourself about that,' said Gilles, looking quite relieved, she thought. 'Nicò has got the better of me as usual.'

Valentine watched Nicolas reach out and slap Gilles on the shoulders. '*Bravissimo, mio amico*! We'll make a swordsman out of you yet.'

A little while later, Valentine emerged through the stone archway leading from the castle kitchens. Over her arm was a wicker basket, piled high with tasty gifts for her family from the Castle cook. As Gilles had rightly predicted, she'd been pampered and spoilt by all the servants and fed with Saint Valentine sweetmeats galore. Contentedly licking some grains of sugar from the corner of her mouth, she glanced up at all the copper pans hanging above her head, guessing there were more than two score.

<<*I think Maître Jacques might have more than that. Even if the Ardres are richer than us...and Papa has no heir*>>

She'd left Nicolas and Gilles examining the wares of a passing peddler who'd visited La Colombe the previous afternoon. Scissors, knives, needles, herbs and coloured ribbons were all laid out on a long oak table.

"*Here, Valentine*," Nicolas had said, handing her a length of scarlet ribbon. "*The perfect gift for your name day.*"

Gilles pretended to look vexed that the ribbon had been given to Valentine and jabbed his forefinger towards himself. '*Avevo il mio occhio su quello, bastardo!*'

"*A ribbonless Valentine would be a disappointed Valentine,*" Nicolas grinned, giving a shrug of his shoulders.

Valentine had no idea what Gilles had said, nor was she interested in a discussion the two of them began (in French, this time) about a different traveller in the area, selling sparrow hawks and falcons.

"*Monsieur Guy is expecting him today and has asked me to help him make a selection,*" Nicolas said.

"*I'm surprised Tristan isn't around. I saw him heading in the direction of the stables before. Let's hope he doesn't help himself to your horse again. Like last time.*"

"*If he does that, he'll find himself with more than a black eye. I don't care if I have to clean the stables for the rest of my days.*"

Hearing this, Valentine instantly decided to go to the stables. Nicolas's magnificent black stallion must be housed in there and she wanted to feed him some oats.

<<*And irk Tristan*>>….

To her relief, she managed to slip away without either young man noticing her. Glancing back over her shoulder to ensure that Nicolas wasn't following, Valentine set off in the direction of the stables. It was his custom to insist on accompanying her back to La Colombe if she strayed far from home. Thankful that he was too preoccupied today, she quickly reached the long building with its thatched roof and pretty diamond-shaped design, above the brickwork running along the bottom. Choosing not to enter through the main door to avoid attracting unwelcome attention from the grooms, she pushed open a side door that had been painted blue. The familiar smell of the stables greeted her: a mixture of hay, animal, and the various potions used to clean the equipment. It was a heady odour she was familiar with from the stables at La Colombe.

It was quiet in there today; perhaps all the grooms were off presenting their valentines with gifts. There was certainly no sign of Tristan. Wandering down the row of stalls, stirring the occupants to interested life as she did so, Valentine suddenly spied Nicolas's horse in the corner.

He'd told her his horse had a different name but for the life of her, she couldn't remember what it was.

'*Je m'excuse*, Minuit,' she whispered, setting down her basket and reaching out a hand to nuzzle him. 'I've forgotten your new name so I'm afraid you'll just have to make do with your old one.'

She quite understood why Nicolas guarded him so jealously; a destrier was a noble beast. A conversation with her father came back to her from the time she'd asked him why such a horse was so valuable:

"*Only royalty and the nobility own destriers. They're the most expensive but worth their weight in gold. Bigger and stronger than all the others, swifter and more agile, they're trained for battle or to take part in tournaments. They're hot-blooded too.*"

"*What does hot-blooded mean?*"

"*It means they're spirited and know no fear. In order to be the best, they're quite capable of biting or kicking other horses.*"

"*Dis donc! I'd better keep Cassandre away from them*"

"*Oui, chérie. Take good care of your little Cassandre because she's perfect for you. A Jennet is bred to walk, not dash across the fields at a fast and furious pace like a destrier.*"

Valentine was halfway across the floor to fetch a pail of oats when she heard a strange noise coming from the end of the stables. It was a kind of moaning sound, almost as if a woman were in pain…but yet not. Curious, she crept along the stables in the direction of the noise. Yes, it was definitely a female voice and the sounds were coming from a stall at the very end of the stables. Noticing a small stool, Valentine climbed onto it and peered over the side of the stall. What she saw was so shocking she almost lost her balance and narrowly missed toppling off the stool. Sprawled out in the hay below her upon a couple of blankets, Tristan d'Ardres was locked in an embrace with her nursemaid. Bonne's head was thrown back and her shoulders were bare. Tristan was holding her around the waist with one hand and was—

'What was that?' Valentine heard Bonne gasp.

'Nothing, *ma jolie*. Just one of the horses knocking against a stall.'

Valentine didn't wait to hear anymore; instead she swiftly eased herself down from the stool and took off up the stables, grabbing her basket as she went. She couldn't let Bonne know she'd been spying on her. And she certainly didn't want Tristan to know either. Still shaking from what she'd seen and heard, she fled from the building and collapsed onto a nearby stone trough filled with icy water for the horses. Almost immediately, Bonne emerged from a door at the other end of the stables, pulling straw from her hair and re-arranging her bodice. When she caught sight of Valentine, her eyes grew as big as saucers and her mouth dropped open.

'*Nom de Dieu*! What are you doing here, Demoiselle Valentine?'

It was just as well Valentine had prepared her speech involving one of the servants at La Colombe. 'Pierre was coming over to the Castle to ask for some grains of paradise for Maître Jacques. I asked Papa if I could go with him and he said yes.'

'Where's Pierre now?'

'*Je ne sais pas*. Dame Grace offered to take me home so maybe he thinks I've gone with her.'

<<Will I be struck down by a bolt of forked lightning as punishment for my lies, even though it's my name day?>>

Bonne's plump cheeks were as red as one of the *Chataignier* apples in their orchard, and her brown eyes as bright as the precious stones Valentine had once seen at La Colombe in a necklace around the throat of the Queen of France,.

'*Allons-y*,' her flustered nursemaid said, pulling her brown woollen cloak around her shoulders, 'let's get you home right this minute before everyone starts to worry. There are plans to celebrate your name day.'

Valentine allowed herself to be led out of the courtyard, but not before casting a rueful glance back at Ardres Castle. With the late morning February sun shining on it in all its splendour, unlike La Colombe, it was a place with no money woes. She loved her home but knew her parents struggled with such matters. With Gilles firmly in place as the much prized Ardres heir, there would be no dizzy-eyed distant cousin no one had ever met coming to live at the Castle.

<<Tristan is so lucky. I wish I lived in a castle too>>

HOUSE OF TUDOR

Chapter Fourteen

15th March, 1513. The gardens of the Palace of Placentia.

S top being so modest, Ned. *"Lord High Admiral of England, Ireland, and Aquitaine"* has a most pleasing ring to it. We only have to wait another few days to announce your appointment.' Henry gave the merest nod of his head. 'Out of respect for John de Vere's family. I have to confess, without wishing to speak ill of the dead,' he said (crossing himself...this action instantly mirrored by Ned Howard), 'that our last Lord Admiral was getting so old I was beginning to think he must have been sipping from the same faery cup as your good father.'

There was a troubled look in Ned's brown eyes, watering from the chill wind that had heralded in the Ides of March (with an early morning mist) and chafed the cheeks of anyone brave enough to venture out. 'I worry I might not live up to your expectations.'

Henry liked nothing more than an initial show of modesty and self-doubt in his courtiers; he took delight in reassuring them as it made his benefaction all the more meaningful. If only Ned's tiresome father (or his two brothers, for that matter) had a little of *this* Howard's hesitancy; but for Ned's sake, he tried not to grit his teeth too much at the sight of the old Earl whenever he appeared at court. <<*Usually to scold me for some expense he deems inappropriate. Well, he's got an entire war to deal with now*>> Henry's irritation had abated of late; he pitied Thomas Howard for the loss of his daughter, Tom Knyvett's widow, and had decided to forget about his own fury on Twelfth Night when the entire Howard clan mysteriously vanished in a puff of smoke. Only to turn up a week or so later, with Thomas Howard the Younger firmly wed to Edward Stafford's eldest girl.

Even so, Henry couldn't help but be cheered by the thought of how vexing the approaching war must be for the Earl of Surrey. He threw his arm around Ned's shoulder. 'You deserve this honour. Think of it as just deserts for your Grandsire John probably dying at the hands of John de Vere, or one of his soldiers, on the battlefield at Bosworth. Even if your grandsire was on the side of my father's enemies, and thereby a traitor.'

'I hadn't thought of it like that, Hal.'

'Well, now you do. And have no fear about my doubting your Howard loyalty to the crown. All I want is for you to give me your word that you'll seize control of the Narrow Sea and its sea lanes. In return, I'll give you eighteen ships, including my very finest—'

'Not "*The Mary Rose*"? I know how much she means to you.'

'Yes. I helped to design her so naturally I take great pride in her. I'll give you "*The Regent*" too.'

Ned let out a whoop of delight, and Henry couldn't help thinking that his friend's boyishness was what made them so close. Who would have guessed that nearly fourteen years separated them? If it weren't for a few fine lines on Ned's face, anyone meeting them for the first time would probably think Henry took seniority.

<<*But then I am the King of England. So it's hardly surprising I'm the equal of a man in his thirties*>>

'You know, Ned, you're the very best of the Howard men. Your father should be proud of you. Your older brother has the skills of a good soldier, but is lacking in heart. Your younger brother does not please me at all.'

Ned held up his gloved hands. 'I am indeed fortunate to be in your band of brothers. It was one of the proudest moments of my life when you invited me to join *"The King's Spears"*.'

Henry could feel tears pricking his eyes, as often happened whenever he was touched by something, or saddened by his own personal plight. 'When my father, the King, and my mother, the Queen, left me alone on this earth to govern, I was most fortunate to have not only Kate but also all of you to support me.' Henry stopped short of saying "guide me". That was down to God and Henry's own abilities, with a little interference here and there from Dame Fortune.

A tear was in danger of trickling from his right eye and he briefly debated whether or not to let it free. But, no. Far better to reassure his Howard friend and move on to other equally exciting topics. He could easily have let it loose by mentioning Ned's dead sister, Muriel, buried in the Palace grounds not a few weeks hence. But he had no desire to dwell on the disturbing topics of death or dying. Especially not on the Ides of March.

He blinked a couple of times to shoo away the no longer needed tear. 'Ned, I have every confidence that you'll prove to be an *"Amiral par excellence"*, as froward Old Louis of France and his court might say.'

Ned pulled back his shoulders, thereby reaching his full height which fortunately fell far short of Henry's own. He put one hand on his heart, and would have dropped to his knees if Henry hadn't put out a stilling hand. 'You have my word that you will not live to regret your decision.'

'Now,' said Henry, steering his friend along the path, 'I want to show you my new stables and tiltyard. I have a mind to build a banqueting hall to outdo every other in Europe. And armouries to produce suits of mail for all my soldiers. Without a doubt, I'll need forges with the best blacksmiths in the land.'

Ned let out a low whistle as they drew nearer. 'Everyone will be able to see those towers for miles around.'

Henry beamed. 'I want the towers and the tiltyard gallery to provide the biggest space for viewing.' He clapped his hands together. 'Just think of all the celebrations we'll have here.'

'Once we beat the pesky French, you mean.'

'Exactly. We'll hunt in the morning, joust in the afternoons, walk our ladies around the pretty gardens, dance with them in the evening—'

'And continue the pleasure at night?' teased Ned, his hands idly tracing the shape of a voluptuous female.

Henry let out a bark of laughter at both the gesture and the image. 'God's Nightgown! I like the sound of that. Do have a particular lady in mind?'

'Other than my own wife you mean?'

'Lady Alice has many charms—'

'But not those of the bedchamber, you want to say.'

'I'm sure she was in possession of those once upon a—'

'Twenty-five years ago mayhap,' interrupted Ned again, giving a wry smile and raising one eyebrow in question.

'I do not wish to insult your wife but as I asked you this past New Year, don't you wish to be with a younger woman who can bear you sons. Not a woman of fifty who cannot.'

Expecting one of his friend's usual jovial denials, Henry was surprised to see a solemn look on Ned's handsome face. And not even the trace of a smile.

'My father was saying something similar recently. As I explained to you before…there was someone once—'

'Who broke your heart—'

'Into so many pieces they were surely scattered to the four corners of the earth.'

'When she wed elsewhere.' Henry always prided himself on his ability to remember facts and figures, particularly where his nearest and dearest were concerned.

'And has another life now.'

'Tell me, is this woman past her childbearing years?'

'Gra— No, no, she's not.'

'Well, then, once this war is over and we're victorious, we'll deal with the matter.'

'Deal with it, Hal? I don't understand.'

'I am Henry Tudor, King of England. Soon to regain my rightful title of King of France. If I say that you and this lady, who captured your heart so long ago and enflamed you, will wed before the year is out, then not even the Pope in Rome can prevent your union.' Henry gave a little shiver from a sudden icy blast of wind, glad that the two of them had broken their fast in (an unusually) princely fashion. He drew his cloak around him, stamped his feet to ward off the cold and looked over at Ned. He was gratified to see an expression of joy and hope in his friend's eyes.

'Yes, not even the Pope in Rome can stop the King of England from getting a marriage annulled.'

The two of them had reached the stables, and were marvelling at the quality of the six destriers sent by Margaret of Austria from her home in Mechelen.

'I'm quite sure I've never seen such a powerful rump on a horse!' exclaimed Ned, standing in front of a stall containing the first black stallion. 'Has Charles seen them yet?'

His enthusiasm delighted Henry; it gave the Archduchess's gift a much greater significance. 'Brandon? No, not yet. I intend to bring him here tomorrow.'

Ned slipped off one of his gloves and reached out to stroke the horse's mane, soothing it when it arched its neck, pinned back its ears and rolled its dark eyes in trepidation. 'Steady, my fine fellow. You have no cause to be nervous. I can see you now in battle or in the lists, coiling, springing, stopping, and sprinting with your master to victory.'

'Little wonder they call a horse like this "a great horse".'

'It's a good thing they're so rare. The greatest horses should only belong to the greatest masters.' Ned turned and gave a mock bow. '"Henry the Great".'

Henry laughed; his friend's comments never failed to please him. '"*Henry the Great*"?' That has a fine ring to it. I'd certainly like to be remembered for my deeds in battle and on the field.'

'Not to mention being the Father of your people.'

Henry tugged at a lock of russet hair that had fallen into his eyes. 'I'm not sure those venerable days have come quite yet. Maybe one day when Kate and I are old, and have strands of winter frost threaded through our hair as we sit joyfully upon our thrones, our sons and daughters nearby, and our grandchildren playing at our feet.'

'I can see the image all too clearly, as if it were a painting on the wall of the great hall in the Palace of Westminster.'

That was exactly why Henry liked Ned and Charles Brandon so much; they made him feel so good about himself: as if his dreams weren't dreams at all…but reality waiting to happen.'

'Now, Ned, what do you say to taking this fine chap here, and his noble cousin next to him, out for a gallop across the common before I have to attend an audience with the Burgundian Ambassador at Eltham. Why not come and dine with us there. How does that sound?'

'Like music to my rider's ears. I'd say the dawn mist has cleared enough for us by now. Race you to the Great Oak....'

❧

'God's Blood, Ned! I think you might have beaten me by a whisker.'

'Never,' panted Henry's friend. 'You won fair and square. My horse would tell you as much if he could talk.'

The two of them had dismounted and were standing beneath the ancient oak tree, said to date back four hundred years. Clutching his side to rid himself of a bothersome stitch caused by riding in the freezing cold, Henry decided he could afford to be magnanimous. After all, he was soon to be a General leading his army into France. 'No, I insist you take the honours this time. But don't think I'll let you take them across Blackheath Common.'

Ned stretched his arms above his head. 'Fair enough. Let's just hope there are no robbers lying in wait there.'

'If I can take on the Pope in Rome, I don't think a couple of dog-hearted thieves are going to stand in my way of a hearty meal at Eltham. Perhaps it's for the best we can't hunt a hart or two until my birthday in June. Or I'd be tempted to stay. The park always gives us such tasty morsels for our supper.'

'You might not be here for your birthday. You might be in France.'

Henry puffed out his chest. 'You're right. Of course I will. I mean, *we* will.'

Next to him, Ned cleared his throat. 'Hal, there's something I've been meaning to discuss with you for several months and now seems as good a time as ever.'

'That sounds grave. Are you trying to put me off my stride for our next race.'

Ned burst out laughing. 'As if I would do that. That's far more Will Compton's style than mine. But I have wanted to talk to you.'

'So…what is it?'

Ned took a deep breath. 'If anything should befall me, I'd like you and Charles to see to the upbringing of my two bastard sons.'

'By the Mass, Ned, I won't hear of such tal—'

Ned held up a gloved hand. 'But…if by some unlucky chance, I don't make it, I want to go to my grave knowing they're taken care of.' Henry saw tears in his eyes. 'I can't think of two nobler, better men to guide them through life than you and Brandon.'

However much he baulked at the idea of losing his dear friends, Henry knew that war was no laughing matter. Look at Tom Knyvett. One moment he'd been riding in the lists in the full vigour of his manhood, and the next he was merely a name scrawled in black ink, on a piece of parchment, travelling back on a ship over the Narrow Sea.

Henry took a deep breath. 'Very well. Although it pains me to think upon it, you have my word that your sons would be cared for as if they were of our own blood. But what of your father? Wouldn't he mind that he'd been overlooked for the task?'

Ned shook his head. 'I have no need to tell you that my father has more than enough sons to look after…and probably more to follow.'

'True. True. But while we're on the subject of sons, I want you to promise me that once we've emerged victorious from this war, you'll seek out your past love and have a boy of your own with her.'

Ned put his hand to his heart. 'I promise that once this war is over and I've avenged Tom Knyvett's death, I will seek her out and we'll have a boy of our own. It would be my heart's desire.'

TRISTAN

Chapter Fifteen

The same day. Ardres Castle.

Wake up, slug-a-bed! The English navy won't wait for us.'
Jean rolled over, blinked once or twice and let out a long yawn of
protest. In the grey light of dawn, my closest friend on earth bore
no resemblance whatsoever to a future Cardinal of the Church; instead, with his
long flowing locks and deceptively innocent expression, he looked every bit an
angel fallen from the heavenly realms. Or an imp of Satan. Part of the reason
for Jean's manifestly dissolute appearance was an excess of his host, my
father's, best (pilfered) Gascon wine while playing Primero and throwing dice
long into the night with several of the young local lords. Only Nicolas hadn't
remained until the end; he stormed out of the great hall in a currish humour
when Jean beat him at cards, muttering something darkly about a perfidious
sleight of hand. To be fair, with Jean anything was possible. The only reason
Nicolas hadn't reacted more vigorously was because he and I were both still
under Father's watchful eye, following our Twelfth Night brawl.

"Heureux au jeu, malheureux en amour!" Jean had said mockingly as he
showed my arch enemy a fistful of grinning aces, while holding out his other
hand for payment. He winked at me when Nicolas - in a fit of ill-temper - flung
a handful of *sous* onto the table. *"Nicolas, you could be a soupçon more
gracious about my victory knowing I've beaten you fair and square. Fortunate
at cards, unfortunate in love. As a free man, you are able to try your luck at
love."* He made a big show of scooping up his winnings, even placing one of
the coins between his even teeth as if to check it was genuine. That was one
thing about Jean: he never disappointed. And nor did he now. He closed his fist

124

tightly and grinned at Nicolas. "*As a man whose future lies with God, an occasional appearance at the card table is all I can hope for.*"

A scowling Nicolas ignored Jean's jibe, bade a swift farewell to the others gathered around the table, grabbed his cloak and left.

That had been a mere few hours ago; there was no conspiratorial wink from my bleary-eyed friend now. '*Ventre Saint-Gris*, Tristan!' he growled. 'What infernal hour of the morning do you call this?'

'It must be five because the bells for Lauds just rang out over at Anderne Abbey. If we don't go immediately we risk being seen.'

Although Jean gave a further groan of protest, I knew he was as eager to go 'English hunting' as I was. We'd been planning this two-day excursion for the best part of a fortnight. I was dismayed to see sleep threatening to overtake him once more.

'*Je t'implore*,' he yawned, closing his bloodshot eyes and turning over, 'give me a few moments longer.'

Hearing a servant or two beginning to stir down below, I lifted my foot and gave him a comradely kick of encouragement.

'*Aie*! That hurt!' he complained, rubbing his right thigh. 'Oh, very well, you base-court dragonslayer. Go down and fetch the food and drink from the kitchens as planned. I'll meet you by the gatehouse.'

'Hurry, then. Or I'll go without you.'

We both knew this to be a falsehood but I said it anyway. I was glad Father had allowed Jean to stay on after Twelfth Night - although I think Mother had far more to do with it than she let on, persuading him that Jean de Lorraine, as a member of the powerful Guise family, younger brother to Duke Antoine of Lorraine (and already Bishop of Metz), was a positive influence on me. In truth, she and I both knew that Jean and I were as bad as each other, but she didn't object because our escapades were fairly harmless. <<*Until now*>>

❧

As I tiptoed down the backstairs from Jean's bedchamber in the direction of the kitchens, guiding myself with a sputtering candle in the half-light, using all the stealth of a Castle cat, I knew in my heart that my mother wouldn't approve of what we were about to do. 'Foolish' and 'dangerous' were just two of the words she might use. As for Father—

One of the actual Castle cats returning from its nightly prowl with a sizeable rat between its teeth, let out a yowl as I accidentally knocked against it on the last few stone steps. It jumped up as if scalded by a pan of boiling water, dropped the dead rat and proceeded to knock over a bucket at the entrance to the kitchen. The ensuing clatter and feline hisses of protest were loud enough to wake the entire Castle. I held my breath and stood stock still for a moment or two. From inside the great hall nearby, a flurry of stray snores followed the disturbance as if the servants had been momentarily stirred from their slumber.

<<*Luckily they're all too bone tired to come and discover the Count's younger son purloining cheese and rolls from the home of his own parents. Like a wastrel on the run from the law*>>

It couldn't be helped, I thought, as I grabbed a couple of leather flasks and filled them with small beer. I was just in time because I suddenly heard heavy footsteps approaching along the corridor outside. I knew they were headed in the direction of the small *galopins* sprawled in a heap in front of the dying embers in the big fireplace, drifting in and out of jarring dreams of stirring the pot or turning the spit until their poor wrists ached. Giving them a pitying glance, I let myself out of the far door and slipped into the frozen arms of a most unwelcoming March dawn. I was glad I was wearing my warmest cloak made of felt and lined with black cloth, as well as my most comfortable soft buff leather boots. I pushed my beaver hat firmly on my head and set off to the agreed meeting place. *En route* for perhaps the most important excursion of my fifteen years.

Jean and I had decided it was up to us to find out what the English navy was doing in the Narrow Sea, off the nearby coast.

"But isn't it like asking you to choose between your right hand and the left...being half-English yourself?" he asked, giving me a quizzical look.

"Not at all. If it were the other way round, and I were standing in the harbour in Dover, I'd be doing exactly the same."

"Suit yourself," Jean replied, giving a shrug of his shoulders. It was perfectly plain that our friendship meant far more to him than which side I was on in the approaching war between France and England. He and I were always going to be on the same side because of the terrible fate our fathers had decided upon at our births: to snuff out our manhood and enclose us in dusty cells within a monastery, until our will to lead our lives as red-blooded knights had ebbed away.

<<*Well, I won't let Father destroy my life! I was born to fight. And have as much right as Gilles and Nicolas. More than Nicolas because he isn't even a true-born son*>>

Naturally that one had been striding around the Castle, acting as though the outcome of the war was wholly dependent upon his participation. My one consolation was that I had Jean by my side who always gave Nicolas back as good as he gave. I was pleased Nicolas had been unfairly robbed of his *sous* last night.

As I waited for Jean, shivering beneath the arches of the gatehouse, I thought about political events hurtling themselves towards us in a fair imitation of a runaway horse I'd seen a couple of days before, in full gallop across the fields of Picardy.

Rumours had begun to circulate since before Christmas that the young Tudor King had warmongering designs on his elderly Valois neighbour. Even though, as Jean had said, I was half-English, I still understood the hardship England had caused France. People hadn't yet come to terms with the legacy of the previous century: during the first fifty years, the English had come and spilt the blood of innocent people, or turned them into starving beggars. My French grandsire, the former Comte d'Ardres, always used to talk about the horror of the year 1420 (just after a treaty had been signed at Troyes, handing over the French throne to the victorious fifth Henry of England and his heirs). I could still recall his stories.

"It was five years before I came into this world, Tristan. My father told me that a combination of wet weather and an extremely cold winter added to people's hardship. Rotting grapes produced rotten wine four times more expensive than usual. It wasn't uncommon for my parents to walk around Paris to be met by the gruesome sight of dozens of dead children piled up in the streets, having perished from lack of food and the cold. My mother said she'd never forget it as long as she lived. However much their families wanted to help them, mon garçon, no one had any bread, corn, firewood or charcoal. Cabbages and turnips could not sustain a body for long and, by Christmas, bread was so expensive that even if you got to the baker's at dawn, you probably wouldn't have the eight blancs to pay for what was usually four for a loaf.

"I know your own dear mother is English but matters didn't improve much after her people left us. There was a struggle to the death between the Crown

and certain nobles motivated by ambition and greed. Strife with Burgundy only exacerbated these problems."

Nearly a hundred years had passed, but it seemed that nothing much had changed, I reflected. Just after Twelfth Night, word began to spread that the new English King intended to invade France with sixty thousand men by Easter.

"*With a royal army...and with fire and sword*," he'd boasted to his Parliament.

That was when Jean and I had come up with the idea of making a secret trip to Cap Gris-Nez, near Audinghen, which was officially on English soil within the Pale of Calais. We knew it would take us the best part of a day to reach it on horseback, but once there we were hoping it would be worth the trouble. The distinctive grey sandstone cliffs of the Cape were well-known to be the best vantage point for the sea below and - at a mere twenty miles - (as many as separated Ardres and Cap Gris-Nez) this was the shortest distance between England and France. I'd been there a couple of times on a clear day with Father, Gilles, and Nicolas. We'd even been able to see the White Cliffs of Dover. But what interested Jean and me the most was the increasing number of ships that (according to visitors to the Castle) kept appearing in the waters; whereas once they'd been mostly fishing trawlers innocently going about their business, now they were much larger vessels...and their purpose clearly far more sinister—

'I hope this isn't a wasted journey,' grumbled Jean as he finally stumbled towards the gatehouse arch - suitably clad for the trip - a knapsack on his back. His blue eyes were watering from the bitter wind, and he was shaking his hands to try and keep them warm while he reached inside his cloak for his gloves.

'You took your time,' I parried back.

Jean grinned, showing a dimple in his right cheek. '*Eh bien alors*, I was hiding from a couple of the Castle maids.'

'What about what you told Nicolas last night?'

My friend adjusted his hat of dark brown sable to cover his ears. 'About being unlucky in love? From what I've heard, Nicolas is far luckier in love than cards.'

'When he's not up against a card sharp like you, you mean?

The Guise eyes sparkled with feigned hurt. '*Moi*? A scoundrel. *Jamais.*'

'Come on, enough about card games, even if you did manage to separate Nicolas from his money. To the stables!'

It was as if the horses could sense they were going on an adventure worthy of their noble breed. I was tempted to take Nicolas's magnificent black stallion from the adjoining stall. The horse was his pride and joy but after what had happened on Twelfth Night, I was a little more circumspect. Besides, Nicolas would be sure to raise a hue and cry if he discovered his precious beast missing for a second time. An image of an incensed Nicolas leaning forward in the saddle, spurring on his horse - hellbent on hunting me down - didn't exactly fill me with delight. Especially when it was accompanied by an image of my father right next to him, his body tensed like a serpent about to strike, his mouth fixed in a thin line of fury. Giving a sigh, I turned back to stroke the mane of my own horse, Tredavoe.

'You're going to get "*an imaginary pebble lodged in your hoof*", my fine friend,' I whispered to him, 'to provide us with an alibi for our absence tonight and tomorrow.' Then I ushered him out of the stall, mounted him in one easy movement and led him out of the stables.

With Jean next to me, we quickly trotted through a second archway and were just about to take off down the hill and make for the fields beyond the Castle, when something made me stop. It was an unexpected glint of gold out of the corner of my right eye. I suddenly had the uncomfortable feeling we were being watched.

'Wait a moment,' I said to Jean, handing him the reins of my destrier and jumping down.

There it was again. Gold. And red. In that moment, I knew exactly what I'd seen. Racing across the courtyard, I threw myself at the corner of the building and stretched out my left arm.

'Got you, you earth-vexing little harpy!' I cried, as with one tug I dragged a protesting Valentine de Fleury out into the dawn light.

Behind me, I could hear Jean laughing. '*Palsambleu*, Tristan! Leave the brat and let's go.'

But I wasn't about to let her off the hook that easily. Gripping her tightly by the arm, I jerked her towards me, not caring if I was a little rough with her. '*Nom d'un petit bonhomme*! What do you think you're doing out at this ungodly hour? Spying on us like one of the goblins on the roof of Notre Dame de Grâce.' I knew she would have a saucy retort; this was no normal child on the verge of tears, terrified at being caught red-handed by the Governor of Picardy's son. Twisting away from my grip, she gave an exaggerated toss of her golden ringlets, her very pale blue eyes flashing fire. 'I'm not a goblin!' she said with great feeling, poking a small finger at me for good measure. 'I asked Pierre if I could come with him to the Castle on an errand.'

'"*Asked*" him? More like *forced* him to bring you, you mean, you little tyrant.' I could well imagine the exchange between Valentine and the poor servant.

This set Jean off laughing again. 'Come on, Tristan, or it'll be too late. Bribe her silence with a doll or something. Anything.'

I glared at my prey. I'd lost count of the number of the times I'd been forced to do the unruly little harpy's bidding because she'd caught me in the middle of some misdemeanour. It was quite uncanny how she did this, almost as if she had an inbuilt knowledge of all my movements. A couple of months ago, she'd caught me and a few of my friends drinking Father's best Beaune behind the stables; recently she'd appeared from nowhere as I was about to go riding on his favourite horse. The time before that, I'd been chasing a giggling kitchen maid around the lake— The list went on and on, and knowing that she was unlike other little girls made me completely lose patience with her. She probably didn't even have a favourite toy I could hide in retaliation. Still, I had to do something.

'*Nom de Dieu*, Valentine! Go and find Pierre.' I decided to use Jean's suggestion. 'And then go home and play with your tickle-brained dolls.' I certainly wasn't going to give her one as a reward for her mischief. 'And if you tell anyone you've seen us, I'll…I'll—'

She fixed me with those extraordinary eyes of hers that surely belonged to the sky in the Italian paintings in our great hall. The ones that all seemed to have enormous downy clouds acting as a resting place for various winged seraphims and cherubs. To my frustration, my very own little demon (who rightly belonged in a nightmare of dark sprites and images of hell) wriggled out of my grasp and ran off, shouting over her shoulder.

'I warned you you'd better be good, Tristan d'Ardres!'

Relieved to see Pierre mounting his horse in the distance while looking around for Valentine, I became aware of the sound of slow clapping from behind. '*Bien joué, ma petite,*' Jean called after Valentine's retreating figure before shaking his head at me. '*Comme c'était amusant* to see you bested, my friend.'

Scowling at him, I stomped back to my waiting horse and jumped on, uncomfortably aware that he was right.

<<I've just let a nine-year-old child - and a girl at that - get the better of me>>

Thankfully, after we'd left Ardres Castle far behind, the rest of the journey was far less eventful. When we stopped to share some bread and cheese, Jean took a swig of the small beer and reminded me that today was the Ides of March.

'Perhaps not the most auspicious days to choose for an adventure such as this.'

I shrugged. 'Let's hope you're not planning the same fate for me as Brutus did for Caesar.'

'It depends how many English ships you manage to find for me.'

For months now, the fleets of the English and French had been a topic of conversation at the Castle, and in Calais, whenever Father and I visited our friends, the Baynhams. Or when, as Governor of Picardy, Father found himself on urgent business with Gilbert Talbot, the Deputy Governor of Calais. I'd heard so many comments from both sides. The French were fiercely proud of their navy: "*The stomachs of those base English sailors will churn more than the waves of the Narrow Sea at the sight of our Breton vessels. Not to mention when the scurvy knaves catch sight of our allies, the Danes and the Scots.*" Or: "*Pardieu! I'd like to see their common-kissing faces when they meet Prégent de Bidoux. Not for nothing is he known as the scourge of La Manche. 'Prester John', the English and Scots call him.*"

The English strolling up and down Lantern Gate Street in the centre of Calais were equally cocksure: *"King Henry won't let us down. Our valiant monarch of the seas. They say he's given Edward Howard twenty-four ships and nearly seven thousand soldiers and sailors."*

Warmed by the thought of Sir Edward Howard, still high on his pedestal in the furthermost reaches of my mind, I stood up abruptly, placed my flask back in the knapsack and prepared to re-mount my horse. Swinging myself up into the saddle, I looked at Jean. 'Come on, you worthless hugger-mugger. Finding ships will have to wait for the morning. By the time we reach Audinghen, darkness will have fallen.'

I was right about that. It was almost pitch black when (saddle-sore and starving) we reached the small village, and made our way to the aptly named *'Ship and Anchor'* where I'd stayed once before.

'Now remember,' I murmured to Jean after we'd handed the reins of our horses to two eager young urchins waiting to tether them to the railings, 'we're English. Keep that folly-fallen Guise mouth of yours closed for once. Let me do all the talking. You're my younger brother who lost your wits when you nearly drowned off Boulogne.' I smirked at Jean's thunderous expression, knowing he had no choice but to agree. With relations between England and France so poor at the moment, the young Bishop of Metz would not be given a warm welcome by a small English tavern in the Pale of Calais, about to go to war with France.

He opened his appropriately named Guise mouth to object but quickly closed it again and followed me inside.

ↄ৴

'We must do this again more often,' I said to my fuming companion as we sat inside the smoky interior, forcing down a rather greasy mutton stew that was an unpleasant grey colour. A strong wind had suddenly sprung up outside, blowing gusts of black smoke down the chimney that made our eyes water and caused us to choke.

'Poor lad,' said Mary, the owner's wife, when I explained about Jean's affliction. How he'd been rendered speechless and had any wise thoughts stripped from his mind after his terrible ordeal. 'Such a beautiful face,' she said, shaking her head. 'All the milkmaids around here would drop their churns in an instant if he came a-calling. With those blue eyes of his, so bright they remind me of the Holy Virgin's robe in the window of the Church of Saint Nicholas in Calais.' She crossed herself several times. I did the same and pulled what I hoped was a suitably mournful expression.

Not daring to look at Jean after this comment about virgins (which I knew for certain he was not), I instead gave him a warning reminder with my foot beneath the table. However, I nearly let the side down (and had to stifle a treacherous peal of laughter) when he obliged by turning his head to one side, giving our hapless hostess a drooling smile. His pitiful action seemed to decide something for her.

'Your supper is on Walter and me, my lads,' she spluttered, lifting up her grimy apron to dab at her eyes.

Almost as if he understood her kindness and was overwhelmed by it, Jean slumped forward, head on table, narrowly missing the evil mutton kitchen slops masquerading as stew. Nearly gagging at the foul stench, I couldn't help thinking longingly of the fare we would have been served back at the Castle. But I was also very appreciative of the kindness of these humble village folk.

Mary gave a loud sniff. 'And your lodgings too.' She looked at me with reddened eyes. 'You, my lad, are a saint and will be rewarded in heaven for your pains. The way you look after your beloved brother as if he were a holy bishop on God's good earth.'

<<If only she knew>> Watching her disappear back into the kitchen, probably to weep profusely at Jean's cruel fate as she re-told it to the servants within, I decided enough was enough.

I grabbed Jean by the elbow. 'Come on, you scurvy-valiant fraud! You've just done these good people out of any profit this evening. To bed with you.'

It was a stormy night; a howling wind rattled the shutters for most of it, and made me curl up into a ball under a thin coarse blanket I prayed was not also home to a thousand fleas. The moment the first chinks of light entered our meagre chamber above the tavern, I leant down and tugged at a lock of Jean's flaxen hair as he dozed below me in the truckle bed Mary and a couple of servants had hastily rolled into our chamber.

"*Your brother deserves his comfort,*" she said. "*And his own bed. He has precious else to be thankful for.*"

'Come on, wake up,' I urged him. 'We have ships to find.'

I thanked the stars that the thought of this spurred Jean onto to greater action than the previous morning and (leaving behind a few *sous* for our gracious landlady, enough to show our appreciation, but not so much as to arouse her suspicions) in no time we found ourselves on the cliffs of Cap Gris-Nez, staring out at a miraculously clear sea, and even more miraculously, the distant cliffs of Dover gleaming pearly white in the dawn light.

'We have that clapper-clawed gale to thank for this,' said Jean, so relieved to have been given back his voice that he'd hardly paused to take breath since we retrieved our horses.

I could see the local fishing vessels going about their daily tasks, but behind them on the horizon was a flotilla of unidentified ships exactly as we'd heard described. Suddenly, an image of a dark-haired nobleman came rushing into my head again. A dare-devil, a worthy buccaneer of the seas, the most accomplished Vice-Admiral Henry Tudor could ever wish fo—

'I wonder if that hero of yours is on one of those ships. The one you never stop talking about. What's his name? Howard.'

I was so startled to find that my 'witless' little brother had somehow wormed his way into my brain that it was my turn to be struck dumb. With the mention of Edward Howard, I found myself back at the table in the great hall of Zennor Castle, raising a spoon of pea pottage to my lips, my cousin, Cecy, by my side....

CECILY

Chapter Sixteen

The same day. Zennor Castle, Cornwall.

I knew he'd come! I knew he'd come!' I shrieked, tearing down the stone stairs from my bedchamber two at a time, the long sleeves of my new midnight blue velvet gown: a pair of angel's wings aiding my descent. In my haste to reach my father, I'd left my long-suffering nursemaid, Gabrielle, tortoiseshell hairbrush in hand, calling after me in vain as she waited to finish tidying my hair and place it a net.

"It's not decent for a young lady to go gallivanting around half of Cornwall with her hair flying around her face like a baseborn hoyden," she'd sniffed yesterday. It was easy for her to say; she always managed to look perfectly turned out. Mother told me it was because Gabrielle was French.

"Frenchwomen are always the prettiest in the room, wearing the prettiest dresses."

With her long shining hair the colour of an autumn chestnut, and her matching eyes, my nursemaid was no exception.

'*Doucement*! *Doucement*, Demoiselle Cecily! *Attends-moi*,' she was calling now.

Defiant in victory, I nevertheless threw back an intentionally placatory rejoinder over my shoulder: '*Je m'excuse, Gabrielle. Mais c'est mon anniversaire*!'

<<*I knew Father wouldn't miss my twelfth birthday*>>

Even though my name day was on the twenty-second day of November (and we celebrated that too), my parents had been so thrilled to have a living breathing baby at last that they decided both that and my day of birth should be a cause for great celebration in the Castle.

'I have news,' said my father, striding into the great hall and throwing off his cloak and riding gloves. He walked over to the fireplace and began rubbing his hands together to get warm. 'But first I need a drink and some food.'

I threw my arms around him and he kissed the top of my head. 'I'll go and tell them in the kitchens right away,' I said.

'Good girl. And then you and your mother shall hear all.'

Giving a squeal of excitement, I ran off in the direction of the kitchens. I loved surprises; the last one had been a new puppy so I couldn't wait to see what this one was. Father had been away for the past two weeks, staying with the Bullen family at Hever, and I was eager to hear news of Nan, Mary and the boys.

However, the moment I came flying back into the great hall, I could see by the troubled expression clouding my mother's face that all was not well. Everything looked as it had when I left earlier: warm light was still flooding through the coloured glass bearing the Tredavoe coat-of-arms in the oriel window above; the ornate salt cellar which divided the raised dais where our family and friends sat (from the rest of the hall below), was still in pride of place; every shield, angel, and mythical beast was in their correct position on the hammerbeam roof. But something was wrong. Very wrong....

'*The Burgundian Netherlands*! You want me to leave here and go and live in the Burgundian Netherlands?' The words stuck in my throat like crumbs from a three-day-old manchet.

My father gave an uncertain smile. 'Yes, my dove. With Nan Bullen. To the celebrated court of the Archduchess Margaret of Austria. At Mechelen. It will be an extraordinary opportunity for the pair of you.'

Tears were blurring my vision as I wildly looked around the hall as if in search of someone or something to help me reject this hateful plan. The portrait of my mother (looking radiant on the day of her wedding) hanging above the enormous fireplace gave no pleasure today, not if I was to be snatched away from her. I looked up at the minstrels' gallery, half-hoping a row of gaily clad knights would appear both to pledge their allegiance to me, and save me from this calamitous turn of affairs. But the gallery remained empty. As empty and drained of hope as my heart. Everything in the great hall was so familiar and beloved: the ornate carved panelling, the chestnut roof above, the unusually tall windows that let in light all year round, the German clock (a wedding present from my Pendeen grandparents), the Tredavoe heraldic arm—

'Cecily, I said it would be an extraordinary opportunity for you.'

Being in no mood to be placated, I whipped my head round back to face my by now grim-faced father. 'You mean "an *extraordinary opportunity*" for Nan's father.'

Being disrespectful to him like this was uncharted territory, and was making my head spin. However, I knew I had to at least try and change his mind.

'To be fair,' he said, ''Tis true the idea might have been Thomas's in the first place. But it's his father-in-law who has managed to push it through.' Distracted, he motioned for two servants who'd appeared with a platter of tasty looking pies and fruit, to set it down on the long table and leave.

Standing over by the window gazing out to sea, Mother turned to stare at him, her crimson and cream skirts making a loud swishing noise. She was extremely pale and there was a fierce expression in her blue eyes. 'The Earl of Surrey? Thomas Howard. William, why on earth would such an important man take an interest in our Cecy? He's only met her twice.'

Clearing his throat several times as he always did in moments of uncertainty or dismay, Father gave an exaggerated shrug. 'I honestly don't know. It seems our daughter made an impression on him over on Saint Michael's Mount at the wedding. And again in London last month. He wants her as a companion for his granddaughter and was the one who obtained the King's approval.'

'That ill-begotten Twelfth Night travesty of a wedding has brought all of us nought but misery!' burst out my distraught mother. 'I thought it was only poor little Lizzie Stafford and Ralph Neville who must suffer. But now it's us too. Do you think the King is punishing us by taking our daughter?'

Seeing that my mother was close to tears, my father walked over and pulled her to him. 'Hush now, my love. I am sure the Howards didn't tell King Henry where the wedding took place. It would have looked bad for them too. Coming so far afield from the court to conduct a clandestine wedding.'

'What about the threat of war? How can the girls possibly go across the Narrow Sea at a time like this?'

I felt a surge of hope. 'Yes, Father, you've done nothing else but talk of war for months.' I pressed home my point, wanting to make him relent. 'I'm sure you don't want to put me in danger.'

I immediately felt guilty for being responsible for a look of abject pain on his face.

'Of course I don't!' He looked at my mother. 'Alys, Tom Bullen told me the King has given his personal assurance for a safe passage for the two girls. After all, Margaret of Austria is a trusted ally. King Henry sees this as a way of forging an even closer alliance in the eyes of the world. And equally a way of showing the French where we send the girls of our noblest families.'

'I'd rather see them go to your sister in France than to a woman I've never met and know next to nothing about.'

My father's voice was both gentle and the quietest I'd ever heard it. 'I couldn't agree more. Grace would take the greatest care of them. And they would improve their French…not that Cecy needs to. The problem is that Thomas Howard has got the King's approval for this and….'

Hearing my father's words trail off into thin air was akin to the final nail being hammered into my coffin of despair, sealing my fate. I was finding it difficult to breathe and tears were coursing freely down my cheeks. 'I don't want to go! Please don't make me go. I don't want to leave Cornwall. Or you and Mother.'

Looking deeply shaken, my mother left my father, crossed the floor and took me in her arms. She clearly felt as helpless as I did. Silent sobs were making her body shake as she held me tightly. As for me, I could feel my own tears drenching her bodice.

I glanced up at my father. There was a look of sadness on his face as if he'd never truly believed in this "*extraordinary opportunity*" either. 'You will be *filles d'honneur* to the Archduchess,' he said eventually, in a flat voice. 'Believe me, the competition for such places is fierce. When Tom Bullen mentioned it to me at Christmas, I thought no more about it, thinking it was but a whimsical idea of the day. I'm not quite sure how he managed to get not one but *two* places. My guess again is that Thomas Howard was the one behind all of it.' He gave a small cough as if the words he was about to utter needed a little help to leave his lips. 'We should be very grateful.'

There was no conviction whatsoever in this last statement. There was also rather a large gap between thinking something exciting was going to happen and it actually taking place. Unlike Thomas Bullen (who'd obviously been plotting the whole thing on Christmas Day when he sent me away from the high table), I knew my father was devoted to his only child. Seeing my tears and my mother's distress, the bright promise with which he'd entered the great hall vanished into thin air in the manner of a hearty blaze in the fireplace that suddenly dies down and splutters into a few faint sparks…and then nothingness. Even though I'd warmed to Thomas Howard during that bracing sled ride, I now hated him with all my being. I almost wished I'd never met my best friend if it had brought me to this. Standing here in our great hall facing my father, any treasured memories of the day on the frozen Thames had turned to slush.

'I want to stay in Zennor Castle forever,' I said, but more brokenly…almost in a whisper. 'I love it here. I love being with you and Mother.'

'I have said yes to Tom now,' my father said, his voice suspiciously thick, as if he had a sudden urge to blow his nose. 'He's relying on us. We cannot let him down. He's answerable to both the Howards and the King.'

I couldn't bear it a moment longer. Ignoring the pleas of my mother to stay, I rushed from the great hall. I almost flew out of the main entrance, through the courtyard, along the drawbridge, following a rocky trail for some distance until I came to the brown hillocks beyond. In the spring and summer they were covered with greenery but today they looked ugly and bare. I ran and ran until I came to the only place I knew would bring me comfort.

To others, this pile of stones leaning against each other, with a large one on top, was merely an ancient burial chamber. But to me, Zennor Quoit was a place of magic and mystery. People said any stone taken from it would bring bad luck, and there were tales of how stones had been known to find their way back here in the middle of the night.

I stood poised on the flat stone, seagulls circling in the sky above me, their harsh guttural cries seeming to mirror my own inner ones of anguish.

Looking over in the direction of the sea, I tried to draw upon the invisible forces around me, as well as my own little army of fairies, elves and mermaids to come to my rescue.

'Please help me,' I whispered to the air, relieved that Gabrielle hadn't yet made an appearance to take me back home. She was good like that. 'Make Father change his mind. Even if it means losing the favour of King Henry.'

The bright-haired young man with the hearty laugh came into my head with all the force of a comet streaking through the night skies. 'Tell him anything. That I'm too weak, too sick, too feeble-minded to go. And let that old man, Thomas Howard, suddenly be struck dumb.' I didn't dare wish him anything more terrible than losing his voice, for fear of offending God. 'Let him keep his ambition for his granddaughters, not me. I'm nothing to him.'

I turned to face the sea. 'You can help me too,' I called out to the water sprites frolicking in the distant waves, beyond the hills in front of me.

As if in answer, a breeze sprang up out of nowhere, gladdening my heart and making me dare to hope that one day very soon I wouldn't be standing on a boat on those exact same waves, being carried away into the unknown....

'I don't care who wants me to go,' I called out, as fierce as the commander of any army. 'Thomas Howard. The entire Howard dynasty. Or the King of England himself. I'm *not* going!'

HOUSE OF STEWART

Chapter Seventeen

March 27, 1513. Easter Sunday. Stirling Castle, Scotland.

James, how many times can you use the same excuse about being busy with your guns and gunpowder? Dr West is growing impatient. You've kept him waiting for days now.'

'Och, hinny, not even the King of Scotland can help it if it's Holy Week, and he's obliged to spend time with holy friars rather than men of politics.'

Maggie put one hand lightly on his arm, the length of ermine on her sleeve brushing against his skin, causing him to smile inwardly at the outrageous cost of such a gesture. 'Husband, no one knows better than me how seriously you take your duty to God. But my brother's man is not going to go away. You know that as well as I.'

'That I do. Verra well. I'll have Forman send word that I'll receive him tomorrow.' He laughed. 'Though my fine Bishop of Moray hasna yet forgiven your brother for refusing him safe passage through his kingdom, to wrestle a Cardinal's hat from the Pope in Rome.'

'Oh, James, sometimes I worry you don't take things seriously enough. My brother means war. That's why he's asked me to prevent you from acting against him while he's absent in France.'

He looked up at the hammerbeam roof above their heads, admiring the fine Scottish carpentry. 'Aye. But ye and I also ken that your fine younger brother hasna handed over your legacy yet.'

Nothing was more guaranteed to rouse his avaricious Tudor wife to anger than the memory of the jewels and plate, bequeathed to her by her dead brother, Arthur, and her grandam, Margaret, but still in the grasping paws of her rabble-rousing brother, Henry. Sometimes, when she looked at the sparkling diamonds and rubies in golden caskets brought to her to peruse (or luxury goods such as the ermine she was wearing, so eye-wateringly expensive that the Scottish lion in the centre of the golden coins given in exchange, had roared extra loudly in protest), she reminded him of a magpie; her blue eyes would turn so dark they almost became black and she had a habit of licking her lips when aroused in this way. She did the same thing naked in his arms in the royal bedchamber.

'What will you tell West?' she asked him now, far more battle-light in her eyes than previously. That's what he needed: his Queen by his side, their son, James, in her arms. There had been no sign of another bairn in her womb since the death of their wee princess back in November. Which was for the best in the circumstances. That one had come much too quickly after the birth of his son and heir in April. But it couldna be helped. As Janet Kennedy had recently reminded him, he needed sons. Strong lads, with the brawn, hearts and souls of the Stewarts, as well as the brains, swagger, and good looks of the Tudors. He could see them now in the courtyard below, racing around using their fists to make a point until scolded by their nursemaid that using words to smite a foe was more effective than raining blows on their head.

Every king in Christendom needed a son and heir. Maggie's brother, Henry, didna have one. Louis of France didna have one with his second wi—

'Will you speak to West of Pope Julius's plan to excommunicate you?'

'Aye, I most certainly will. And inform him that I have every intention of sending my man, Forman, to the new Medici Pope, Leo. I want him to tear up any incriminating evidence against me the other auld fool might have left behind on his death bed.'

Maggie walked over to the large bay windows through which he could see the Elphinstone Tower beyond. He was glad his haughty Tudor wife was housed in a castle earning it the envy of half of Europe. And certainly one worthy of her dead father's palace at Eltham.

She turned back to him. 'But what if the new Pope refuses?'

James shrugged. 'Then I'll take my chance with the French Admiral, Prester John.'

A little frown puckered her brow; he knew from experience that these Tudors were not best known for either their humour, or their willingness to be teased. 'I hope you won't jest like that with Nicholas West. I fear he'll be as little amused as Harry would be.'

'My English rose, ye need to have a little more faith in me. My spies in Edinburgh gave West a wee dram or two too many of our verra own *aqua vitae* in *'The World's End'* tavern by the city gates, on Wednesday night. They wormed it out of him that he's planning to offer me a thousand marks to compensate me for all the plunder the English have taken in border raids. As well as persuade what he clearly considers to be my sorry hide that peace with your brother is worth a plume-plucked bribe like that.'

'I do have faith in you, James. I imagine that West has been sent up here with all kinds of misleading messages from Harry.'

'Then I'll be ready for every last shrill-gorged one of them.' He lifted her hand to his lips and kissed her fingers, one by one. 'Dinna fear, I'll be asking for what's owed to ye. And it willna depend on me behaving like some unwilling calf being towed by its scrawny neck to the market place in Berwick, by your rump-fed brother. He's the one seeking war with me, not the other way round.'

'Berwick. I know that's still a thorn in your side.'

'Thistle, more like. Thirteen times has it passed back and forth betwixt England and Scotland, as if we were playing a game of *"La grosse boule"*.'

'You can't blame yourself. Your father brought it upon himself by alienating so many of his lords. Making it easy for Grandsire Edward to send up troops and take it.'

'Aye, it was lost on my father's watch. I was but a wee bairn of five, but I can still recall the loss. I swear, my sweet Maggie, upon my sainted mother's life, and upon every hogshead of fine wine and ale in my cellars below, that I willna rest until I win back those lost two and a half miles, gobbled up by that sheep-biting hell-hole, Northumberland.'

Maggie grimaced. 'Hold your nerve. I'm sure Harry has asked West to return with written proof that you intend to keep the peace while he sails off across the Narrow Sea to do the exact opposite.'

'Then he'll have a verra long wait. I see relations between England and France as a tricky game of chess: both looking for support from the player off the board.'

'Oh, I'm sure you have an excellent chance of winning, my lord King. I've rarely heard tell of a better chess player than you.'

James caught hold of Maggie's wrist and pulled her to his chest. He put one hand under her chin and tilted her face up to his. 'I'm good at other games, Madam, as well ye know.'

Bending down, he kissed her hard upon her English mouth, deciding that if he couldna best her brother for now, he would take the greatest of pleasure in doing just that to his older sister.

'James!' she exclaimed as he grabbed her left breast with the assurance of a lover who knows his advances are welcome, confident he's never had any complaint about his caresses. 'Not here. Not now. We're about to leave for

High Mass in the Chapel Royal. The Dean himself might walk in at any moment.'

He could tell from the brightness of her eyes that the idea of Queen Margaret of Scotland being ravished on the floor of the King's audience chamber didna match her coy protests. He imagined he'd find her as delicious and slippery to the touch as one of the oysters attached to a shiny black rock, in the Firth of Forth. The verra thought of this excited him as much as any foray into the bedchamber with his spirited red-headed mistress, Janet Kennedy. His Maggie knew she had the ability to draw him to her bed. For pleasure...not merely to beget a new heir. Over the past ten years, he'd tamed and trained his stubborn wee Tudor mare, breaking her in with a mixture of tenderness and mastery, unfailingly taking her to the heights of pleasure.

Or its depths, he thought now, as he skilfully put one knee behind hers and brought them both tumbling to the wooden floorboards beneath.

'We're in the King's House now. God can wait!' he gasped as he seized the heavy skirts of her crimson damask gown and, without further ado, swept up her hem in search of his English prize....

HOUSE OF HOWARD

Chapter Eighteen

The same day. Portsmouth.

E dward slammed his tankard of ale against mine, spilling half its contents and most of mine as well.

He gave a great bellow of laughter, his dark eyes crinkling with humour. 'Your very good health, Father! Thank you for coming.'

I glanced down at the ale pooling on the gnarled surface of the oak table, watching it drip onto the stone flagstones below. I smiled at my beloved son's attempts to mop it up with a handkerchief he'd drawn out of his pocket. How comely he looked this morning: a vest of green and cream brocade complemented his breeches of scarlet and yellow velvet. It wasn't lost on me that he was as comfortable in a private chamber in the interior of '*The Dolphin*', a High Street tavern not far from the water's edge, as he was seated opposite the King of England playing a fast and furious game of dominoes. He had inherited his easy ability to cross borders between men and women (and put them at their ease, however high or low born) from me. I, too, happily supped in Greenwich at Number Ten, Turnpin Lane, as a guest of the Warners, but I was equally at home in the nearby Palace of Placentia where I'd expect a welcome worthy of the powerful Earl of Surrey. By contrast, Edward's newly-wed older brother, Thomas, and his younger brother, Edmund, were quite content to look down their long Howard noses at anyone they considered unfit to breathe the same air.

<<*Not for nothing does Henry Tudor call out for 'Ned Howard' whenever he needs a little cheering*>>

My middle son was fêted wherever he went; a loud cheer had gone up amongst the sailors in the tavern (lit by acrid-smelling tallow candles in wrought iron sconces) when the two of us walked in. Of course, as Lord High Treasurer of England, I was celebrated in my own right, partially in recognition of my success in weathering many a long year on this earth. But in his thirty-sixth year of life compared to the whisker off seventy of mine, Edward was *à la mode*. He was from a different era to me; others saw him as youthful, strong, agreeable to the eye, and brave. With so much to occupy his time right now, I was grateful he'd granted my request for a private conversation before he marched up the gangway to his first commission as Lord High Admiral of England, Ireland, and Aquitaine. I knew it would seem sound beef-witted to some but I sometimes muttered his title aloud in private, intoning it as if I were mouthing a prayer whilst kneeling upon a hassock (decorated with the Howard coat-of-arms, naturally), next to the almost completed nave of the Abbey of Westminster. I savoured the way the words rolled off my tongue as if they were honey upon a pewter ladle in the kitchens in one of my homes (perhaps Ashwellthorpe Manor), trickling into a saucepan below.

'Give us two more tankards of the same,' Edward said to the innkeeper who'd timidly knocked and entered the room, eager to please the most powerful man on the seas. I watched him blink a couple of times as his eyes alighted upon the famed admiral's golden whistle (encrusted with jewels, including a large ruby at the centre) hanging about my son's neck. I wondered how many times a similar admiral's whistle had been blown by its owner in the last three hundred years (ever since the third Henry, a Plantagenet, appointed Richard de Lucy as the first Lord High Admiral of England). The whistle's shrill tone (some said as loud as a trumpet) had been designed to call sailors to arms, commanding them to clamber up to the poop deck in order to do battle.

'Right away, Your Excellency,' the man said, happy to oblige my son while tugging at a non-existent forelock; I think he would have licked the soles of my son's high, tawny leather boots if asked. Instead, he knelt down to mop up the small puddle of ale at our feet.

'This is an excellent brew,' Edward said, by way of apology.

My Edward. Always the charmer. Robert Warner, that most discerning of men (his years on the Thames making him a practised reader of a man or woman's character), had once said of my son:

"Edward is that rarest breed of man. A born crowd-pleaser. Forsooth, he was born to please. My only concern is that he forgets to please the most important person of all. Himself. And he's too hasty by far. In his daily tasks…and in judgement, I fear. I've seen more cuts and bruises on your boy, and a broken bone or two, than in both your other sons put together. Many a time have I watched him hand over a treasure into Thomas's jealous, outstretched hand, not because he feared retribution, as Edmund would. But because he wanted to keep the peace. Objects don't seem to carry the same weight for him."

Thinking of his words now brought to mind my terrible secret.

<<I made Edward give up the one thing in the world that pleased him most. If only I could tell him—>>

"You did what you had to, my friend," had been Robert's only comment when I told him about Edward and the Cornish girl. But the sorrowful expression on his face had belied his words of reassurance.

I forced myself back into the present, leaving behind a past that could not be undone, however much I occasionally wished it could. I needed to grasp at common sense, in the same way a drowning man might claw at some slippery reeds on a river bank. With difficulty I tried to form my thoughts into a helpful argument:

<<*If you unpick a tapestry, you'd still be left with the same silken threads as before. The same needle. And the same hands to stitch once more. Who's to tell that God and Dame Fortune wouldn't arrange matters so you produced exactly the same work again*>>

In front of me, the tavern keeper stood up and straightened the apron around his waist. He gave Edward a slightly toothless grin so wide I feared his cheeks might split.

'I'm glad you like my ale, Your Excellency. I order it from the new brewery up on Saint Nicholas Street. "*The Dragon*". There, they're turning out over five hundred barrels a day.'

It was as if he were reciting a passage from God's own Bible, or had done all the work alone.

<< *But why not be proud? Every man deserves his day to bask in the sunshine - like that tabby cat curled up in front of the fireplace opposite us*>>

It wasn't every day that men like us walked through the front door into our host's low-beamed tavern: a couple of Howard aces (holding two of the most important positions in the land). We would tip him well but it would be nothing compared to the stories he'd recount of our visit. Tales that would grow taller with each telling.

<<*Who knows, at some point I'll probably become King Henry himself, accompanying his Lord High Admiral to the harbour*>>

Whichever way, brandishing our names about in the manner of a flamethrower at a masque would keep our toothless friend in good standing (and flush with coins) with the locals for the next decade, at least.

'I can offer you fine gentlemen some warm manchets from the new bakery up the road. Several of your officers are very partial to them. As well as some tasty, hard cheese delivered this morning from Southwick Priory a couple of miles away.' He made a little flourish with his hand. 'The exact same kind, Your Excellencies, that the monks served to His Majesty, our gracious King when he visited the priory three years ago.'

As Lord High Treasurer of England, I could have made a sharp retort about using the most expensive flour in the land for anyone wearing less than a lieutenant's badge. I had a sudden vision of the sailors below decks flinging away their dry biscuits and considering a mutiny to get their hands on the precious manchets. However, for Edward's sake, I kept my counsel.

The tavern keeper was looking as pleased with himself as if he were offering us a reclining Cleopatra. Indeed, at this very moment, I fancied the dainties far more than the fabled Queen of Egypt.

<<*Or any other female*>>

There had only been one woman I'd ever truly desired with every fibre of my being.

Matilda de Lac—

❧

'You know, Father,' said Edward leaning back in his chair and looking pensive, 'I've been wondering what Mother would say if she were here. Wishing she could be.'

'Your mother would be the proudest woman in the whole of England to be able to call her son Lord High Admiral.'

'Yes, I think she would.'

The tavern keeper returned with our ale, and while Edward exchanged pleasantries with our host, my thoughts wandered back to the woman I'd met the day before my marriage to Edward's mother. In my head, Matilda and I were holding a conversation every bit as real as the one in progress next to me:

'Lord High Treasurer, Matilda. Lord High Admiral. We Howards have done well for ourselves, haven't we?'

I already knew the scathing response to such flap-mouthed bragging; like me, she'd never suffered fools gladly.

'Thomas Howard, you've always been a man to play the game. Any game. The King's. Your own. Wedlock. Elizabeth Tilney wasn't enough for you. You had to have me in your bed.'

'Not only in my bed. In my heart.'

In my mind's eye, her face softened and her slanting eyes seemed to become pools of liquid blue. 'Oh, I know that. On that August day we raced across the causeway to Saint Michael's Mount, I knew your heart was mine. Do you recall the dolphin we saw when we were seated upon Saint Michael's Chair, swinging our legs over the cliff's edge, looking down at the summer sea below?'

'I only remember feeling terrified that you were going to fall to your death. I couldn't let that happen. Not when I'd just found you again. My right hand ached from holding onto your hip so tightly.'

She ignored this show of weakness. 'The creature was all alone, poor thing. Separated from its kin. I told you it had come with a message. *"What is that?"* you teased me, holding me fast, your dark eyes fever-bright from the lovemaking that couldn't wait until we reached the top.' Her voice grew low and husky. *"It's come to sing us a song of love"*, I told you. *"Of our love."'* She paused and looked down, her eyelids fluttering, before continuing in those breathy tones of hers: '"*What are the words?"* you asked m—'

'Father! Father.' Edward waved a hand in front of my face. 'You're very far away. Were you dreaming of manchets?'

Startled, I didn't have time to invent anything. 'No. Dolphins.'

'Dolphins?' He grinned. 'Let's hope a few choose to swim alongside '*The Mary Rose*'. To bring us luck. And that we don't see any mermen or their treacherous maids, quite capable of luring a good man onto the rocks.'

⋄

The tavern keeper re-appeared, this time bearing aloft the promised manchets, although the delicious aroma of the added ingredients of rosewater, cinnamon and nutmeg had already wafted into the chamber ahead of his entrance. They were a sight to surpass even the most extravagant treasure of a fearsome pirate. As he laid down the platter with a grand flourish, I recalled how Matilda's husband had sworn the Damask roses I sent her every year on the first of May were from a pirate.

"*He's not far wrong,*" she'd once sighed, lying sated in my arms after a particularly energetic bout of lovemaking: perhaps even the one that produced our lost boy. The babe whose death after a mere few months signalled the end of our love affair.

Matilda. My Cornish mermaid.

I suddenly saw another face, a very young one, so similar to the one I'd loved so well that my heart had almost stopped on that Twelfth Night at Saint Michael's Mount.

'Do you recall the Tredavoe family from Cornwall?' I asked my son. <<*God's Nightgown*! *What was I thinking?*>> I wished I could swallow back the folly-fallen question. There was no help for it. Like someone inching along a narrow ledge above a precipice, I couldn't turn back now. 'Oh, forgive me, Edward. Of course you do.'

He gave a shudder, and I knew it was because the memories of that area were still so painful.

'I've tried to banish everything from that dreadful episode in the chapel from my memory. Especially as it brought back so many memories of Grace.'

'I understand, son.' I swiftly changed the subject, away from the Mount and all its secrets. 'I'm only happy this war will give your brother something to do…and perhaps give little Lizzie Stafford a respite from his unwanted attentions.'

Edward looked pained. 'For her sake, Father, let's hope they're a little more "wanted" now. I can't bear the thought of that innocent girl at my brother's mercy, day in, day out. He must be seething about my appointment.'

'"*Seething*" doesn't quite do it justice. Seeing your younger brother being handed a plum appointment by the King would be hard for any man. And even as a child, Thomas was anything but forgiving. I sometimes wonder whether he was conceived during a dark moon.

<<*Or because I was in love with another*>>

Edward closed his eyes. 'Poor little maid. I hope she can visit Nan and Mary while he's gone. They seemed so distressed at the wedding. So did the other one. The one who came with us to Greenwich.'

'Which one?'

'William Tredavoe's daughter. Cecily. My Grace's niece. A fetching little thing. She put me in mind of the King's sister. Almost more Tudor than the Tudors.'

<<*Except that she's a Howard*>> I wanted to blurt out. <<*And your niece too*>> Instead, I tried to keep my voice neutral.

'I have some news about her. Tom Bullen spoke to me after Muriel's funeral about some hair-brained idea to send our Nan to the court of Margaret of Austria.'

'As a maid-of-honour?'

'Exactly. I told him she couldn't possibly go alone. And as he wanted to keep Mary back because she's nearly of marriageable age, I suggested the little Tredavoe girl. Of course, I'd only met her briefly on Saint Michael's Mount. Before that day on the Thames.'

<<*If only he knew the truth about Cecily Tredavoe*>>

'That was a good idea.'

'Yes. It worked out very much to my advantage. By the time I saw the King, he'd read my letter explaining that losing Muriel had broken my heart, and that the only reason Thomas married Lizzie Stafford in such haste was so she could witness the wedding before the end.'

Edward crossed himself. 'God rest my poor dead sister's soul. May she be spared any knowledge of such an untruth.'

'The King seemed to have forgiven - if not forgotten - our absence at Twelfth Night and could only think of offering me comfort. He instantly approved of my suggestion for Nan and the Tredavoe girl to take up their places at Margaret of Austria's court. He said it would show the French how much we valued the Burgundian Netherlands.'

I knew this wasn't the right time to start being honest - not with my son about to embark on the most important voyage of his life. By removing the burden of the past from my own shoulders, I would be placing it on his. 'Believe me, Edward, I don't like telling falsehoods either (<<*may the good Lord forgive me*>>) but you might not be fingering that whistle around you neck if I hadn't.'

My son leaned across the table and put one hand on my arm. He looked me straight in the eyes. 'Father, I know. All your life you've only done what's best for all of us. And this time was no different. You're still the phoenix that rose from the ashes of Howard despair.'

I could feel my eyes threatening to well up with womanish tears at this. If his words were gouging out a hole in my heart, it was no more than I deserved for my scurvy behaviour. But that was my lot now. I had to live with my past actions…and their consequences.

The two of us left the tavern and walked across the cobbled High Street to where our horses were tethered. It was a sight to warm the cockles of a true Englishman's heart. Portsmouth had come out in force to give our men a fitting send-off: every house was gaily decorated, and on all sides, men, women and children - some holding the flag of Saint George - ran out to cheer and yell words of encouragement to their new Admiral. Dressed in all his finery, there was no mistaking him in their midst.

'Put the fear of God into those pesky Frenchies, Sir Edward!'

'Yes. And bring back the French crown to its rightful owner.'

'God save King Harry!'

'God save England!'

'God save Sir Edward!'

As we mounted our horses, a pretty young maid ran up to Edward, reached up and shyly handed him a bunch of snowdrops. 'I picked them myself, Your Excellency,' she said, bobbing a little curtsey.

For some reason, this gesture pierced my heart anew and allowed guilt to come rushing into the wound. Edward's wife, Alice, now in her fiftieth year, had declined my invitation to accompany me to see off her husband. *"The ague has kept me to my bed this past month,"* she'd written. *"The ague"*, be damned! Edward needed a beautiful young girl like this to be waiting for him as he drew back the curtains to his bed. Not an old woman complaining of aches and pains, however heavy the purse around her waist. It prompted me to speak.

'Son,' I said as we slowly wended our way through the crowd, smiling and waving at all the loyal townsfolk, 'I've been thinking about your marriage to Alice.'

Edward turned and laughed. '*Again*? Have you been talking to Hal?'

I was surprised. 'No. What's he said?'

'It seems you are not alone in your desire to find me a younger, prettier wife. I assume that's what you were about to say?'

I opened my mouth to say something, then closed it again.

<<*How to choose my words without giving anything away that could spoil his send-off?*>>

I knew I had to tread carefully. 'What exactly is the King proposing?'

Edward took several more bunches of bluebells, daffodils and sweet violets, all the time melting a score of delicate hearts with his dazzling Howard smile. 'Hal has promised me the earth, the stars and the sun.'

I was at a loss. 'The moon too?'

'Ha! Yes, that too.'

'And are you going to tell me what exactly our gracious King is proposing to give you.'

'My heart's desire.'

I edged my horse nearer. 'Son, you speak in riddles.'

'Forgive me.' Edward gave a shrug and lifted the sweet violets to his nose. 'Hal is convinced he can turn back time for me and bring back my first...and only love.'

I could feel the manchets churning in my stomach as I pretended to be distracted by the boats in the harbour.

'Father, it is of no matter. I will keep him to his promise and come searching for my reward later. But first of all, I have a war to win. Look at *"The Mary Rose"*. Did ever a more beguiling female await a man?'

He was not wrong about that; I let out a whistle as I estimated the cost of the ship, and keeping a crew aboard. With its streamers in the Tudor colours of green and white; red and white flags of Saint George; and Henry's very own coat-of-arms (featuring the three golden lions of England on a red background, and the three golden fleur-de-lys of France - England's rightful property - on a blue background), the jewel of King Henry's fleet looked as colourful as a castle garden decked out for May Day. Named for the Virgin Mary, Mother of God, from where we were standing, its design was a nod to the carrack developed over the last two centuries, with what looked like castles placed in the bow and stern, and low decking in the middle. For all its appearance of Maytime gaiety, the guns positioned in their ports were deadly serious in their intent. I took note of the bronze culverins and sakers.

"Manufactured by Hans Poppenreuter in Belgium," Edward had told me before.

I turned to my son, preparing myself to embrace him before I left to hear the Easter Mass back at Domus Dei. Pointing up at the Howard coat-of-arms flying above the guns, with its own ferocious lions in place, I gripped my precious boy by the shoulders, never wanting to let him go. Keeping in mind his recent comments, I drew him to me and wrapped my arms around him. 'Edward,' I murmured in his ear, 'remember this. Unless God or Dame Fortune decree otherwise, what a Howard wants, a Howard always gets.'

CECILY

Chapter Nineteen

April 26th, 1513. Dover, England.

'Cecy, can you believe we're finally heading for France?' Nan grabbed my arm in excitement as we stood on the swaying deck of '*The Swallow*', bound from Dover to Calais. 'I can't wait to feel my feet sink into French sand. Can you?'

I closed my eyes to shut out both her questions and the startling sight of the quay at Dover slowly beginning to fade into the distance. I couldn't answer because I was fighting back the tears that were threatening to overwhelm me. Sadly, not even my beloved fairy folk had been able to prevent this journey, although I kept the hope alive until the very last moment. But I'd always known deep down that my ethereal friends were no match for Nan's father, or her powerful Howard grandsire. My own wishes were of no consequence to ruthless men like that; my role as Nan's companion was all that mattered to them. It reminded me of a game of chess (at which I had no mean skill), except that here I could only play the part of a mere pawn, with the court of the Burgundian Netherlands: the chessboard. Both the Bullens and the Howards believed that a fluent French speaker accompanying their young pawn could only enhance Nan's chances of speedy advancement at the court of the Archduchess Margaret.

"*Please do this for your father, my darling daughter*," my mother had pleaded with me in the end. "*None of this was his doing, but when this particular King of England favours an idea, it seems no man nor woman can change his mind.*" She clasped me in her arms and wiped away my tears (while shedding more than a few of her own). "*It might be the King's will that you go. But you have my word,*" she said, a fierce expression on her face, "*that if you're wretched - no matter what Tom Bullen, Thomas Howard, or King Henry himself say - you're coming straight home to us."*

Weeks of frantic activity had followed, filled with gathering suitable clothes for a maid-of-honour to go into a travelling coffer: for all seasons, it appeared. Gowns of velvet lined with satin; one furred with ermine to see me through until summer; French hoods, kirtles of satin, nightgowns, a new ruby pendant, the list was endless.... No mention was made of how long I'd be forced to stay; it seemed as though time was indeterminate. There then followed a search for the right man to accompany the two of us to Margaret of Austria's palace in Mechelen. Messengers rode back and forth 'in post' with relays of horses (on an almost daily basis) between our castles of Zennor and Hever, carrying anxious letters between both fathers - well, from my father (ably helped by Mother), at least. The Archduchess was to provide an escort: a diplomat from Flanders (Captain of the Guard to Prince Charles of Castile) called Claude Bouton, Seigneur de Courbaron. Thomas Bullen also sent word that he'd managed to track down a local Frenchwoman who was going to go up to Hever Castle.

"To give my Nan a little more than her present grasp of the rudiments of the language," he wrote.

How I hated picking up his discarded letter and reading his spidery writing dictating my future. I might love my friend like a sister. But she was neither my sister, nor any kind of relation for her father to behave in this high-handed way.

In the end, I felt as though I'd hardly had time to come to terms with what was happening to me - let alone say my goodbyes. I wasn't even allowed to wait for the traditional Zennor Castle May Day celebrations

"I am sorry, Cecy," my father had said, *"but Margaret of Austria's escort has already arrived at Hever. And with talk of imminent war with France rife, both families are aware that the tiny window of opportunity to ensure a safe passage through French territory for you, is dwindling as quickly as the last grains of sand in an hourglass. It is now or never."*

"Then let it be never!" I cried, and would have continued but for the haunted expression on my father's drawn, white face. I stopped short. What was the point? I knew that no miracle was forthcoming, and as soon as the tides were right, Nan and I would be leaving with Seigneur de Courbaron to begin a journey…into the unknown.

"At least you'll see Tristan and your Aunt Grace soon," said my red-eyed mother, biting her lip to ward off further tears. As if a brief stay in Ardres Castle, *en route* for the Burgundian Netherlands, could sweeten the bitter taste in my mouth.

To my increasing annoyance, Nan wouldn't stop chattering nineteen to the dozen about all the possibilities that lay ahead. She seemed oblivious that there was only one of us in the conversation; her incessant prattling and obvious glee made me fear I'd get one of my megrims. Unlike me, she wasn't overly concerned about leaving her family. Only Thomas Bullen had accompanied her to Dover, and neither father nor daughter had shed so much as a single tear on parting. I'd heard him lecturing her about the proper way for a young girl to behave abroad as she rolled her eyes at me the moment he turned his head away.

<<*I wouldn't be concerned either if he were my father. And Nan's mother, Lady Elizabeth, spends more time looking at herself in her hand mirror than she does keeping an eye on her children*>>

As Nan had pointed out an hour or so earlier when we stepped onto the boat, one moment she'd been playing an energetic game of hide-and-seek with her two brothers and sister in the gardens of Hever, and what seemed like the next, the pair of us were standing here on an unknown ship, with an unknown man by our side who wasn't related to either of us. I didn't state the obvious: that both our fathers would probably be making the same journey to France within a very short time. The thought was enough to make me feel more homesick and fearful than I could ever have believed possible.

'Just think, Cecy, we might pass my uncle's boat on the way over. Father said "*The Mary Rose*" is in the area somewhere.'

'Which uncle?'

Clasping her hands together, Nan's eyes were sparkling. 'My Uncle Ned, silly.' She puffed out her chest a little. 'The new Lord High Admiral of England.'

I remembered Father mentioning something about Edward Howard's appointment. And my thinking how pleased Tristan would be.

<<*But I'm not happy. At this very moment, I hate every single member of the Howard family. Even Nan. For she is one just as surely as her mother, grandsire and uncles. I wouldn't care a jot if they all ended up on the bottom of the Narrow Sea, with seaweed and pebbles in their mouths*>>

Thinking such a wicked thought instantly made me feel as guilty as if I'd ordered their deaths myself. I quickly crossed myself, hoping that God hadn't been listening. Despite my best efforts, a lump formed in my throat and my vision became blurred as I watched the white cliffs growing smaller and smaller...until they dwindled into a tiny white dot in the distance. Next to me, Nan was still praising her oh-so-important uncle: 'They say he's the handsomest Admiral eve—'

The only thing left to me was to hope the future wouldn't be as bleak as I imagined. Standing here on the deck, I was unable to look beyond our watery voyage, and the few days on horseback immediately afterward that would lead me...to Tristan...Aunt Grace. A terrifying uncle I'd never met. Tristan's brother, Gilles. And Nicolas - that ward of his parents' - whom Tristan disliked so much. I certainly hoped I wouldn't meet him at this unknown castle in France....

PART THREE

THE MERRY MONTH OF MAY

'The month of May was come, when every lusty heart beginneth to blossom.'

Sir Thomas Malory 1415-1471
'Le Morte d'Arthur.'

VALENTINE

Chapter Twenty

The first of May, 1513. The library, La Colombe.

Wait until I catch you, Valentine de Fleury, I'll— Oh, *je m'excuse,* Monsieur le Baron. I was looking for Demoiselle Valentine.'

From her hiding place behind one of the bookshelves on the upper floor of the library, Valentine clapped a hand over her mouth to stifle her giggles. Bonne was vexed with her because she'd refused to wear the plain blue gown - insisting, instead, on the dark green satin one with popingay-blue and pearl-white striped sleeves.

Valentine imagined how flustered her nursemaid must have felt rushing headlong into her father like that. <<*Serves her right for trying to make me wear that old blue thing*>> She started to make her way over to the stairs leading down to the main part of the library, but at that moment the door below opened and several of her father's friends entered the room. She suddenly remembered what her father had told her mother:

"*I'll join all of you later, in time for the crowning of the Queen of the May. With the threat of war hanging over us, I'm staying behind to discuss plans with some friends. And then we'll speak to Guy.*"

Valentine frowned. <<*Oh, non! Now I'm trapped in here. It's all Bonne's fault. She was the one who started chasing me down the corridor*>>

Inwardly sighing, she hastily backed away from the stairs and settled down once more into her little hiding place. Outside the mullioned windows, she could hear all the laughter and merriment of the May Day revellers at the bottom of the drive, passing by La Colombe on their way up to the Castle. She could hardly make an appearance in front of her father and his friends after

Bonne's outburst. She would seem like a common eavesdropper instead of the dignified eldest daughter of a baron.

Down below, the men had arranged themselves into some chairs and she could hear her father pouring something liquid into goblets for them.

'Some of my finest claret, Messieurs,' he said.

By sliding along the wooden floor, Valentine managed to manoeuvre the men into her line of vision (but still remain hidden from view).What did it matter now if her green and white dress got dirty; she already knew she wasn't going back to the festivities for at least one turn of an hourglass.

There were about ten of her father's friends seated around a table, men she knew: some of them neighbours. The conversation had turned to money…or lack of it.

The task of administering his lands, coupled with the financial uncertainty, was starting to give Valentine's father a frown line in the middle of his forehead that hadn't been there before. At nearly ten, she was old enough to be aware of his struggles. She understood from snatches of conversation she'd overheard that it took a lot of money to keep La Colombe running: in the kitchens alone, the Baron had to pay everyone from Maître Jacques to the lowliest spit-turners and pot-stirrers. Although Valentine always thought of it in her head as 'the kitchens', she knew it comprised the Pantry, the Buttery, the Spicery, the Bakery and the Larder. All these different areas were served by various merchants, such as those who sold wine and fish (her least favourite item): regular visitors to La Colombe.

<<*And all of them demanding instant payment for their wares*>>

Valentine was aware that her father not only received a certain percentage from any sales transacted within his domain, but also rents for the use of the oven, press and mill, as well as a toll he enforced on any wagons passing through his estate. But this was not enough. Valentine had recently overheard her mother talking to a friend. *"All this worry is giving my poor Charles nightmares. He frets about the girls' futures."*

'*Que le ciel me garde,*' he was saying to his friends now, as if he could read her thoughts, 'if I can't manage to find dowries for my girls. Can you imagine what Athénaïs would say if I turned up with the son of some wealthy merchant for one of our girls? *Mordieu*! It would finish me off too if I had to shake hands on a deal like that.'

'Charles, every single one of us has had to soil his hands from time to time,' replied Robert de Sapincourt, one of their neighbours.

Valentine had learnt that whenever the old '*noblesse de l'épée*' came into contact with the '*noblesse de la robe*', families such as the Fleurys and Sapincourts would look down their well-bred noses in contempt. In return, the land-hungry bourgeoisie of the towns regarded families like theirs, at best, as intruders and, at worst, as enemies.

'I've had to deal with one of the wretched little *parvenus*!' another neighbour (like the others, a nobleman of the sword) exclaimed. 'Just because he's an up-and-coming young lawyer, he suddenly thinks he's one of us. *Bon sang de bon Dieu*! I can imagine the scoundrel strolling around Guy's May Day celebrations, acting as though he's lived somewhere like Ardres Castle or La Colombe all his life...when we all know he hasn't. Last month, he had the impertinence to offer to take my daughter, Gillette, in exchange for a couple of my best pastures. But if he thinks buying a position at court is going to make him one of us, he's completely mistaken.'

Valentine was unimpressed. <<*Gillette Thureau has the face of a pig. If I were that young lawyer, I'd need at least a score of Seigneur Thureau's pastures to tempt me to the church door*>>

✍

Nevertheless, she knew it was the ultimate humiliation for a nobleman to be forced to surrender, not merely a field or two, but several *seigneuries* to his social inferiors. Her father was always complaining to her mother how prohibitively expensive life at court was, as were the skirmishes which the nobility were expected to support wholeheartedly. *"After all, what good is a coat-of-arms if there isn't enough money to feed the family?"* she'd heard him say on more than one occasion.

'It's all very well telling us we don't have to pay taxes,' Gervais Thureau was now grumbling as he took a gulp of his claret, 'and that we should be grateful for all our privileges. But if we can't make enough from our estates to live on, and we don't want to go into the Church, then what are we supposed to do?'

'Become full-time soldiers or turn to the nearest rich lord, I suppose,' her father replied.

Robert de Sapincourt rubbed his chin ruefully. 'In that case, *mes amis,* expect to see me hammering on Guy d'Ardres' door too. I might be a wealthy man now, but not for long, I fear. Just take this May Day, for example. A pretty young wife like my Ysabeau seems to need more new gowns and fripperies than I'd ever dreamed possible. Not to mention a pendant in the form of the letter Y, pearl brooches, rubies and emeralds. Last month, I ordered a new headdress with several diamonds set in a border of gold. I swear I've spent a hundred times more on her in one year than on my poor dead Denise in our entire twenty-five-year marriage. *Qu'elle repose en paix!*'

One of her father's other friends, an older man like Robert de Sapincourt, shook his head. 'You have to make a stand, Robert, or else she'll ruin you.'

Another called Pierre Vizet held up one hand. 'Next she'll be asking for a diamond for every finger. And all her toes too.'

A ripple of not unkind laughter echoing around the room made Robert de Sapincourt put his head in his hands. 'I know. I know. I'm a rich old fool, more than twice her age: a ridiculous greybeard who cannot hope to capture her affections. With her, I feel jealousy like I never felt in all my years with Denise. It eats me up on a daily basis and makes me want to die. Or lock her up and throw away the key so no one else can have her.'

Valentine watched her father smile and give their neighbour a sympathetic squeeze of the shoulder. 'In time, I am sure Ysabeau will prove to be a good wife to you, *mon ami*. She's very young, and so beautiful it's hardly surprising she has her admirers.'

'Too many for my liking,' sighed Robert de Sapincourt. 'The three boys up at the Castle would take her in a heartbeat, I'm sure. Even the youngest one singled her out on Twelfth Night. And he can't be more than fifteen or sixteen. But I must remember that only four years separates him from her, not the twenty-four that separates her from me.'

Valentine had to agree with her father that Ysabeau de Sapincourt *was* extremely beautiful. Up until now, she'd always pitied her for being wed to such a gorbellied old man. But now she wasn't sure that it was Ysabeau she should be feeling sorry for. She'd once heard Béatrice and Maître Jacques gossiping about the Sapincourts, unaware that she was hiding around the corner, hoping for a tidbit from the stove.

Béatrice had sounded most disapproving. "*I think she's a saucy baggage, myself. Seigneur de Sapincourt needs to keep an eye on her. I've seen the way she looks at our young master.*"

"*Which one—*"

Unfortunately, the pair of them had been distracted by a nearby pan bubbling over so she hadn't heard the rest of the conversation. It was probably Nicolas, she'd decided at the time. She'd heard a few of the Castle maids squabbling about who was going to serve him at supper. From what Robert de

Sapincourt had just said, it seemed that the two Ardres brothers also admired her.

<<That can't be right. Tristan is so dog-hearted I can't imagine him falling in love with anyone. Or anyone with him>>

ॐ

The conversation below had changed from Robert de Sapincourt's wife back to complaints about their financial situations.

'There's not even much we can do about it,' said Pierre, wringing his hands.

Valentine knew he was referring to how, if a gentleman had money problems, farming his land became well-nigh impossible because of the high cost of labour. And if he stooped to become involved in business, he risked the loss of his class privileges. Charles de Fleury had thus far survived by a mixture of soldiering and family connections, as well as being occasionally employed by the King as a roving ambassador.

Tired of listening to them bemoaning their lot, Valentine managed to stifle a yawn that threatened to expose her. In the distance, she could hear the faint strains of music. She was hoping that the men would hear it too and want to join in. And hurry to watch the crowning of the Queen of the May. But regrettably, none of them were nine years old and, to her dismay, instead of getting up to leave, she heard more wine being poured into goblets as the conversation turned to the latest news from England.

'Now, *mes seigneurs*, we have work to do,' said her father. 'Preparations to discuss. A war is upon us.'

<<Not that peevish old topic again>> Valentine closed her eyes, hoping that merciful sleep would at least transport her to another place....

❧

She must have got her wish and dozed off because she jerked awake to the sound of the scraping of chairs.

'I promised Ysabeau that we'd be in time for the crowning of the Queen of the May,' Robert de Sapincourt was saying. 'My wife won't take it kindly if we miss it. And then I'll have to endure one of her fits of ill humour.'

After all she'd heard today, Valentine decided that any man would have his hands full if he went anywhere near the mercurial Ysabeau.

'*Allons-y*,' her father replied. 'I promised Athénaïs…and my Valentine I'd be there in time for it.'

NICOLAS

Chapter Twenty-One

Ardres Castle.

From his vantage point high above on the Castle battlements, Nicolas could see everyone gathered to watch the crowning of the Queen of the May. For once, he felt curiously detached from the proceedings. For the first time in three years, he had no intention of pursuing the pretty girl with a garland of flowers in her long fair hair, dressed in a gown of virginal white. In reality, since Twelfth Night he'd pursued no one at all. Not since Tristan had thwarted his amorous intentions. Scanning the crowd, Nicolas was able to make out the culprit standing next to his mother, the Countess, cheering and clapping. A little further along, he could see the newly-arrived, portly Robert de Sapincourt greedily clutching his young wife's hand: the achingly winsome Ysabeau who was clad in silver and pale blue. The cause of Nicolas's heartache and sleepless nights had taken on the part of Jean Chartier's '*La Belle Dame sans mercy*'. If she were *La Belle Dame*, that would make Nicolas '*le plus dolent des amoureux*', a role that did not sit easily with him: he did not consider himself the most unhappy of lovers.

His only consolation was that Tristan stood almost no chance of success with the fair Ysabeau either; the swag-bellied Sapincourt guarded her more closely than King Arthur and his Guinevere. There was no doubt that she was interested in Tristan; on each occasion she'd visited the Castle since Twelfth Night, Nicolas had noticed her giving his enemy enough deceptively coy, sidelong glances of encouragement to reassure him that his attentions were far from unwelcome.

Replacing unfulfilled love with thoughts of a far more war-like nature, his spirits immediately lifted once more, aware that war was not an area in

176

which Tristan would ever be able to partake. Instead of joining the honourable ranks of soldiers, he would be reduced to standing on the sidelines, limply administering the last rites to those that had fallen in their country's name. He might be able to fawn and prance at the May Day festivities, join in activities that prepared all the local young men for a tournament, or even (heaven forbid) encroach upon Nicolas's love life...but he would never know how it felt to compete in the greatest tournament of them all. Bored of watching a Queen of the May whose beauty he had no wish to sample, and determined not to torture himself any further by drinking in the merciless Ysabeau's beauty, Nicolas threw himself down on the ground with his back against the stone wall, stretching out his legs in front of him.

A short while later, it became obvious that however much he tried to shut out the May Day festivities, it was an impossible task. The strains of music, raucous shouts and laughter drifted up to the battlements: a sign that the dancing had begun. No doubt Tristan was taking full advantage of the chance to dance with the fairest young maids in the region. The thought that it would almost certainly involve Ysabeau was enough to force an irritated Nicolas to his feet, resolved to flee from such torture. Striding purposefully towards the door, he seized the iron ring, turned it and began taking the stone steps two at a time. He knew full well that the only remedy that could soothe his extreme agitation was a punishing ride on his beloved horse, across the green fields gently washed earlier that morning in May Day dew.

As he galloped at full pelt, freeing the cobwebs of love's despair from his mind, far ahead of him he could see the ramparts of Guînes Castle: a sombre reminder that the French and English were soon to be at war. How strange to think that their near neighbours in Calais were now to become their sworn enemies. He wondered how Dame Grace must be feeling, especially as she was presently expecting English visitors *en route* for the court of Margaret of Austria. She was fully English unlike her toad-spotted son who was only half an Englishman. Or rather a perfidious lurdane. Nicolas could well imagine Tristan d'Ardres happily betraying both England and France, depending on which side of the Narrow Sea he happened to be.

He wondered what Dame Fortune made of the worsening relations between the two countries. She hadn't entered his head since his conversation with Gilles about that manuscript he brought back from Venice: '*Le Prince*' (which Nicolas had since read twice over). That same night, he'd dreamt of an alluring woman, even wondering if it might be the terrifying Dame herself - although afterwards, he attributed it to several goblets too many of Monsieur Guy's favourite red wine from Orléans while debating the merits of war with Gilles, long after the ashes in the grate had turned cold. In his dream, he'd seen an unknown woman (not Ysabeau, he was certain of that); although her face was indistinct, he had the impression of a pair of eyes in which a man could easily drown, a sultry mouth to bring him to his knees, and a body he'd gladly die to possess.

Scattering a few terrified rabbits in his path as he and his horse charged through the undergrowth into a forest, Nicolas narrowly missed a large fallen branch, probably brought down during a recent storm.

'*Whoa!*'

Thankfully his reactions were fast. Digging his heels hard into his horse's flanks, man and animal flew up into the air, avoiding the treacherous obstacle at the last moment…as if by magic.

The violent jolt brought him to his senses.

Bigre! What kind of elf-skinned apple-john am I turning into, he chastised himself, as he silently praised his horse for saving him from a terrible fall that could easily have resulted in a broken neck…or death. Nicolas's heart was thumping against his ribcage and his breath was coming in great gasps.

Ever since leaving the Castle battlements and saddling up his horse, his thoughts had been straying to love. What's the matter with me, he continued to scold himself. I'm becoming as soft as some moonstruck maiden or squire, my head crammed full of flowery words of love. Not to mention muddled thoughts as sweet as honey. Well, such feebleness of mind had nearly cost him his life. Not one of these thoughts was remotely worthy of the clear-thinking warrior he aimed to be in the forthcoming war. Conjuring up words of love he'd spoken to the unknown woman in a dream was the last straw that broke the horse's back. Nicolas gave his dark curls a vigorous shake as if to expel any further idiocy from his mind.

Au nom de Dieu! I'm no better than that fool-born ninny Tristan was talking about on Twelfth Night: the one who wrapped himself up in a wolfskin to impress a woman.

Better to be a real wolf…than a spineless wooer any day.

Jumping from his horse at the bank of the river Hem which was just north of the village, Nicolas was glad for the coolness of the water as he waded across to the other side. At least it seemed to do the trick of dispelling any foolish thoughts of love and lovemaking. In the distance, he spotted the weathercock on the roof of the manor house belonging to their neighbour, Guillaume Gouffier, Seigneur de Bonnivet (and his bitter rival from the days of François of Angoulême's little band). Frowning, Nicolas mounted his horse again and urged it onwards, lightly digging his heels into its flanks as they effortlessly cleared ditches and small streams.

'Faster…faster, Machiavelli!'

He turned his eyes skywards. 'Let war commence!' he yelled at a flock of birds as if they might lead him to the battlefield.

HOUSE OF HABSBURG
Chapter Twenty-Two

Later that afternoon. Ardres Castle.

'He loves me, he loves me not...'

The clear, imperative tones of a little girl carried the length of the sunlit gardens (heady with the scent of honeysuckle), catching the attention of a man and two young girls strolling along the leafy *allée* beyond. Somewhat curious, Claude Bouton stepped into an arbour and pushed aside the vines, taking care not to prick his fingers on any stray thorns of the intertwining roses. What he found beyond made him smile, and he immediately drew his companions closer so that they might see too.

Standing a few yards away on a green lawn, tugging at the petal of a daisy she was holding in her left hand, was a girl of about nine or ten dressed in a green and white striped gown. She was an exquisite child, wide-eyed with small even features. Her angelic face was framed by waist-length ringlets, the colour of ripened wheat, which she was now shaking with a certain amount of vigour.

'Tristan, are you asleep?' The child did a little twirl, clutching the petal in her right hand. 'Knowing you, you're probably dreaming about stupid old war.'

Claude followed the girl's gaze to a boy, a few years older, who was lying prone, several feet away. It was hard to tell whether he was sleeping or awake. He was on his back with his feet stretched out in front of him, seemingly oblivious to the world around him. It was only when he reached up to swat a passing fly that had landed on his cheek that Claude guessed he must be feigning sleep.

'That's my cousin,' whispered one of the girls next to Claude.

They all watched as the little girl crept forward and sprinkled the petal onto the boy's nose. '*Il m'aime un peu*,' she chanted in a loud sing-song voice.

'*Arrête*, Valentine! *Je t'en supplie*,' the boy growled as he sat up and ran one hand through his unruly, dark blonde hair. He glared at his tormentor. 'Surely that's enough now.'

In answer, the child stamped her foot. '*Non...non...non*! It's not nearly enough.' And as if to prove her point, she swiftly tore off two more petals:

'*Il m'aime beaucoup*

Il m'aime passionnement.'

Closing her eyes, she lifted her face upwards in the manner of a lady expecting a kiss from a suitor, her rosy lips shaped into a perfect little bow. There was a look of ecstasy on her face as she carefully plucked another petal with her finger and thumb.

'*Il m'aime a la folie*,' she breathed.

This polished display was enough to bring forth an unintentionally loud chuckle from Claude in his hiding place in the arbour...which in turn caused the boy sprawled on the grass to sit bolt upright, a look of alarm on his face.

'What was that?'

Happily, his small friend, lost in her thoughts of chivalry and romance, was far too busy to notice. 'N-o-thing,' she replied dreamily, gazing at the flower in her hand as if it were the face of her future husband.

The expression on her face suddenly seemed to bring the boy to his senses. 'Oh, this is too much!' he cried, snatching the daisy from her.

'*Il ne m'aime pas du tout*!' he finished for her, flinging the denuded flower onto the ground in disgust as he stretched out once more, a look of satisfaction on his handsome face. 'See. He loves me not at all. And that's exactly what'll happen to you, Valentine de Fleury, if you go running after boys. Besides, you're only nine years old. And shouldn't even be thinking of such things. You're far too young.'

In front of Claude, the little girl was staring at the discarded daisy as if she were contemplating the lifeless body of her beloved. Then putting her small hands on her hips, she vigorously shook her head while going quite pink in the cheeks.

'I'm nearly *ten* years old, Tristan d'Ardres! And you…and you.' Here, Claude could tell she was struggling for the right words which - when she found them - he guessed would be delivered with great aplomb. 'You're dog-hearted. And *"will never be any good to any woman*!" That's what my mother says about you.'

ळ

This time, the black-haired girl in the arbour next to Claude burst out laughing but the pair beyond were far too preoccupied to notice.

'She says you can never be a soldier and go to war like the others. And you won't be able to get wed, but will be locked up in some stupid old monastery with only monks for company. A beautiful woman like Ysabeau de Sapincourt will never give you a second glan—'

'Silence! You fork-tongued little termagant!' yelled the boy, rising to his feet. 'I knew I should never have agreed to this nonsense in the first place.'

The girl's expression was one of triumph. '*Dis donc*! You had no choice. I meant it when I said I'd tell your father what you and your friend were up to that day outside the stables.' She paused for effect. 'And I still might. Unless you play with me some more….'

Behind the hedge, Claude was filled with admiration for the enchanting little tyrant. As Captain of the Guard to young Charles of Castile (and implicitly trusted by both Margaret of Austria and her father, the Emperor), he'd come across many a scheming minx in his forty-three years. But very few as engaging as the one in front of him…in spite of her tender years.

'What a beauty,' he murmured. 'Even now,' he added, almost to himself. 'In several years' time, no man's heart will be safe.'

He glanced at the two girls beside him, noticing how the Cornish girl was clutching both hands to her heart, clearly thrilled at the thought of being reunited with this poor, browbeaten cousin of hers….

CECILY

Chapter Twenty-Three

I was so happy to catch sight of Tristan again on the other side of our fragrant hiding place, in the bower of roses. As well as the famous Valentine who appeared to be every inch the firebrand Tristan had described in Cornwall. With her cherub's face and sweet smile, it seemed that appearances could be deceptive. I found myself assessing my cousin through Nan's eyes. I'd noticed a fulgent smile appear on her hitherto serious face. Knowing her as well as I did, I could imagine her thinking that if this was how boys were going to look on the opposite side of the sea the French named '*La Manche*', or 'the Sleeve', she would no longer give a single thought to Hever, her parents, her sister, or brothers. Although Tristan was still an unformed youth of fifteen, already his height, broad shoulders and strong facial features showed signs of the man he would become.

'Oh, here you are, Claude,' said a voice behind us, interrupting these thoughts.

Turning, I saw a comely, fair-haired man who was slightly breathless as if he'd been running. '*S'il vous plaît, excusez-moi*,' he began, bowing to Nan and me as he spoke to our companion, 'but I had to check on Athénaïs. She's not having it so easy this time,' he added in a lowered voice.

Claude Bouton clapped the man on the shoulder. 'Take it as a good sign, Charles. My wife took far worse with our son.' He made a flourish with his arm in our direction and we bobbed a little curtsey to the newcomer.

'May I present Cecily Tredavoe, niece of the Governor's wife…and young Tristan's cousin. And her travelling companion, Anne Boullan. And this,' he said to us, 'is Baron Charles de Fleury. A neighbour of the Governor's. And an old friend of mine.'

185

Niceties over with, Claude Bouton turned his attention back to the Baron, picking up their conversation where he'd left off. 'Getting a boy needs more effort,' he told him.

I watched the man give a wan smile and run a hand through his blonde hair. 'Up until now, Claude, I've had five girls... and five disappointments. So the appearance of a male heir a few months hence seems almost too good to be true.' He suddenly cleared his throat rather noisily as if he realized this might seem rather insulting in present company. And...could that be a hint of a tear in his pale blue eyes, I wondered.

'Not that I don't dote upon all my girls,' the Baron went on. 'And Valentine, in particular, possesses every quality I could ever wish for in an heir - except for the fact that she's a girl.' He let out a sigh. 'Such is my fate, that in order to protect my house and my girls, and ensure everything doesn't one day pass to a distant cousin of mine I've never even met, I need a boy.'

'I'm weary of doing nothing,' the little girl was complaining, as if in answer to Charles de Fleury's thoughts about his eldest having boy-like qualities. Her high-pitched voice carried through the hedge with piercing clarity. 'I command you to play a game with me. Remember if you don't, I'll-'

'I remember, merciless wretch! What d'you want to play?'

'"Kings and Queens"!' came back the unequivocal response.

'Oh, not that game again, Valentine, *je t'implore.*'

'*Mais si, si, si*! I am the Queen of France and you are the King of England. On your knees right now, impudent cur!'

'*Aie!*'

I noticed the smile the two men exchanged; it was becoming obvious from Tristan's howl of pain that the imperious '*Queen of France*' had probably just given the outraged '*King of England*' a healthy kick on the shins.

'That hurt, you little demon. Don't be motley-minded, Valentine! Kings and Queens don't talk to each other like that. And they certainly don't kick each other.'

'Of course they do. Especially when one of them's trying to steal the other's country.'

Valentine's father threw a nervous glance in our direction, probably praying that our French was so basic we wouldn't be able to understand this insult.

'Time to intervene, I think,' said the Baron, addressing Claude Bouton in rapid French, 'before we have to witness "*the Queen of France*" and "*the King of England*" coming to undignified blows. 'Come, Demoiselles,' he said in a kind voice, speaking French more slowly for our benefit. 'I'd like to introduce you to my daughter, Valentine.'

Our smiling escort nodded over to the sparring pair in the garden. 'I have no doubt, Charles, that your little Valentine will bring young men flocking to your door before very long.'

I glanced at Nan who suddenly seemed shy at the prospect of meeting my cousin. Smoothing down the skirts of her new green gown, her hands fluttered up to her headdress in a coquettish gesture.

'Don't be afraid,' I whispered. 'He won't bite.'

VALENTINE
Chapter Twenty-Four

Rather put out that her precious game of 'Kings and Queens' had been interrupted, Valentine was studying the two girls and the older man whom her father was introducing. Both girls were *très jolies*, with one of them - Tristan d'Ardres' cousin, it turned out - having creamy skin, green eyes, and hair of an unusual red she had only seen once or twice before. So these were the two young English girls who'd just landed in France and were on their way to the Burgundian court. How important that sounded and how Valentine envied them. She watched as Tristan and the girl called Cecily first bowed and curtsied with mock formality, before falling into each other's arms, clearly delighted to be reunited.

'*Whegyn ow holon*,' said Tristan, in a language that very much resembled caterwauling to a listening Valentine.

'I believe that's Cornish,' said the stranger to Valentine's father.

Whatever it was certainly seemed to be causing Tristan's cousin much mirth. She also seemed to be poking fun at a nearby marble statue of Tristan and his mother, erected by Guy d'Ardres in front of the large fountain in the Castle gardens.

"*As fine a craftsman to be found the entire length of Italy*," Valentine's father had recently remarked, referring to the Milanese sculptor who'd travelled all the way to northern France to fulfil his commission.

Becoming bored by the cousins' antics, Valentine's gaze moved to the other girl left standing alone. Intense dark eyes in a thin pale face returned her own gaze, not unfriendly but questioning. It was definitely not a beautiful face, Valentine decided, at least not as beautiful as the other girl, or Tristan's mother who also came from this strange land across the water. Beneath an elaborate headdress, the girl's thick dark hair had a reddish sheen as she moved in and out of shafts of the midday sunlight. There was something appealing in her elfin looks, and when the girl who was called Anne gave a shy smile, it was almost impossible not to smile back.

"Enchanté, Demoiselle Valentine," the English girl had murmured awkwardly a few moments ago when Valentine kissed her on both cheeks, after a prompting push from her father.

If Valentine had not been used to the ugly accent of some of the English friends who came to visit the Comtesse d'Ardres, she would have laughed out loud. *Bah*! If this Anne Boullan had come hoping to find a husband, someone ought to tell her that she would never capture a Frenchman's heart unless she learnt not to massacre his precious language.

She was still feeling superior when, to her extreme annoyance, Tristan - who'd been doing a perfect imitation of a dying slug for the last hour - was led over to the new girl by his cousin and, as if miraculously re-born, started enthusiastically addressing her in what Valentine assumed was her mother tongue. Valentine saw all hesitancy flee the English girl's face to be replaced by a vivacity that even the unworldly Valentine could see would make every man for miles around come running. She gave a sideways glance at her father and the other man, and saw her suspicions confirmed by their rapt expressions.

'Naturally Demoiselle Anne is happy to converse in her own language again,' she heard the stranger saying to her father. 'And it's good to see Demoiselle Cecily with family again.'

'Poor mites!' replied Charles de Fleury. 'They're too young to be sent so far away from home. And at such a time as this…when our two countries seem to be on the brink of war.'

The other man shrugged. 'I agree. I tried to tell Demoiselle Anne's father I had fears for our safety. But he wouldn't listen. He was so desperate to send the two girls off to live at a foreign court. It seems to be the way of the English to send their children to live with strangers. Not something I can understand myself.'

'Nor I.' Valentine's father agreed. 'I would never contemplate it.'

'Especially when one of them can hardly speak a word of French. It's been very limiting so far.'

But there was clearly nothing limited about Anne Boullan's English, thought Valentine crossly as, over the men's conversation, she listened to Anne's tinkling laugh interspersing snatches of horrible sounds made by Tristan's cousin: what an ugly language English was. At times, it sounded like snakes hissing at one another; at others, like dogs barking. One thing cut her to the quick; *she* had never been able to make Tristan laugh like that. Hurt and jealousy made her want to kick his ankle very hard again but she dared not in front of her father. Thankfully, a reprieve of sorts came in the guise of Tristan's parents, the Comte d'Ardres, and his English wife who stepped from the arbour just as Tristan and the two girls burst out laughing for about the hundredth time.

Valentine could see that Tristan's mother looked pleased at the little scene in front of her; after all, according to Charles de Fleury, it had been her suggestion for the English girls to stop off at Ardres Castle on their way to the Burgundian court, guessing they might be suffering from pangs of homesickness.

Valentine frowned. Thanks to Tristan, melancholic thoughts seemed to be the last thing on the mind of either of them....

CECILY

Chapter Twenty-Five

Slowly but surely, I could feel a lessening of the dreadful pangs of longing for Zennor; the delicious fragrance of lavender, thyme and marjoram, mingled with marigold and violets had filled my nostrils when I first entered the gardens. They must have been planted by my aunt as they were all so reminiscent of home. I might be feeling more at ease but I couldn't quite shake off a feeling of foreboding that something momentous was about to happen - whether good or evil, I couldn't make up my mind. But hugging Tristan immediately changed all that. He never failed to make me laugh, and I was delighted to see Aunt Grace who bore such a strong resemblance to her brother, my father.

Wrapping her arms around me, she pulled me close. 'Little Cecy, you have no idea how pleased I am to see you here. And to meet your friend,' she added, smiling at Nan. Knowing that Aunt Grace - now a golden-haired countess in Picardy - had spent her childhood in Zennor Castle with my father, was a comfort. Her delicate, almost fey beauty, had translated itself into something far more rugged in her son; he had a longer nose too. I was amused by how completely mesmerized Nan was by him. But then even I could see his appeal with those mischievous green eyes of his and dulcet voice, low and teasing as he spoke to my friend: a winning combination of fluency in Nan's own tongue, tinged with the charming accent of his mother's native Cornwall, overlaid with *his* native Picardy.

'I am so relieved you speak English, Tristan,' she was saying. 'I am afraid I only have scant knowledge of French.'

'I would happily teach you some while you're here,' Tristan replied. 'We can start with your name.'

'*Je m'appelle* Anne Bullen,' said clever Nan, diving into a new situation with her customary courage and confidence. Probably because she knew her brains would never let her down. '*Je suis anglaise et j'habite au Château de Hever.*'

'*Bravo!*' cried Tristan, 'I can see you're going to be the best pupil a tutor could wish for. *N'est-ce pas*, Maman?'

Aunt Grace laughed. '*Certainement.* By the time you and Cecy leave here, I am sure you'll speak French fluently. Or as we say here: "*tu parleras couramment le français*".'

Even though I'd lived a comparatively sheltered life at Zennor, without robustious brothers such as Tom and George Bullen as companions, and had only just passed my twelfth birthday, I was able to recognize a knowing air in my cousin that would bring a blush to the cheeks of many an experienced chit about the court. I watched as Tristan let his eyes wander to Nan's lips and keep them there for longer than was proper. In return, Nan let out a little giggle and at least had the grace to blush. But there was also a new sparkle in my friend's hazel eyes.

<<*She's not even twelve for another month*>> I felt very grown-up in my disapproval even though there were only a few months between us, not a decade. As for Tristan, there was no denying it: he'd matured since last May Day when that prank in Cornwall had nearly gone so badly wrong. This new Tristan might be as friendly as ever to me, but in the intervening year he'd acquired airs of which I felt I understood little.

'Come, Cecy, let me introduce you to your Uncle Guy,' Tristan's mother said. 'Nan, you come too.'

After the stories Tristan had told me about his father forcing him into the Church, I didn't go willingly to the other side of the garden where the Governor of Picardy was talking to Claude Bouton and Valentine's father. However, for the sake of politeness, I let my aunt guide us. I thought Guy d'Ardres looked rather fierce. Father had told me that the Governor of Picardy had an outstanding military reputation. On the way into the Castle, we'd passed beneath the Ardres family coat-of-arms; there was something about the Count that made me think of the black and gold eagle on the crest. Perhaps it was his slightly hooked nose. He was undoubtedly personable with his jet black hair and dark piercing eyes, but his haughty manner and bearing reminded me too much of Nan's frightening grandsire, Thomas Howard, Earl of Surrey.

'*Enchanté, mes demoiselle*s,' my new uncle said as we bobbed a little curtsey, his smile reassuringly reaching his eyes. While the Countess laughed and joked with Claude Bouton and the Baron, I noticed her husband's eyes lovingly resting on her tiny slender frame - pride written all over his face. And it was obvious that she felt the same. I noticed the warm smile that lit up Aunt Grace's dainty features, as well as the great tenderness in her luminous green eyes whenever she looked at her husband. Realising that Tristan's father was bewitched by his lively wife, I began to relax about the prospect of spending a week at the Castle. Before today, I'd always thought there was an air of sadness about my aunt I couldn't quite put my finger on: a distant memory that had perhaps cast a shadow over her life. I recalled the French song she'd sung at Zennor Castle: one so sad that tears seemed to cling to every word. However, seeing her so contented here in France with her husband, I realized I must have been mistaken.

I wondered where Tristan's older brother was as I was eager to meet him. And where was his parents' ward, Nicolas? The one he'd once described as "*a toad-spotted varlet*"? Perhaps it was just as well that one hadn't turned up....

I took a deep breath and felt at peace for the first time since leaving the harbour at Dover. My joy at being reunited with Tristan and his mother at this castle on French soil was making me feel as though I'd arrived at a little piece of home.

NICOLAS
Chapter Twenty-Six

Following the sounds of a May Day in full swing, Nicolas boldly rode through the front gates of Guillaume Gouffier's stone manor house in Brêmes. If the master of the house had an inkling of the identity of the latest reveller to arrive, Nicolas knew no invitation would be forthcoming. Quite the opposite. But he didn't care; in fact, it made his visit all the more entertaining. With its twin towers and matching turrets, crowstepped gables on either side of the main house, as well as its symmetrical windows, it was a house of which *Gascon* must be proud. Best friends with François d'Angoulême, now Duc de Valois and old King Louis' heir - with no sign of a male heir from Queen Anne of Brittany, *Gascon's* star was definitely in the ascendant.

Nicolas slid off Machiavelli and handed the reins to one of *Gascon's* grooms.

'*Avec plaisir*, Monsieur le Baron,' the boy said, taking the reins while bowing and scraping to the stallion's master. Nicolas found it quite amusing that he'd been given a title he didn't deserve; undoubtedly, Machiavelli's noble appearance had convinced the boy that his master must be similarly endowed. He had no intention of owning up to the truth - and being reduced to a simple '*Monsieur*'.

Nicolas brushed some blades of grass from his doublet. 'Where's your master?' he asked, hoping to remain *incognito* a little longer.

'He's gone inside the house. We were about to crown our King and Queen of the May when some men entered the gate in search of him, riding as if their lives depended upon it.'

'*Ah bon?*'

The boy looked proud to have some important information to pass on. He straightened his brown jerkin as if he were the King's own messenger. '*Oui.* They said they'd come straight from Brest and needed to speak to the master. They looked travel weary. It's over four hundred miles away and they said they'd been on the road for days.'

'Brest? And you have no idea why they're here?'

'*Hélas*! They took their grooms in with them to eat and drink in the kitchens so I got no chance to ask them their business. But I'm guessing it's something to do with the English.'

Nicolas frowned, wondering what had happened in Brittany. 'I think you're probably right.'

'They said some riders had gone straight to Paris to find the King. Others have gone locally to the Governor of Picardy over at Ardres Castle. Oh, look, Monsieur le Baron, it's—'

Turning at the sound of a horse's hooves on cobblestones, Nicolas heard a familiar voice shouting his name: '*Wolf.* Is that really you? I was going to send a messenger over to the Castle tomorrow.'

With that, the Duc de Valois, clad entirely in Maytime green, leapt from his horse and threw his arms around Nicolas in a typically enthusiastic greeting.

Behind them, the groom's jaw was hanging open (Nicolas saw him mouthing '*Ventrebleu!*'), no doubt thinking that after all the comings and goings today, the stables were the place to be, not the gardens with the pretty demoiselles and the dancing.

'Come, let's go and see if we can find a tasty morsel,' said François, flinging his arm around one of Nicolas's shoulders and steering him in the direction of the painted maypole, decorated with pretty ribbons. The villagers had obviously been busy bringing in wildflowers, as well as branches of hawthorn (with their highly-scented pink and white flowers, and tiny red haws), not to mention making floral garlands to wear about their necks.

'Are you talking about food or ladies, François?'

'What do you think? Although if I'm with you, I'm probably robbing myself of any success. Choosing between your perfect straight nose and my long "foxnose", I know who'll lose out. Perhaps I should have washed myself in the early morning dew earlier. Isn't May Dew supposed to make your complexion radiant?'

Nicolas laughed, pushing his failure with Ysabeau to the back of his mind. 'I wouldn't know. These ladies you're talking about might enjoy my flattery until they find out which of us has a good chance of ending up as the next King of France.'

'Not if the wife of my cousin, Louis, has anything to do with it.' François pulled a face of *faux* horror. 'Every time Anne of Brittany starts cradling her belly for the slightest reason, even after a heavy meal on a feast day, my mother is instantly beside herself with worry. She's still hanging onto to the prophecy that hermit made all those years ag—'

'That you'd be king against all the odds.'

'That's right.'

As they neared the merrymakers, François turned to Nicolas 'Where's *Gascon*?'

'Inside. Some horsemen came with news. Something to do with Brittany. The crowning of the May King and May Queen has been delayed because of it. Is *Gascon* alone or is his wife with him?'

'*Gascon* never brings her here.'

Nicolas remembered Twelfth Night, seeing Gascon disappear with a woman who certainly wasn't Bonaventure du Puy-du-Fou. 'I'm sure he doesn't. Why were you out riding when I got here?'

François grinned and tapped his long nose, his brown eyes dancing with mischief. '*Foi de gentilhomme*! That would be telling.'

Nicolas stared at his friend. 'I know that expression and it usually involves a woman.'

'*Eh bien*, you're right and you're wrong.'

'So now I have to guess a riddle. Let me see. I'm right that you went out searching for one and wrong that your search was fruitful.'

'*Wolf*, you're too clever for me. I arranged to meet a certain young lady at the entrance to the woods but I fear her nursemaid guessed my intentions.'

'*Nursemaid*, François? *Sacristi*! How old are we talking here?'

'Fifteen. But I'm only eighteen myself. So it's hardly a crime.'

'Nicolas shrugged. 'I always forget you're three years younger than me.'

'Yes, but we're both to be husbands. Sooner than we'd like. Wed to "the cousins". As the farmers in the fields say; "*when the sun shines make hay. Which is to say…take time when the time comes, in case time wastes away.*"'

François was looking very pleased with himself at his proverb; next to him, Nicolas had that sinking feeling in the pit of his stomach whenever he thought of his own freedom being curtailed one day in the not so distant future. François had taken to calling their brides: Claude de Valois and Robine de Croisic: "*the cousins*", to let Nicolas know he wasn't alone in his dismal predicament. Two vigorous young men entering the prime of their lives, tethered to girls neither healthy nor graced with good looks, but heiresses in their own right. Claude: to the Kingdom of Brittany; Robine: to her father's fortune.

'Why don't you stay the night, *Wolf*? I've told *Gascon* I want to go hawking tomorrow. It might be the last chance we get if *Henri d'Angleterre* invades and this war goes ahead. It seems there's an abundance of herons nestling on the banks of the Hem this year. It would tickle me to watch you beat *Gascon* as usual.'

Nicolas was about to reply when he noticed a commotion near the entrance of the house. Some men were running up the steps and calling out to others to follow them.'

'*Par Dieu, Wolf*!' exclaimed François. 'Let's go and find out what's so important that the King and Queen of the May are still waiting for their crowns.'

TRISTAN

Chapter Twenty-Seven

The Castle gardens.

God's Teeth! Why did Father have to turn up now? He'll only blight everything.

Since my punishment on Twelfth Night, he and I had been polite but very distant. That first night, as I lay tossing and turning at the unfairness of it all - sweet memories of Ysabeau de Sapincourt temporarily forgotten - an invisible dagger had floated noiselessly through the air down the corridor to my parents' chamber and hovered over my father's heart. But to no avail. I'd awoken in the morning, no nearer to a solution to my problem. It was time to take Guillaume Gouffier's 'godfatherly' advice to "*act so disgracefully*" that my deeds would get back to Father; accordingly, once my chores in the church and kitchen were finished, I put my new campaign into action. Beginning with my scandalously overt flirtation with Ysabeau on Twelfth Night, right under Father's very nose, this was swiftly followed by every other act of defiance of which I could think. He would have needed to be blind, deaf and dumb not to see his younger son had no calling whatsoever to enter the Church. And he was certainly none of those things.

All my hopes for a second public dalliance with Ysabeau on this May Day had been dashed. One moment I noticed Nicolas was nowhere to be seen, gleefully hoping he'd left because he knew his cause with Ysabeau was lost. The very next, I turned back to see that Ysabeau's swag-bellied husband, Robert, had appeared from nowhere and was now standing next to her in the manner of a gaoler guarding a highly prized prisoner. To make matters worse, the Fleury brat sought me out, tugging at my doublet and threatening with me with all kinds of terrible torments unless I went off to the gardens with her. In the end I agreed, seeing that the situation with Ysabeau was hopeless…at least for today.

May Day was traditionally a time for lovers, with its celebration of the return of spring and its association with fertility rites. After my first magical encounter with the exquisite Comtesse de Saint-Séverin, my interest in the fairer sex was increasing by the day. Of course the English girl in the garden, Cecy's friend, was far too young for me but I'd quickly learned to discern dormant passion. And she had plenty of that. I knew Father was watching me but good manners would prevent him from reprimanding me if I went too far, owing to the presence of Valentine's father and the visitor from Flanders.

I was delighted to see Cecy again, making me think of all the exciting visits to Zennor Castle which was set in the perfect surroundings for an adventurous young boy. Even if Cecy always teased me mercilessly for not being able to swim as well as her - or for my non-existent knowledge of Cornish.

"You don't deserve to call yourself a Cornishman of any kind," she would mock. *"Even half a one."*

Once again, the only fly in the ointment (apart from Father) was the irksome Valentine. She kept pestering me to talk to her, attempting to interrupt my conversation with the girls and pulling on my sleeve. Seeing this, Cecy tried to help me out by speaking French to the little monster.

'*Enchanté* to finally meet you, Valentine. Tristan has often spoken of you.'

There was suspicion and belligerence in Valentine's pale blue eyes when Cecy said this, and her reply when it came was abrupt. I knew she guessed exactly what kind of things had been said about her.

After a while, I lost patience…especially when I wanted to keep speaking English in order to make myself understood to Cecy's friend, Nan. 'Oh, *nom d'un nom*, Valentine! Leave me alone, will you.' As if to prove I meant it, I turned my back on her completely, relieved that this time it seemed to have done the trick. That was obviously what she needed: a firmer hand.

Thoughts of Valentine soon faded to the back of my mind as I pointedly continued to laugh and joke with the girls, and Mother, who'd come over to join us. The fact that Father had never bothered to learn Mother's native tongue was making the whole experience even more enjoyable.

'Cecy's parents, the Count and I once visited Eltham Palace,' Mother told Nan, after overhearing Father asking Claude Bouton about his recent stay at the English court. 'When the old King was on the throne. We were staying as guests of William Blount, Baron Mountjoy, in Greenwich. That's where my husband and I first met friends of ours - two scholars - Desiderius Erasmus and Thomas More. We also met young King Henry. Or the Duke of York, as he was called then.'

'What was he like?' asked Nan. 'Cecy and I met him on the Feast of Candlemas this past February.'

Mother smiled. 'You did? How interesting. I want to hear all about it. He was just a boy then, about the same age as little Valentine over there. So well-proportioned, lively and gifted. The royal tutor to the Tudor children was there too. John Skelton. A talented poet—'

My father's voice cut across Mother's words. '*Malheureusement*, I fear war is exactly what lies ahead. As you both know, we've been expecting an invasion for months now.'

Able to switch from English back to French with infinite ease, hearing my father use the word '*war*', '*la guerre*', halted me in my tracks; I was troubled by his undeniably grave tone...although the idea of war opened up endless possibilities for adventure and excitement. Mother had mentioned Desiderius Erasmus. What was it he'd said to me in that darkened corridor on New Year's Eve? Oh, yes. "*Dulce bellum inexpertio*". '*War is sweet to those who have not tried it.*' Ignoring the wisdom of the Dutch humanist's words, I instantly stopped listening to Mother's story of England's boy king (I would ask Cecy about her meeting with the King of England later); I was far more interested in Father's story of what this same 'man' king was up to at the moment.

I wandered off towards my father and the other men, leaving Mother on the other side of the lawn still regaling the girls with stories of the young prince. Turning, I saw her leading Cecy and Nan down the steps to her rose garden below: her pride and joy, filled with blooms from cuttings she'd brought back from Zennor. In particular, her prized Damask roses gifted to her once by Cecy's grandam. I would lay down my life for my adored mother and had no wish for her to be frightened unnecessarily by any talk of the threat of war.

'At least wolves no longer roam our capital devouring the corpses,' I could hear Valentine's father saying to the other two men as I drew nearer. 'Surely, *mes amis*, that must be counted as a small mercy—'

&

As I threw myself down on the lawn near the bench, hearing this made me think of my very own 'wolf' that resided in Ardres Castle. I was glad Nicolas hadn't made a re-appearance at the May Day revelling; not only would he be vexingly strong competition for the attentions of Nan but he'd be able to join in the discussion on war, knowing he'd be part of it soon enough. I, on the other hand, had to loiter on the edge like a starving bird seeking crumbs of bread from the loaf of life. Since Twelfth Night, Nicolas and I had been circling around each other like a pair of wild beasts, hardly speaking unless strictly necessary. I knew I shouldn't have taken his horse that afternoon but the stables had been empty, apart from Minuit or 'Machiavelli', as he was now known. How folly-fallen and typical of Nicolas who fancied himself as an expert on all manner of subjects, a budding warrior, and seasoned lover. His horse had snickered at me the moment I walked in. As if to say: '*Take me, Tristan. No one will ever know.*'

I'd succumbed to temptation thinking that, in a way, the horse should rightfully have been mine. Then, after our fight and my harsh punishment, I'd decided to attempt to take my revenge on Nicolas in a way I knew would hit my enemy the hardest. Although I'd found Robert de Sapincourt's new young wife extremely alluring, the fact her husband was one of our neighbours might well have put me off, causing me to seek my pleasure in pastures slightly further than home…had it not been for Nicolas's clear interest in her.

Immediately, it had turned into one of our customary battles. As Lord of Misrule, I seized the moment to impress Ysabeau with some mournful song about the woman in an enormous painting hanging in our great hall. The day before, I'd heard some of the maids chattering in an animated fashion as they polished the painting's frame. They were discussing the romance between this Loba, the She-Wolf of Cabaret, and a wandering minstrel. I noticed their secret smiles and wistful voices, and used this as inspiration on Twelfth Night. It was the first time I'd challenged Nicolas in this particular sphere (of love, in which I knew my rival excelled), and victory tasted sweet. Even a couple of venomous remarks by Nicolas the next morning hadn't been able to spoil things for me. Back in March, Jean had more than repaid him for his malice by cheating him out of that goodly sum at cards.

I couldn't help thinking how much I missed Jean, wishing he were here to meet Cecy and Nan. Our visit to Cap Gris-Nez had ended abruptly with our being chased by some English men-at-arms after we came upon them unexpectedly, both of us caught off-guard speaking excitedly in French: the language of the enemy. We'd just spotted about twenty ships, including a fair few, long low ones, with oarsmen at the helm. Being young and drunk on adventure, the fact that we were pursued as far as our horses (and the frisson of fear that came with that) only added to our enjoyment. Thank goodness Mother never found out or Fa—'

'You saw my son doing *what*?'

Father's angry question pulled me out of my memories and made me jerk my head upwards. Charles de Fleury was staring at his little daughter as if he dreaded to think what she'd just said. *Diantre*! How could I have missed Valentine creeping around the garden like an evil sprite on a mission to mischief. Sidling up to Father. Beckoning him to crouch down so that she could whisper in his ear.

All eyes were now on the little fiend, including mine; I was so wishing I *had* pushed her into the lake that day last month when she forced me to take her riding. Her cheeks were flushed and I could see defiance written all over her face. As the grinning vixen opened her mouth to speak, I suddenly knew that what was about to come out was going to cost me dear.

Very dear.

'I saw Tristan kissing Bonne's *tétons* in your stables on Valentine's Day,' she intoned in a singsong voice as if it were a child's lullaby. 'And yesterday I heard him telling a friend about his trip to Cap Gris-Nez in March. How he and his friend, Jean, were lucky to get back safely after nearly getting caught by some English soldiers.'

She finally stopped to catch her breath, in the manner of a marauding army pausing to assess the devastation it has caused.

There was a stunned silence, apart from a suppressed cough from the Flemish visitor. Then Father took a deep breath and glared at me. Although his face was an implacable mask, beneath, I knew his emotions would be churning; glancing down, I saw his fists were curled into two tight balls.

'*Nom d'un chien*! You witless young fool! Whatever were you thinking? If the English had caught you trespassing on their land, in their current mood they would probably have strung you both up. Have you any idea what it would have done to your poor mother if we'd found you dangling from a rope in Audinghen?

'And what exactly, Tristan, would you have had me say to the Duke of Lorraine? That his younger brother, entrusted into my care, accidentally wandered onto English soil. And wouldn't be coming home again. Ever.'

I was stunned into appalled silence; my only consolation was that Mother, Cecy and her friend weren't here to witness my humiliation.

'*Je m'excuse, Père*,' was all I managed eventually as Charles de Fleury reached out and pulled the cause of the pandemonium towards him.

My father opened his mouth again, no doubt to berate me about my dissolute behaviour with Bonne, but the words died on his lips. Curious, I turned and followed his gaze. A stranger was striding across the lawn towards us with great purpose, perhaps a messenger of some sort? A wave of relief flooded over me. It was as if Hermes himself, the cleverest and most mischievous of all the Olympian gods, had arrived to rescue me from an impossible predicament.

TRISTAN
Chapter Twenty-Eight

I watched as Hermes (as I'd gratefully christened him) walked up to my father who, by now, was on his feet. My saviour, who was holding two rolls of parchment in his hand, was dressed in the King's livery: dark blue…with Old Louis' badge on one shoulder, depicting a porcupine standing on the lower part of a letter L. In Latin, this creature was called a 'quill pig'; I knew the quills usually lay flat unless the porcupine felt threatened and then they would stand on end, as formidable as any pikes gripped by soldiers in battle. As a show of support for King Louis, and to prove he was being well-guarded, all the quills were upright and upon them, at the very top, sat the royal crown.

Hermes gave a little bow as he handed over one of the rolls of parchment, bearing the royal seal of the porcupine. 'Monsieur le Comte, His Majesty asked me to bring you this.'

I watched my father quickly undo the ribbon and break open the seal. As he read its contents, I watched the enraged expression on his face from his recent dealings with me gradually change to one of grim acceptance.

'*Messieurs*,' he said in a controlled voice, devoid of emotion, 'the King has sent grave tidings. He writes that he has it from a very reliable source - namely a Norman priest from Argentan who has been living at the English court - that *Henri d'Angleterre* intends to invade us next month.

'It seems we are finally to be at war!'

Charles de Fleury was the first one to find his voice. 'Guy, may I suggest we go up to your study where we can discuss matters further. And you, Valentine,' he said, turning to his not at all penitent looking goblin daughter, 'will go and find your mother right away.'

Valentine looked as though she was going to protest but then thought better of it; instead she sulkily retraced her steps across the lawn. I watched her go, rewarded for my efforts by the sight of an impudent pink tongue as she turned the corner.

The Flemish visitor was stroking his chin. 'This news changes everything. The English girls and I need to leave at first light.'

My father nodded, a little distracted. '*Oui, oui, naturellement*. My home will no longer be safe for those considered to be enemies of France.'

<<*Charming! Does that include Mother and me?*>>

Hermes handed my father the second roll of parchment. 'This one is from some riders who have come straight from Brest. We met on the road near Ardres and they asked me to bring it to you. It is from the Captain at the Château in Brest.'

Father took it from him and unrolled it. This time his expression was one of surprise that turned to pleasure. 'A great sea victory! There's been a French victory off the coast of Brest.'

'*Bravo!*' cried Charles de Fleury, punching the air with his fist. 'What else does the letter say?'

My father paused for a moment. 'That the English Lord High Admiral tried to board our own Admiral's ship but Prégent de Bidoux's pikemen surrounded him, pushed him against the rails and then toppled him into the sea.'

I could feel myself going hot and cold. 'Is he dead?'

My father looked at me oddly. '*Oui.*'

'And are you sure it was the Admiral and not the Vice-Admiral?'

'What is this *absurdité*, Tristan? It was the English Admiral.'

I felt like leaping up and hugging him. 'That's wonderful news!'

He looked perplexed 'While I am surprised you see the victory as quite the cause for celebration, I cannot say I am disappointed.' He managed the hint of a smile. 'We'll make a Frenchman of you yet.'

Relief that it wasn't Edward Howard made me unusually gracious: '*Bien sûr, Père.*'

'Now,' said my father, 'You have the opportunity to prove yourself a worthy son rather than a reckless varlet. As much as I love your mother, it wouldn't be right for me to give her such calamitous news about her countrymen. Please go down to the rose garden and break the news of the French victory. Gently, mind.'

I needed no encouragement; I knew it was a task I was more than suited for. Leaping up, I dashed across the garden in the direction of the steps to the rose garden.

My mother looked confused. 'A French victory?'

'Yes, a considerable one. And a huge defeat for us. Unfortunately, we English lost our Admiral.'

'The Earl of Oxford? John de Vere.' My mother crossed herself. 'God rest his soul. The only consolation is that he was an old man and had seen out a long life, not to mention a worthy career at sea.'

'The Lord High Admiral?' Nan repeated slowly, her eyes almost black in a white face. 'Are you sure it wasn't the Vice-Admiral?'

It seemed strange to be holding a mirror image of the conversation I'd just had with my father. 'Quite sure. It was definitely the Lord High Admiral.'

Nan let out a wail and dropped to the ground. 'No! No! Not Uncle Ned!' she cried. 'Not him.'

'It wasn't him,' I reassured her, crouching down to put one hand on her shoulder. 'It was the Admiral, not the Vice-Admiral. I made sure of that.'

Cecy stared down at me, her face stricken. 'Tristan, Edward Howard *was* the Lord High Admiral. The old one died at the end of March and Nan's uncle replaced him. Living here, you haven't heard.'

I couldn't believe my ears but I could believe my eyes; the niece of my very own Edward Howard was prostrate on the ground, sobbing her eyes out. I stood up to say something to Mother but as I straightened up, her eyes fluttered, her head rolled back and she fell into my arms in a dead faint.

VALENTINE

Chapter Twenty-nine

S till gripping some daisy petals in her hand, a disgruntled Valentine very slowly made her way back up to find her mother and sisters, dawdling every step of the way in the vain hope her father might catch her up.

Shard-borne Tristan d'Ardres!

It was all his fault her father had sent her away, forbidding her to stay longer and spend time with the Countess and the two English girls.

'Shard-borne Tristan d'Ardres!' Valentine repeated out loud, and with great feeling. She was angry with herself that she'd let her father down. Charles de Fleury was not a man easily given to complaint but he was out of sorts today, and she knew herself to be the cause.

Or rather…Tristan d'Ardres.

She so wished her father was with her now to reassure her that all would be well. Her nursemaid, Bonne, was sure to be in a fury when she heard that Valentine had given away her shameful secret. Oh, why did her father have to spend his time talking about pribbling old England anyway? Valentine already hated the language with its harsh sounds, and the English themselves seemed hardly better - even though Grace d'Ardres was always very kind to her, and both Tristan's cousin and the girl called Anne had smiled in a friendly enough manner when they left.

But then again, Tristan was half-English which only went to prove her point.

'England, England, England!' Valentine railed out loud, flinging the squashed daisy petals into the air. 'I hate the country! I hate the language! I hate the people!

'But most of all…I hate the King of England!'

THE HOUSE OF HOWARD

Chapter Thirty

The same day. Framlingham Castle, East Anglia.

W hy? Why? Why, oh Lord, did you have to take him? My boy. My golden boy. My Edward. Edward.'

I rasped the words out loud; to my ears, my voice sounded strained, harsh…broken. Kneeling on the step beneath the altar with its backdrop of a recent purchase of a Flemish tapestry, depicting the Adoration of the Magi, I was aware I was quite undone. Normally I would be drinking in the reds, blues and greens, appreciating every last thread of the scene. Today, with all the colour washed from my life, all I could see was grey, more grey, and even more of it.

No colour at all.

The cut-purse responsible for the loss of my earthly joy had come creeping up the drive yesterday morning in the guise of a messenger, on his way to bring my life crashing down around my ears, with the same momentum as the earthquake that took down the buildings in Vesuvius in olden times. He brought with him two letters: the first - in a final twist of the knife by a cackling Dame Fortune, and to break my heart quite completely - was from Edward himself. Seeing the Howard lions standing up straight and proud on his own personal seal, I'd picked that one first. In a touching gesture, he'd cut a lock of his dark hair and carefully placed it beneath the beeswax, tinted with vermilion. The second was a missive from the King, telling me my precious boy was now lying at the bottom of the Narrow Sea. Making mischief at the court of King Neptune instead of that of Henry Tudor, exchanging May Day garlands for strips of seaweed.

I forced open my eyes, swollen from the rainstorm of tears I'd shed since opening the heinous letter, with the King's own red seal of him gaily out hunting (without a care in the world), a greyhound by his side. This image was accompanied by the obligatory Tudor rose in the background. Red. The colour of blood. The lifeblood of my second-born son. And white. The colour of heaven and its angels. The King could have used a black seal: the traditional colour of mourning, but if I'd laid eyes on that I truly believed my heart would have stopped mid-beat. Already on the first reading, the terrible words written there had blurred before my eyes, transforming themselves into ugly black spiders on the page, intent upon bringing destruction and despair. Twenty-four unbearably long hours later, the pain of reading had dulled into a constant ache rather than the unbearable agony that had ripped through my entire body at the beginning. I unrolled the parchment, noting a few smudges here and there where the tears of a loving father had left their mark on the page....

'*Thomas,*' the King wrote, the pleasingly bold flourishes undeserving of their place on a page of doom. '*News so grave I can scarcely find the words. Our Ned was honourably killed in battle off the coast of Brest on April 25th. Captured on a ship of the enemy while giving fight, he was thrown over the side by some common sailors and most tragically drowned. I have lost a precious brother. And you a son.*

Edward Etchingham, a captain and a witness, described our boy thus: "There was never a noble man so ill lost as he was that was so full of courage and had so many virtues. He who ruled so great an army as well as he did and kept so great order and true justice.'

I let the parchment slide through my fingers, knowing the rest *verbatim*: how King Henry praised Edward and said for his sake we must all carry on and wage pitiless war against France in his name, as a way of avenging his untimely death. The other letter still set my heart beating as I could almost imagine Edward beside me, uttering the words. It was dated April 23rd (by a fine irony), the Feast of Saint George, patron saint of England. I was sure if someone asked me I would also be able to recite these words by heart; it was as if a branding iron had seared them into my memory. I pulled apart the second letter, my throat already tight at the prospect of meeting my son again one last time on this earth, even if it was in the form of a letter and not face to face:

'*Father,*' Edward wrote in his beautiful hand. '*I trust this finds you well and in better spirits than me. Since we bade each other farewell on Portsmouth Harbour, matters have not gone as smoothly as I hoped. As you know, I already had to turn my ship back to Plymouth for lack of victuals. I fear I need your help most urgently. With every passing day, our supplies are dwindling to nothing and we cannot last much longer. I have begged the King for help but to no avail—*'

A noise from the back of the chapel startled me. Who would dare to interrupt me in my darkest hour of grief? A great wave of rage swept over me. 'Get out!' I yelled without turning around. My voice was hoarse and cracked through grief. I wasn't going to let anyone in the world see my cheeks mottled red and damp with womanish tears. Not Agnes, not my other children. There was only one child I would have welcomed with open arms but he was lost to me forever. If it was a messenger from his widow, Alice Parker, I wasn't interested. The woman had brought him material comfort, not happiness. Or heirs. To my increasing fury, I could hear footsteps getting ever nearer. Not only would I have my servants outside the chapel flogged but I would do it myself—

A hand came to rest on my shoulder, not forceful but firm…even gentle. Bitterly resenting another human touch (the wrong human touch), I jerked my head round and found myself looking into the concerned blue eyes of—

❧

'Y-you!' I stuttered, hardly able to believe who was standing there. Dressed from head to toe in Cardinal Red (even though he hadn't even reached the rank of bishop), apart from a white shirt and black riding boots, it was as if I were staring at an apparition. No hair shirt for this one. Hardly knowing what I was thinking or doing, I distractedly appraised the man before me, if only to give my mind a moment's respite from the grief that threatened to engulf me entirely. There was no denying he was a comely figure of a man with the appealing features of someone who took delight in all the senses: far more preening than priest-like. His mouth alone, full-lipped, absurdly shaped to form a smile or bestow a kiss, was enough to give the game away. This was no mealy-mouthed, fitful, fasting ascetic, raising a belt for self-flagellation - intent upon denying himself the pleasures of life. The blue eyes, usually dancing with humour and intelligence, were today sorrowful and filled with compassion—

<<*God's Fury! What on earth is wrong with me? How can I think of anyone else but my Edward*>>

Even with the King's Almoner standing right next to me. My arch-enemy, my….

Snake!

For some absurd reason, I didn't immediately send him away. After all, it was possible he'd come with a message from the King. Saying that it was all a terrible mistake and my Edward wasn't dead after all.

'May I sit?' Tom Wolsey asked. 'I've ridden post horse from Westminster to reach you as if the very Devil was on my coat-tail. My sore backside is

217

presently showing its great displeasure, complaining that it no longer belongs to a young man of twenty-four, but to a far more mature one that's recently turned forty.'

I gestured to the front pew behind us and, in spite of my better judgement, I allowed Tom to help me to my feet and guide me to my place. My heart was in my mouth as I eased myself down, waiting for the words that would free me from my torment. What did it matter if my old enemy noticed that my eyes resembled dog piss in the snow, frozen in grief. Or perhaps twin red hot coals in a furnace, burning up with despair.

<<*Tell me, tell me it's not true. Tell me my Edward's coming home*>>

Tom looked at me for a long moment, then he reached up and removed the heavy gold crucifix from around his neck. He took a deep breath and turned to me. 'Thomas, I'm not here in an official capacity.'

<<*So, it's true then. So help me dear Mother of God. 'Tis true*>>

'I'm not here as a representative of God or the King. I'm here as...' Here he hesitated. 'As a man. And a friend, if you'll let me be one.'

He put out a hand and grasped me by my right shoulder again, giving it a little squeeze. 'And I'm here as a father, though I know I have no right to be one in the eyes of God. But how can I dare come to you who's lost so much these past months unless I declare myself weak and frail. God has seen fit to take two of your children from you, while deigning to place another in my arms shortly. Tom is three and thriving, thanks be to God. And Dame Fortune.' He closed his eyes and made the sign of the cross. I couldn't quite bring myself to follow suit, not on this day of bitter loss. Tom opened his eyes and looked at me. 'But my heart would still be sore to lose little Tom.' His voice was soft and full of pity.

I let out a long sigh, trying to rid myself of the sorrow within as if I could exhale it in the manner of air being released from a football. Eventually I managed to speak. 'The pain of losing a child is like losing an eye or a limb.

Especially when you're so attached to them. As I was with my Lizzie and Ed-' The words suddenly halted, dried up in their tracks at the back of my throat, waiting to be watered by the tears I was trying so hard to prevent. 'D-did he have a good death?' I burst out, willing myself to be strong and act like a man, not a snivelling child. 'I only know he climbed onto an enemy ship and was thrown overboard by common sailors—' I couldn't go on; the muscles of my stomach were so tight I feared they'd snap with the effort if I clenched them for a moment longer.

Tom squeezed my shoulder a third time. 'That is why I have come, my friend. To try and ease your pain and soothe your poor soul.'

'It seems your Edward launched his attack at around four in the afternoon on the 25th, the Feast of Saint Mark.'

'In broad daylight? What was he thinking? No wonder he said to me the last time I saw him in Portsmouth that: *"never did seaman any good if he wasn't resolute to a point of madness."'*

'I have no doubt that Edward did whatever he thought was necessary. It was a miracle his leading rowbarge even reached the ship belonging to the Admiral of France. To get to the galleys, Edward had to steer through shallow water filled with treacherous rocks and heavily armed bulwarks. The excoriating crossfire of guns and crossbows he travelled through would have turned the bowels of most men to water. Clambering aboard was an extremely brave act—'

I put my head in my hands. '"*Clambering aboard Prester John's ship?*" God's Pity, Tom! Show some respect to your King's most experienced military commander. Taking on a man as formidable as the French Admiral was like walking up to a ravenous lion and expecting it to hold out its paw for you to shake. How many men were with him?'

'Forgive me, Thomas. I am well aware of the excellence of your skills as a commander. I was merely trying to find a chink of light in the darkness in which we find ourselves. One Spaniard and around sixteen sailors accompanied him. It seems they tied their small boat to the French ship but it was either cut loose by the enemy, or slipped away by itself. So they were left stranded with no choice but to fight for their lives.'

'Oh dear God! What led Edward into such an act of folly?'

'Desperation, I fear.' Tom's voice was quiet. 'The French were in their own waters and always had the advantage. Edward had been trying to set up a blockade for some days, but lack of immediate supplies meant that he either had to attack or to—'

'Return to England in ignominy. Like his brother, Thomas, and Dorset, crawling back from Spain last year with their tails between their legs, and an enormous F for failure stamped on their foreheads. He couldn't risk a Howard offending the King again.' I clasped my forehead. 'So he died to spare all of us. As well as honouring his oath to avenge his brother-in-law, Tom Knyvett.'

'Yes, I'm afraid that's about the sum of it. Supplies were on their way but didn't reach him in time. He risked everything in order to secure for Henry the greatest prize of all.'

'Well, "*everything*" turned out to be his own life,' I said without rancour. What was the point? Any more than it would help holding the King to task for being so tardy with the necessary victuals. This was war. I steeled myself to ask the burning question as if I were wearing a gilt shield upon my arm, in the same way as my lost boy must have done.

'And his last moments?'

'He made it onto the main deck but by then matters were hopeless. Some of Prégent's pikemen forced him up against the rails and then pushed him over the side.'

I groaned. 'The weight of his armour meant he would have sunk like a stone.'

'Sadly, yes. But even in his last moments his mind was on honour. He threw his Admiral's whistle over the side so it wouldn't fall into enemy hands.'

'His whistle,' I repeated dully, thinking of it golden and gleaming in that Portsmouth tavern not so very long ago.

Next to me, Tom shifted a little and then reached out to take hold of my right wrist. I felt something in the palm of my hand and looked down.

<<Edward's whistle!>>

'By the Mass! How on God's good earth—'

'It was found in his cabin on 'The Mary Rose'. I believe it's the one he favoured. And wore more than any of the others.'

Seeing the large ruby in the centre, I knew with complete certainty that this was the one Edward had been wearing around his neck when I pulled him into my arms, that final day we were together on earth. Holding my precious son's whistle and realizing that this golden object, together with a few shining strands of his brown hair, was all that I had left of him in the world, proved to be my undoing. Suddenly without warning, my shoulders began to heave and a great tidal wave of grief was unleashed somewhere deep within my being. In that moment, as I threw myself against Tom Wolsey's shoulder, head in hands, I was as much at sea as my poor, dead son.

After what seemed like an age…at least an hour, but probably was only minutes…Tom respectfully handed me a handkerchief. As if returning from a long voyage, I began to blow my nose noisily, surprisingly grateful I had washed up onto the shore of the living once more. I didn't even attempt to excuse my behaviour; in the womblike surroundings of the Howard family chapel, Tom had seen the very core of my being. Whatever we would be to one another in the future, this was a moment frozen in time when he'd stood shoulder to shoulder with me outside the gates of heaven, holding me steady as I stared at the place harbouring my dearly beloved, foolish...foolish son.

I looked at Tom and gave a couple of loud sniffs, wiping away a stray tardy tear or two that had arrived too late to join their comrades in the fast-flowing river of grief. 'Tell me honestly. What is the King saying in private? Not in public where he's respectfully mourning England's Lord High Admiral. I need to hear what he's saying about my son.'

I could see that he was hesitating. 'He said he's lost the only Howard with a heart.'

In normal times, I would have smiled at this telling comment, proud that one Howard was so valued by the King - but not today. 'What else? Tell me. I have to know.'

Tom pursed his lips together and folded his hands neatly over each other in the manner of a priest hearing a confession. 'Very well. He was angry at what he saw as Edward's recklessness. At the failure of the blockade, and the shameful return of the fleet to Plymouth...rudderless. But - most importantly - that his fleet had slunk back...leaderless.'

I was both chastened and grateful. 'Thank you for being so honest.'

'Thomas, you and I both know Henry is but a boy. He's lashing out because he's lost a dear friend and doesn't know what to do with his feelings. Anymore than he did when he lost his beloved mother as a boy of eleven. So he's hiding behind fury because he feels it's the kingly thing to do. Trust me, inside he's howling with pain as he mourns your son.'

I knew he was right. 'I, too, am mourning a life that might have been. For everything that lay ahead for Edward on his future path.'

Even though Tom said he hadn't come in the name of God, I felt as though I were in the confessional stall and needed to get my sins off my chest. My voice was barely audible. 'About the sons he might have had.'

Tom stared at me for a long moment. 'But he did have them. Two if I'm not mistaken.'

I gave a low chuckle that instantly turned into a rasping cough in my parched throat. 'Is there nothing in the Kingdom of England you don't know, Tom Wolsey?'

'Very little, I must admit.'

'Edward wanted another son. And he might have had one but for me.'

'I don't understand'

'You see, there was once a girl, a very beautiful girl from Cornwa—'

'*My lord*! My lord.'

A young boy, one of Tom's servants, came running up the aisle, feathered cap in hand, an apologetic look on his face. 'Excuse me, my lords but the grooms are saying that if my master is to ride before the light fades, we need to leave immediately.'

Tom nodded at the boy. 'Tell them I'll be there anon.'

I was mildly surprised. 'You're not staying the night?'

'I cannot.' He motioned for the servant to leave then stood up and straightened his clothes. 'You know how it is with the King. Everything in his life must be done at breakneck speed. It is a mark of youth. When old age starts to creep upon us, it is the exact opposite as the body prepares for its final journey.'

'Edward was only thirty-five when he went on his final journey,' I said, bitterness creeping in again. 'Not a greybeard like me. No father has the right to outlive his son.'

'Try not to chastise yourself, Thomas. You were a good father to him. Always remember that. He was lucky to have you. Now I must make haste. Trust me, not a single word that we have spoken here today will ever leave my lips. I swear they'll follow me to my tomb.' He spread his hands wide and smiled at me. 'However, I am sure 'ere long we'll be goading each other again. You calling me: "*Snake*", and I calling you: "*that accursed Thomas Howard*!"'

Discovering that my old adversary knew my nickname for him wasn't exactly a startling revelation. He clearly stored every little detail of court and country on those chock-full bookshelves in his head. I nodded my head and held out my hand for him to shake. 'I couldn't agree more. But please know, Tom Wolsey, I'll never forget this day either until they seal me in *my* tomb. How you rode day and night to reach me because your father's heart heard the cry of anguish of another's, across the miles in Framlingham.'

PART FOUR

'A MAN'S HOUSE IS HIS CASTLE...'

'et domus sua cuique est tutissimum refugium'

{'and each man's home is his safest refuge'.}

Sir Edward Cook, 1628.

WOLSEY

Chapter Thirty-One

June 1ˢᵗ, 1513. Saint Bride's Rectory, Fleet Street.

By the time the harvest comes this year, I'll be King of England and France."

'That's what Henry said to you?'

'His exact words.'

Standing behind him on the red and gold Damascus carpet, wearing only her shift, Joannie gave a little shiver. 'France will never let that happen without a bloody massacre. You know how I worry for your safety, Tom. Especially when I hear something like that. If only you, as a man of peace, could turn the King's thoughts away from war.'

'Sweeting, as I once said to the Earl of Surrey about our new ruler, "*Be very careful what you put into that head for you will never ever get it out again.*" Trust me, I stand no chance of removing what others around him have put in. Or of dissuading him from pursuing a course of action of which he's dreamt his entire life. All I can do now is advise him to the best of my ability and try to win for him what he desires so ardently.'

Leaning back against the plumped up linen cushion (painstakingly stitched by Joannie using green, red, blue, and cream silk thread) on the wooden chair in their bedchamber, Wolsey found himself melting under her soft but determined fingers as she kneaded the tight knots in his neck, with all the skill of a baker smoothing out the most unyielding dough. Coming home from court to his beloved girl was the only time in his life he could truly relax.

'Who is it today?' she sighed, pushing down on a particularly sore spot on his left shoulder.

He knew exactly what she meant. His aches and pains always increased or decreased depending on what was happening at court. Or who was making his life a misery. 'Thomas Howard,' he said simply.

'The son or the father? Although as far as I am concerned, one's as bad as the other.'

'The Earl.'

'What's he done now? Surely he's still grieving for that son of his? The Admiral.'

'It's not what Thomas has done to me. It's what I'm going to have to do to *him*.'

'My lord?'

'The King has asked me to tell him that he won't be accompanying us to France but will instead be staying behind to protect the northern border from the Stewart King.'

'Tush!' Joan lifted her hands from his shoulders. 'The King always gets you to do his dirty work. The tasks he would never do himself.'

Wolsey gave a little laugh. 'That's the fate of the slave, my love. And the privilege of the master.'

'From all I know about the Earl he's going to be vexed in the extreme.'

'Oh yes, indeed. In the extreme.'

'You're too kind, Tom, by half,' she said, stroking his hair. 'The way you rushed up to his home in Suffolk to be by his side last month. He doesn't deserve such tenderness. But what do you expect from a man who calls you "*Snake*"!'

'Trust me, I've endured far worse insults than that. In fact, I take it as a compliment that he thinks I'm a match for him. It's better than being sneered at and dismissed as "*a butcher's cur*". Or reviled for being "*the King's creature*".'

'You have the patience of a saint, my lord.'

Wolsey chuckled at the absurdity of this but was quite content not to contradict her - and instead bask in the admiration of youth. The seventeen years that separated them was never a problem: he gloried in her joyful exuberance and, in return, she respected his experience.

*

'Soon the babe will be too big for you to do this,' he said, reaching back to place one hand on her swollen belly. He left his hand there for a few moments, thrilled to feel an answering kick. 'Another boy, do you think? A playmate for little Tom.'

'Mother thinks it's a girl this time. Because I'm carrying high. And felt so wretched first thing in the morning.'

Wolsey considered this. 'A daughter? I like the idea of that. If she's as beautiful as her mother I'll be a proud man indeed.'

Joannie leant forward, gently placed her two hands on his shoulders and planted a kiss on his cheek, her long hair tumbling around his shoulders like a velvety golden mantle. The touch of her lips and the welcome weight of her full breasts on his upper back brought the usual stirrings of desire.

'How blessed I am to have you, my Joannie,' he murmured. 'I am both grateful and full of humble remorse to God for His holy gift to me.'

Joannie slowly straightened up. 'How many times have I said to you that a love as pure as ours can't be wrong. What about the Borgia Pope, Alexander? Think how disgracefully he behaved.'

'Rodrigo de Borja.'

'Yes, him. I've heard terrible tales about that family - of murder, bribery and poisoning - even incest.'

'He certainly sired many children.'

'Exactly. So enough of these regrets, my lord. What about the King? I worry that he disapproves of us.'

'As long as I continue to please Henry in my daily life, he won't interfere with my nightly one. Besides, as I've told you before, having you makes me seem more of a man in his eyes. One with whom he feels he has more in common.'

Joannie gave a little snort of laughter. 'More than with those dusty old clerics, you mean.'

'Perhaps. He and I share a passion for the good things in life. I can serve food and wine of the highest quality; arrange for the best musicians and mummers to entertain him; enchant him with my possessions: for example, paintings and tapestries; accompany him when he goes hunting and hawking; seek out the most skilled jousters to challenge him. As for your "*dusty old clerics*", I'm not sure Richard Fox, the venerable Bishop of Winchester, also the King's Lord Privy Seal, would appreciate your description of him.'

'But it's true. The Archbishop of Canterbury is no better. One of William Warham's sermons is enough to send anyone to sleep for a thousand years. As for John Fisher, confessor to the old King's mother when she was aliv—'

'My love, is no one safe from your contempt?' Wolsey was highly amused and not displeased to hear how the young regarded the old guard from another era. After all, Joannie was only a year older than his royal master. The combined ages of Fox, Warham and Fisher added up to nigh on two centuries. If they were out of touch with what the young King wanted, then Wolsey intended to remain very much in touch. Besides, in some ways they were alike: both possessing enormous reserves of indefatigable physical energy (even if Henry used his on tiring out eight or ten horses a day when out hunting) and mental agility. It was a magical combination: as if each recognized a kindred spirit in the other. At times, it felt as if together they could truly conquer the world…not just France.

෴

'What about the Earl of Surrey? He's so old shouldn't he be confined to his bed at least? Yet still he keeps going.'

'That's precisely why the King values Thomas. For one so young, Henry has an uncanny knack for choosing the right people.'

'You mean like you. So he can go off and make merry.' Her fingers tiptoed across his shoulders. 'Not caring if he leaves my lord with a burden that would have felled a lesser man long ago.'

'My angel. Always thinking of my welfare.'

'Someone has to. You have so many wild beasts circling you at court. Consumed with envy and thinking of ways to bring you down.'

He reached up and grasped her hand. 'Let them. The only one who can do that is the King.' His voice dropped to little more than a murmur. 'And trust me, one day he will.' Catching himself in a rare moment of self-pity, he shook it off and cleared his throat twice before carrying on in a normal voice. 'People say Richard Fox promoted me to keep Thomas Howard from gaining too much power. And I have repaid his kindness by a ruthless climb to the top in a bid to usurp him.'

'But that's unfair and untrue!'

'Of course it is. I am willing to work with anyone, including Richard. At the moment he's giving me invaluable advice, learnt from the time he helped Henry's father take an expedition over to France back in '92.'

'I was toddling around our garden in a long dress then.'

Wolsey laughed. 'Don't make me feel old.' He picked up a letter on the table next to him. 'Richard sent me this yesterday, telling me to press our new Admiral of the Fleet—'

'The Earl's eldest son. I wonder how he feels now that Thomas is Admiral and not Edward.'

'Relieved I would think that it's remained in Howard hands. I don't relish having to tell the new Admiral to find escorts to protect our victualling ships, on hand to feed the hungry crews. He and I are of an age, and he is a very different proposition to his younger brother. Not one who takes orders easily. I also sense cruelty in him.'

Joannie pressed her fingers into his shoulders. 'Didn't he wed that young girl a few months ago? The one who was in love with a boy her own age.'

'Lizzie Stafford. The thought of her with him sends shudders through me. Edward Howard was far too impetuous for his own good and, at times, behaved badly towards his prisoners but still he was worth ten of Thomas.'

Joannie let out a small noise of exasperation. 'Can't you ever do anything right in the eyes of these men, my lord?'

'It's not evident. And every day I do battle with Old Father Time. Even I, with the best will in the world, can't find enough hours in the day. Richard is helpful but expects to be kept abreast of every last detail. And is slightly vexed if he is not. However,' he said, nodding his head, 'as a man who's shouldered a great deal of responsibility, he does appreciate my burden.' He picked up the letter again. 'Listen to what he says here:

'*If you are not delivered soon of your outrageous charge and labour, you shall have a cold stomach, little sleep, pale image and a thin belly cum rara egestione, all of which, as well as becoming as deaf as a stock, I had when in your case.*'

232

'That fills me with fear. Is there nothing you can do to alleviate your situation?'

'Sadly not. Especially when others carp that I slithered along - snake-like - to convince the King that it was better to put the running of the kingdom in one pair of hands, rather than several.'

Joannie tutted. 'So what you're saying is that you can't win either way. Whatever you do, there are those who will condemn you.'

'It's the lot of every successful man who isn't born into privilege but has to make his own way. He leaves himself exposed to the envy of those stranded on the shore behind him, as well as to the contempt of those he now joins who see him as both unfit and a threat.'

Abandoning her post as physician, Joannie slowly walked around to face him, one hand on her belly, the other on the small of her back.

Seizing her hand in his, he carefully tugged her giggling and protesting onto his lap to take up her position of adored mistress. As always, he was a drowning man, unable to resist her womanly charms as he cradled her in his arms: truly a Venus straight from the canvas of the masterly Florentine painter, Sandro Botticelli, who'd died a couple of years before. Burying his face in Joannie's bosom, he inhaled her familiar delicious scent, a mixture of rose and civet: a perfume the Venetian Ambassador had ordered at Wolsey's request.

"For my dearest sister, Elinor," he'd lied when he took the package from a questioning Andrea Badoer, confident that the busy diplomat wouldn't go out of his way to seek out a non-existent sibling.

'Oh, sweeting,' he whispered now, reaching up to tug at the neckline of her cotton shift. As he bent and pressed his lips against her creamy skin he decided he was the luckiest man alive. He reached down to stroke one of her breasts and closed his eyes in bliss, knowing from long experience exactly what it took to arouse his willing mistress. There are other far more pleasurable uses for a man's lips and tongue, he decided, than engaging them in talk of war. He couldn't help but marvel at the way his tongue could already taste a hint of the sweet nectar being prepared for their child by Mother Nature.

God's ways were both mysterious and wonderful. To allow him: a man of the cloth, to feel and experience the same joys as a man of the court. Or indeed, as the King himself.

'Take me to bed, my lord,' Joannie murmured, her narrowed eyes dark with desire, her cheeks flushed.

'But I don't want to har—'

She put a finger to his lips. 'I know you don't. And you won't. But you've taught me there are other ways to find pleasure....'

Later, when she was lying in his arms, both of them sated, he brushed a lock of damp hair (the hue of ripened wheat) from her eyes.

'You're perfect,' he breathed. 'My sunshine.'

'I love it when you call me that,' she whispered, reaching up to touch his face. 'Do you remember the first time you said it to me?'

'Of course I do. I chose "*sunshine*" rather than "*concubine*". I know the latter is the commonly used term for such as you to me but it conjures up an image of a lascivious, scantily clad woman, stretched out on a gaudy yellow velvet couch to match her harlot's hair, feeding sweet red grapes to her lover. Not the fresh-faced young girl I met exactly four years ago.'

Joannie teasingly put her hand to her belly. 'Not so fresh-faced now.'

He shook his head. 'Oh, but you are, my love. You came to meet your brother, Thomas, who'd recently become my chaplain. I knew almost nothing

234

of his family, only that your Uncle John was a rector in Bishopsgate, here in London, and that your father, Peter, a country gentleman in Huntingdonshire. You were akin to a divine revelation when you walked through that shaft of light outside my chapel: an angel come to offer me salvation.'

'You were thirty-five years old and working yourself into an early grave.' Joannie sat up and looked down at him, flashing him that sweet smile of hers. 'All work and no play makes Jack a dull boy.'

'Or Tom too,' he replied, lifting one of her delicate hands and kissing the palm.

She eased herself down again next to him and put her head on his chest. 'I wish I could keep you here forever. Keep you prisoner. *My* prisoner.'

He smiled. 'You already have my heart captive, sweetheart. Have no fear, it will remain yours til the end of my days.'

'And yours mine,' she yawned, suddenly sleepy and reaching out to grasp his hand in hers.

A short while afterwards, he could tell by her even breathing that she'd fallen asleep, leaving him quite alone with his thoughts. Why sleep when you could think? After all, there were only twenty-four hours in each day. As he'd said to Joannie, that wasn't enough for him by half.

WOLSEY

Chapter Thirty-Two

O utside, it was particularly dark with the merest sliver of the moon visible. A keen observer of the night sky, Wolsey knew she was deep into the waning crescent phase that preceded a crisp new moon. And would be at her best a couple of hours before sunrise. Around the time he would reluctantly rise from the warmth of their four-poster bed and make haste down to the landing stage at the bottom of the garden, in order to hail a wherry to take him to Greenwich. Maybe it would even be one of the Warner boatmen (Thomas Howard's excellent spies), their conversation always good value for the fare of half a groat. A few times, he'd deliberately spun a far-fetched yarn to cause mischief at court and, in return, they'd spun a few back courtesy of the irascible Earl of Surrey. He pitied Thomas Howard. Lately, with his son's sudden passing: a soul in despair. Even if his first son had stepped into the shoes belonging to the second.

Wolsey could hear the lapping of the water against the wooden posts, a soothing sound that always brought him tranquillity. He'd chosen the house because of its excellent location just outside the city walls, not far from the Dominican friary: Blackfriars. It also sat rather snugly on the banks of two rivers: the Thames to the south, and the Fleet to the east. Their bedchamber was south-facing to capture the morning rays of sunlight, and to give them a view of the Thames. Little Tom loved to be held up gurgling and pointing as he watched the King's fine ships proudly sailing up the river. A lover of water like his royal master, Wolsey had also taken the house to be able to entertain Henry there. As befitted a Royal Almoner, he decided to name his new home 'Bridewell' after the nearby well of Saint Bride. He had great plans for it; apart from serving his king which took up most of his time, and spending precious hours with Joannie, his other main passion in life was altering houses to his liking, and buying beautiful objects and furnishing to decorate the interior. He favoured large, costly houses: the kind he'd never lived in as a boy but did as a man. Sometimes Joannie gently mocked him as she had last week when he told her that one courtyard wasn't enough.

"I'm going to ask your brother to take charge of the works," he'd announced.

Joannie had grinned and reached up to tickle the back of his neck. *"You're like an eagle, the way you know exactly how a place should look. Soaring high in the sky, seeing it first from above before swooping down and changing it from below. In order to delight a king."*

"Not just a king," he'd replied, reaching down to kiss the top of her head. *"To delight the Queen of my heart too."*

By the light of the remaining candles on the table by their bed, he could just about make out the fine panelling, the Flemish tapestry on the wall depicting a maiden and a unicorn, and (could imagine if not see) his initials T.W. carved above the fireplace, something upon which Joannie had insisted.

"You are an important personage and it is right your initials are there for all to see."

"But it is you," he'd replied, *"who adds the most important thing of all - a woman's touch. If I create the body, my love, you add the features: the eyes, the nose, the mouth. Without you, my creation would be nothing."*

Wolsey wondered what the 'King' in question was doing now. He imagined the twenty-one-year-old perhaps restlessly pacing his bedchamber, his brilliant mind buzzing with preparations. All Henry could talk of from dawn to dusk was his pursuit of the most glittering prize of them all: the crown of

France. No wonder Andrea Ammonio had written to Erasmus two years ago that every day the new King showed himself in a *"more godlike guise"*. He already had a general's eye for detail, right down to the very last biscuit consumed by a sailor on one of his magnificent new ships. Wolsey was bombarded with a myriad of questions at every hour of the day and night, often by way of a messenger urgently hammering on the front door of his house - if Henry's need was great enough:

"How long will it take to reach Dover?"

"Have you received the final list of provisions?"

"Are all my suits of armour ready?"

"Has my bed been readied for travel?"

"What's the latest from our spies in Calais?"

Determined to shut out the endless round of royal queries which would deprive him of any sleep this night, Wolsey glanced down at Joannie's sleeping form. She had her fingers curled around her belly containing the fruit of their love, as protective as any lioness with her cub. Unfortunately for his beloved girl who wanted to keep him here with her, the desire for war coursed through the second Tudor's veins as forcefully as the desire for peace had coursed through those of (Wolsey's benefactor) the first Tudor before him.

A different Henry was now on the throne of England. He was young. He was healthy. He was finally freed from the apron ties of his indomitable grandam, Margaret Beaufort, in whose household at Eltham Palace he'd spent the first seven years of his life, away from his gentle mother and the overly watchful eye of his cautious father who (after the death of his eldest son) had forced young Henry to occupy rooms next to the royal bedchamber, with only one private door leading outwards…much to the amusement of the Spanish ambassador at the time.

"His father treats him as if he were a young virgin maid," he'd scoffed. *"And has given him as little instruction on how to rule as he would a daughter."*

అ

This Henry was rich. Far too rich for his own good…or the good of the country, thought Wolsey. All this thanks to the frugality of the father whose trials and tribulations during his twenty-three-year reign had prematurely aged him. Wolsey had been present at a banquet at Eltham with King Henry, Queen Elizabeth, and the royal children. He could still recall the King's words at the high table: "*As a young boy, I never knew what it was to feel safe. I was either a fugitive or a prisoner, living in fear in both England and Wales. I was forced to leave my mother's side at the tender age of five to go and live in an unfamiliar castle with unfamiliar people in Raglan, Southern Wales. Then at fourteen, I had to flee for my life to the Kingdom of Brittany where I was forced to change the tongue I spoke from English to French. I was to remain there for as many years as I'd lived on this earth.*"

Henry Tudor (like Wolsey himself) had rarely spoken of his humble antecedents - especially his disgraced Welsh great-grandfather, a brewer, who'd been on the run for murder - and certainly never in public. Nor did the family ever refer to themselves as 'the Tudors'; only their enemies used this name out of malice, wishing to remind the world of the King's lowly origins. But Henry had not been without humour. On a different occasion over at Greenwich, he'd chosen to share an amusing anecdote with his children which Wolsey could still recall:

"*Even when I had the crown securely on my head, there were those who whispered behind my back that I was nothing but an upstart. The grandson of a lowly Welsh squire named Owain ap Tudur whose claim to fame were his extraordinary good looks, and the luck he had in falling headlong into the lap of the widowed Queen of the fifth Henry of England. The beautiful Catherine of Valois.*" In the darkness, Wolsey could almost hear Henry Tudor laughing softly as he told his story. "*My grandam was watching her servants dance. It seems my grandsire performed a particularly energetic leap. Landing right in the arms of his Queen...whom he quickly made his wife.*"

I fully intend to share anecdotes of my childhood with my own children, mused Wolsey now. I have no need to feel ashamed of my origins, not when both William Warham and Richard Fox come from yeoman stock. And the good Bishop of Rochester, John Fisher, is the son of a merchant from Beverley.

His thoughts turned to his own beginnings in Ipswich, as the son of a successful innkeeper and butcher. He'd been clever enough to attend Magdalen College, Oxford (paid for by his father), and from there set foot on the path to royal grace and favour. It would be his job to show his children that any man...or woman, to a far lesser degree...could rise very high in this world with enough hard work. That is, if God and Dame Fortune were smiling on them as they went about their daily tasks.

His mind drifted back to the candlelit bedchamber down the river at Greenwich, almost as if he could hear his master's (at times) querulous voice calling out to him across the water. The first Henry Tudor's son had known no such fear or financial deprivation in his own childhood. Of course, his life had been torn apart by the loss of his beloved mother; although he'd been brought up away from her loving influence, her death still hit him very hard. But for now, reflected Wolsey, all such dolorous thoughts had been pushed to the back of the wilfully profligate son's mind as he prepared his country for war. With the cost of gunpowder amounting to four pence a pound and a brass cannon, thirty-five pounds, it was just as well Henry had nearly two hundred thousand pounds in the royal coffers. And By Saint George, he was as eager for what lay ahead as a hunting dog waiting for the scraps of the day. Fighting in the lists had only whetted his appetite for the real thing on a field of battle. As Baron William Mountjoy had once proclaimed to Desiderius Erasmus with such pride, the new King had his sights set on: "*virtue, glory and immortality*".

Joannie might not like the idea of war now it was upon them but she'd enjoyed hearing how the eighth Henry in the royal line yearned to follow in the footsteps of his boyhood hero (his spirited great-grandmother's first husband), the victor of Agincourt. The fifth Henry's deeds had been faithfully chronicled in '*Gesta Henrici Quinti*', and every word repeatedly devoured by this aspiring warrior-king. It was barely a hundred years since he'd returned home from Agincourt to a tumultuous welcome in the streets of London. In the darkness, Wolsey could hear '*The Agincourt Carol*' with its rousing chorus, playing in his head:

"Deo gratias!
Deo gratias Anglia redde pro victoria!"

"*Little wonder*," he'd explained to Joannie, "*it still remains one of England's most popular folk songs. The fifth Henry was extremely well-liked.*"

Wolsey recalled how Henry's subjects were supposed to have chanted: "*Long live the King!*" And on an optimistic note: "*Long live the King of England and France!*" In their eyes, he was a living legend, claiming the hand in marriage of the lovely French princess, Catherine of Valois, and then becoming Regent of France, as well as heir to the French throne.

"*I wish I could have been at the wedding!*" Joannie had exclaimed, her eyes shining with excitement. She hadn't enjoyed the next part of the story. Sadly, when the Lancastrian Henry died he left a nine-month-old babe, another Henry (the sixth of this name), on the throne of England: the same infant who inherited the throne of France just weeks later.

"I would hate to think of our Tom without his father to guide him," she'd said, looking fearful as she clung to Wolsey's shoulders.

Wolsey knew that his current master (whose Beaufort grandam had instilled in him a hatred of France as a very small boy) had every intention of equalling all his ancestor had achieved and more. As the one with many more years of experience beneath his belt, as well as a formidable appetite for hard work, and equal attention to detail, Wolsey saw it as his duty to work with others to turn the present situation to England's advantage. After all, what better way to guard against civil unrest in the kingdom than to give the warlike nobles (particularly the younger ones who, like their King, had never seen active battle) a worthwhile military cause. In order to boost the war effort at home and gather vital taxes, the King's advisors had ensured that rumourmongers were working day and night, spreading (mostly false) tales of French attempts at invasion upon the English coast. It was essential to garner as much home support as possible to justify the war upon France to the general population. Proclamations in favour of the war were being read out in every market place in the land, denouncing Louis of Valois' hostile acts against the sainted Pope in Rome but more importantly, pondered Wolsey, drawing attention to his warlike intentions upon England.

Then the tax collectors would roam the land with outstretched hands, taking thirty shillings from a knight but not forgetting those who only earned two pounds a year…and taking sixpence from them. A knight might be able to afford this, as could those such as labourers, journeymen and servants who earned forty shillings a year and paid a single shilling in tax. In stark contrast, for those at the very bottom of the social scale, sixpence was the equivalent of a week's wages.

'And to what purpose?' Wolsey whispered to his sleeping mistress. 'To support a campaign that must seem as remote to them as the moon in the sky above.'

He was struggling to keep his eyes open, knowing that the arms of Morpheus were waiting to transport him to a land where often turbulent dreams would triumphantly conquer his waking army of thoughts. As he sat up to blow out the candles on the walnut dresser (smiling at the pair of ruby earrings he'd given Joannie as proof of his love this past Valentine's Day), the thought came to him that at least he was going to a place where he didn't have to decide how to deliver bad news to Thomas Howard.

THE HOUSE OF HOWARD

Chapter Thirty-Three

Friday, June 3rd 1513. Framlingham Castle.

A peal of deep masculine laughter at the back of the great hall made me snap my head around. For one heady moment I was convinced it was *him*. As I was almost every day. A passer-by in the distance taking on his form would make me lunge forward…on the point of calling out. Once, a visitor, one of Edward's friends coming to pay his condolences, was wearing a scent favoured by my son: a blend of musk, ambergris, sugar and rosewater. The effect on my senses was so strong I began to feel dizzy and, making my swift excuses, I was driven from the room by a visceral despair. How could my Edward, my vibrant, golden son be reduced to a mere wraith, a fleeting shadow in the darkness, a cruel trick of the light, consigned to uncaring oblivi—

'Some more ale or bread, Your Lordship?' asked a servant with a crisp white linen napkin slung over one shoulder, appropriate deference in his demeanour and voice as he pointed over at the dozen warm loaves of the finest bread, placed nearby on the top table. A large platter of pike, plaice, roach and eggs took pride of place next to them.

I held out my goblet, jolted back into the present as if blown back by the rage of a howling gale. Taking a moment or two to recover, I knew I should welcome the distraction and force myself to take in my surroundings, therein gaining some comfort. I stared beyond the servant, taking satisfaction (despite the cloak of grief weighing me down) in the sight of a small army of servants at my disposal, knowing that a further hundred or so were bustling around in other parts of the Castle, working up an appetite for their midday dinner of beer and mutton. There was plenty for my household to do: from the steward who oversaw the running of it; the chaplain who tended to our souls and safeguarded the religious relics; the grooms cleaning out the stables; John, the head cook in the kitchens, in charge of his own little kingdom; Agnes's personal maids dressing her upstairs and combing out her long hair in readiness to come down to the great hall; the nursemaid in the nursery, perhaps training the newest wet nurse soon to begin her work, while keeping half an eye on William, our two-and-a-half-year-old scamp; right down to the small page boys flying around the house, in the manner of winged cherubs, ceaselessly on some errand or another.

I'd forgotten which Chief Justice said that each man considered his house his castle. <<*Whoever it was never spoke a truer word*>> Seated alone in the great hall very early on this fine Friday morning, with only my dogs and servants for company while I broke my fast, I knew I still had things to be grateful for. We Howards had waited long and patiently for Framlingham, once in the possession of my cousins, the de Mowbrays of Norfolk. Just when it looked as though it might come to us, the Yorkist King, Edward, had snatched it from our outraged Howard hands by marrying off his son, Richard of Shrewsbury, to Anne de Mowbray, daughter of John, the late Fourth Duke of Norfolk. However, with the death of Anne at only eight, and the seemingly mysterious disappearance of young Prince Richard in the Tower, the Castle was once more within the Howard grasp. This time, the throne of England was occupied by a Yorkist brother...not a son. Gifted to my father, John, by King Richard in '83 for his loyalty, we regarded it as the jewel in the family treasure trove.

I took a slug of small beer, determined not to start my morning thinking of Edward of York's lost boys in case I was taken straight back to another lost

Edward. *My* Edward. That way led to another day shut up in my study, refusing to eat, drink or see anyone. A day of anguish that tore at my heart and innards. Far better to rejoice in my good fortune at finally being the owner of Framlingham. Our crushing defeat at Bosworth back in '85, resulting in Father's death, and my own sojourn in the Tower, had put pay to those two brief years of playing Lords of the Castle. I could still taste the bile in my mouth as I paced the battlements of the Tower upon hearing it had passed to my old rival, John de Vere. That one had deserted the Yorkist camp in favour of the Tudor interloper, my *Goose*.

Now Henry Tudor was gone, and I was left to deal with his hot-headed son, I only had fond memories of him; even the way he'd packed me off to the Tower didn't rankle when I thought of how he paid the Lieutenant, Sir James Radcliff, forty shillings a week for my upkeep, and an extra seven shillings and sixpence to cover the expenses of my three servants. Hardly a pittance when the normal cost of a forced sojourn within the Tower's four walls was between three and six shillings. In a world where a gentleman needed an annual income of fifty pounds a year to earn the right to be addressed thus, my own expenditure was quite in keeping with my position. After all, I'd entered the Tower as the son of the First Howard Duke of Norfolk (now that the Fourth Mowbray Duke of Norfolk had breathed his last). Even if I did have to wait three long years both for my freedom, and to reprise my role as Earl of Surrey. Looking back, I had no complaints. Sir James once offered me the chance to quit the Tower in '87 (having received faulty information about the probable outcome of a battle) to join the Earl of Lincoln against *Goose*. But I chose not to. My message to Sir James and *Goose* had been crystal clear: "*I will not depart hence unto such time as he that commanded me hither should command me out again.*"

I was rewarded for this seemingly folly-fallen declaration by my freedom, the return of my title, and the lands of (my now long since departed helpmate) Lizzie Tilney, my first Howard wife. I leant down to pat the head of one of my spaniels at the memory of my decision. 'You know don't you, boy, that a Howard's loyalty will always be to the one seated upon the throne of England wearing a crown.'

Gazing around the hall now and reaching for another kipper, I contemplated how my forbearance and patience had been well worth the wait. The moment Elizabeth de Mowbray, the Dowager Duchess of Norfolk (born the same year or thereabouts as me, but not as robust), left on earth without a husband or a daughter, had (finally) gasped her last breath back in 1507, I knew I only had to wait a matter of months before the Castle passed to me. Of course I had to pay John de Vere an annuity for the remainder of his life. <<*Nothing in life is free except for the air we breathe*>> I remembered the day the Dowager died very well; an unseasonably cold November ushered out the last remaining obstacle to the East Anglian lands upon which I'd set my heart. It also meant that I was now the equal of de Vere, in lands and status in the county: the same Lord High Admiral who'd so recently died to make way for my precious second son (<<*would that he'd lived beyond this war, if only to spare Edward's life*>>).

It took a gargantuan effort for my mind not to remain tethered to the spot on the Narrow Sea where my son had perished, but to set off in the direction of the Castle grounds.

Our Howard coat-of-arms was displayed in triumphant fashion (intended as the flourish of an imaginary drum roll) above the gates at the entrance of the Castle: the upright lion roaring its approval at how far I'd brought the family since Bosworth. Few could fail to be impressed by the large orchard within the extensive park: excellent hunting ground that I fully intended to become a favourite of the young King. The two meres, striking in their beauty, had long ago been formed by damming a local stream in order to provide the Castle with fresh fish such as carp and pike. Agnes and I often took our three girls and three boys for a walk around it, admiring the lady's smock, ragged-robin, and marsh marigolds that grew in such abundance nearby. On other days, a couple of servants would row us out to the small island that my father had built in his very brief period of residence, with a pretty dovecote in the centre.

It gave me great pleasure to be head of such a thriving concern; for the last two hundred years, Framlingham hadn't merely relied on its own resources: a bakehouse for its bread and pies; slaughter house to provide meat and poultry; horse mill to grind its grain; buttery to store its wine, ale and beer; and even its very own vineyard. No, previous owners had looked outwards to the famed annual Stourbridge Fair, held on a common in nearby Cambridge, for their salt and other goods; to the Far East for their spices; wine from across the Narrow Sea in France; venison from distant parks.

I fully intended to continue the work my father had begun, and add many improvements of my own. Agnes, too, as mistress of our household, was following in the familiar footsteps of her Tilney cousin before her, and had plans for the improvement of the Castle. I welcomed her feminine tastes. Whereas I might build a set of stables beyond compare (flattering a mercurial young Tudor king by telling him they were built especially for his visits), or line the corridor outside our bedchamber with highly-polished suits of armour proudly worn by the Howard men, she would be thinking of tapestries from the Low Countries, silk hangings above our bed and a velvet coverlet to spread over it.

"*After all, my lord,*" she'd said after the birth of William, giving me a mischievous grin, "*my most important work is done within our bedchamber. And I deserve a little luxury as a reward.*"

She was cleverly reminding me how she'd provided me with another son to grow up alongside his older brothers, Henry and Charles. Even though I was losing sons and daughters much faster than I could bear, I still had more to fill their places. Henry, Charles and William had three older...no...two, half-brothers, I quickly corrected myself. I sighed. <<*How slow the mind can be to catch up with life's tragedies*>>

Quick! Best to return to how I was going to improve my home, I thought, vigorously buttering some bread, trying with all my might to blot out the image of Edward's beloved face. I intended to use the same modern brickwork I'd seen in other castles; build ornamental chimneys; link the great hall with the chapel; perhaps replace the drawbridge. Agnes wanted a pleasure garden with ornamental ponds and paths beneath a latticed roof to shelter our guests from the all too frequent inclement weather; a large herb garden to supply the kitchens; a whole host of fruit trees: apple, pear, cherry, walnut; a fountain—

'Dada, Dada!'

I looked up from my plate to see my small son, William, charging towards me with all the determination of a knight in the heat of battle. Except that this red-cheeked miniature version was wearing a long cream embroidered gown with gold trimmings, and was being hotly pursued by a flustered nursemaid.

It was quite clear the poor girl didn't know whether to catch her determined charge or curtsey to me. In the end, she did neither. William reached his target and clambered up the steps to the raised dais, leaving her to fall to her knees, abject terror in her eyes. Understandably fearing instant dismissal, loss of earnings for her family, and public disgrace.

'Your Excellency, I beg your pardon. Lord William ran off before I—'

I raised one hand to halt her in mid flow. 'Peggy. Go no further. Please get up. I know you.' I looked down at my son and smiled. 'And I know him. Take a few deep breaths and then go and find a bench over there. When you've recovered, you can take William back to Charles, Henry and the girls in the nursery.'

The gratitude in Peggy's tear-filled brown eyes brought me up short; it was as if she'd walked up to the executioner's block and received a last-minute reprieve. I reached into my pocket and found a couple of silver groats nestling at the bottom. I held them out to her. 'Here, take these and spend them on your brothers and sisters.'

Peggy gave a gasp of joy and turned on her heels but not before I saw the tears beginning to spill down her cheeks. Pleased I'd done a good deed before the sun was fully up, I watched as she walked towards a bench at the back of the hall, thankfully not colliding with Agnes as she eased herself through the door. Squeezing the warm squirming bundle on my knees who'd just spat out a piece of kipper, I waited for his mother, now great with child, to join us. <<*I am indeed blessed*>> I thought, as she slowly made her way to us, one hand on her distended belly and the other on the small of her back. <<*What other man in the whole of England has just celebrated his seventieth year, and will soon be rejoicing as the family cradle in his nursery welcomes its newest occupant*>>

Agnes and I had already used Henry, Charles, and William, to name our other sons so now we needed another. <<*If it's a boy I'll call him Thomas. If for no other reason than to irk my eldest son and heir*>>

Agnes might not be the young girl I'd lusted after so much I'd taken her to bed and board with hardly a penny to her name, but well into her thirties she was still a handsome woman, quickly losing the weight she gained with each child. I'd recently commissioned a painting of her by Hans Baldung, a gifted German student of the renowned Albrecht Dürer. Known for his perspicacity, he'd painted her with sharp lines, perfectly capturing her small features and oft serious expression. I approved of Baldung's composition showing her holding some rosary beads in her long slender fingers, indicating suitable piety in the wife of the Earl of Surrey. Her long hair was plaited and flowed down her back in the manner of a young girl, reminiscent of how she looked when we first met. Baldung didn't disappoint and more than lived up to his reputation; he clearly saw a hint of something else in her, normally hidden from public view. Painting her from the side, he highlighted her long swan's neck dipping into an enticing show of flesh where her bosom was partially exposed…but not to the point of immodesty. He'd noticed the slight pout that had drawn me to her in the first place, as well as the knowing look in the shrewd brown eyes, suggesting that she'd be a willing pupil in the bedchamber. So there she was for all the world to see: my Agnes. A worthy successor to her cousin, Lizzie, whose likeness now resided in a stained glass window in the Holy Trinity Church in Long Melford, Suffolk. She'd also been immortalized in some lines of poetry written by John Skelton when he was our guest at Sheriff Hutton Castle, back in '95.

Of course, neither Tilney cousin would ever equal the charms of their predecessor, Matilda de Lacey. I loved beautiful women and it gave me a thrill to see their features vividly brought to life in swirling colours on a canvas. As if I were showing them off to the world but keeping a part of them back for myself: their husband or lover. I'd arranged for a sitting for Matilda in the autumn of '72, not long after her marriage to Richard Pendeen, planned for when he was up in London on business. She was carrying my child and was furious to find herself married off for the sake of propriety to a man she'd never met. To add insult to injury, she was whisked away down to the wilds of

Cornwall. As a result, she fully intended me to pay for her situation by whatever means available to her. Hardly surprisingly, I'd been almost driven out of my mind with jealousy when I walked into the artist's studio and found her in a blue velvet dress so low it was shameless. I'd paid handsomely for the services of the same painter who did such a fine job with King Edward and Queen Elizabeth. As usual, the merciless Matilda knew exactly how to torment me.

"I hope you like what you can see," she'd purred in the manner of one of the cats stalking around the studio, tail high in the air, while tossing back her long red hair and pulling down the bodice of the blue dress (a perfect match for those damned sapphire eyes of hers) a further half inch.

Seeing the deep blush staining the cheeks of Hans, the young man from Flanders, who had the happy task of being forced to look at my love's bosom for several hours a day, much to Matilda's amusement I snapped at him: *"How long does it take to paint one of these infernal things?"*

I could no longer remember his reply but the afternoon probably finished in a more than usually passionate embrace with my exasperating mistress. I'd often wondered what happened to the portrait that initially hung in Pendeen Manor, her marital home (a surprise gift from her to her cuckold of a husband). When I used to visit her there, it gave me fierce pride to know that the arrogant beauty staring out of the gilt frame was far more my wife than that of the man who owned the house. Perhaps it ended up in Zennor Castle, in the hands of our daughter, Alys. I supposed I would never know.

After Matilda and I parted ways, my love life was set on a much more even keel. Just as with Lizzie, Agnes and I had served each other well: I raised her up from being the penniless daughter of a country gentleman from Lincolnshire and turned her into a countess. In return, she endured many a year of childbearing, mingled with heartbreak, in an attempt to fill my nursery at Framlingham, and before that, at Ashwellthorpe. It wasn't exactly a fair exchange but she rarely complained. I treated my women with respect, never seeing the need to stray from the marital bed. Perhaps it was because I'd known paradise with Matilda that no other illicit liaison could ever compare. Agnes had come into her own, from a hesitant girl barely out of her second decade, to an accomplished lady of the castle exuding calm and confidence. Today she was glowing in a kirtle of green silk, with a jewelled placard fitted in the centre. There were special ties in place to loosen it: in order to accommodate another son preparing himself to come and be a playmate for the little bundle of mischief on my knees.

'William,' she scolded as she sat down next to me, 'what are you doing here?'

Our son stubbornly put his thumb into his mouth and turned away from his mother. It was hard not to laugh at such spirit. He reminded me of Edward at the same age - so full of life and mischief. Swallowing hard, I looked up at the sound of a disturbance by the entrance of the great hall. He certainly bore absolutely no resemblance whatsoever to his two older half-brothers who'd just appeared at the doorway, newly arrived last night from London: each one jostling to enter first, a study in surliness and lack of charm, the pair of them.

THE HOUSE OF HOWARD

Chapter Thirty-Four

I watched as first Thomas, then Edmund, pushed their way into the great hall, followed by Thomas's wife, Lizzie Stafford, as she was so recently known. Life as a Howard wife wasn't easy at the best of times, having to deal with the often tumultuous events in our lives, but it was even harder when you were only fifteen. Even from where I was seated, I could tell from her bowed head that all was not well. When she raised it as she drew nearer, I could see her face was white and tear-stained. I turned to look at Agnes, raising my eyebrows.

'Her courses came last night,' she whispered. 'Thomas was not happy at all.'

I frowned. 'God's Mercy! What's the man thinking? A woman is not a farm animal, able to produce a babe at will. Perhaps he should begin with a little tenderness.'

Agnes pressed my hand against her lips. 'I'm the most fortunate of women, my lord.'

Thomas must have seen this gesture as he drew level with the dais because he threw a furious look in Agnes's direction, and curled his lip at the sight of little William snuggled up to me, usurping him, a forty-year-old man.

'Father...Mother.' The second greeting to Agnes was fairly spat out; he'd never warmed to the idea of a stepmother several years younger than himself.

'Lizzie, Thomas,' Agnes mimicked back, making sure to bestow one of her most beatific smiles on her sorrowful daughter-in-law, at the same time as pouring a world of admonishment into the two syllables that made up my firstborn's name. She'd certainly never said my name in such a disapproving way. She leaned forward. 'Edmund, how are you this morning?'

I looked at my third son who, as he approached his thirty-fifth year, was gathering lines on his face faster than a child's game of Hopscotch scrawled in the dirt. And he wasn't even wed yet. Unappealing in appearance and character it pained me to admit, I supposed at least he wasn't as sour as his older brother.

'Preparing myself for France and for battle, Mother. It can't be long now.'

I knew this comment was aimed at me as an attempt to win over my affection, like a mangy dog in the street knowing itself to be unwanted and unloved. God help me, I'd tried my very best to love Edmund but I saw nothing of either his mother, Lizzie Tilney, or myself in him. He simply wasn't a man to whom people warmed. Besides, Howards weren't born to fail. And Edmund had entered this world as if it were his main mission in life.

I could still remember how my cheeks had burned with a mixture of humiliation and rage as I watched him shame the Howard family name in the lists of Westminster, that day back in February, 1511, shortly after his scurvy-valiant failed attempt at a legal career in the Middle Temple. The mood was jubilant following the birth of little Henry Tudor on the first day of January: the tragically short-lived New Year Prince. Everything was looking good for us…and for Edmund in particular. A born sportsman like his two brothers, the King had put him in charge of the defenders which included Tom Bullen and Charles Brandon. *Goose* would have blanched at the extravagant display that day, but undoubtedly excused it on account of a brand-new Tudor cradle being rocked back and forth in Richmond.

The day should have been perfect: the Howards doing what they did best. *<<By the Mass! We were riding high in the Tudor favour once more>>* Looking back now, the details became a confused blur: Queen Katherine, triumphant in her status as mother to the heir of England, seated with her ladies in a box draped with cloth of gold. Beneath them was an artificial forest built by workers appointed by the Revels Office: green velvet and silk covered rocks and hills to which real grass had been added. Fresh flowers and newly picked ferns completed the wondrous effect while, in the centre, was a small golden castle in all its splendour. I remembered men in the guise of foresters dragging in the replica of a golden lion, its colour replicated by using the finest damask. A silver antelope was similarly adorned. Horns sounded, and lo and behold! Four armed horsemen were revealed inside one of the pageantry pieces, including my Muriel's dashing young husband, Tom Knyvett, and my Edward, both of them selected by the King as his challengers.

<<Oh yes, it was a day for the King - or Coeur Loyale - as Henry called himself>>

Katherine, our Spanish-speaking queen from Aragon, no longer had to fear any potential mistresses creeping along the shadowy corridors of the court, fluttering their eyelids, hoping to keep the King's bed warm at night; Henry's heart was all hers.

Everyone was in fine fettle. *"I think my name, 'Ardent Desire', is better suited to my codpiece,"* joked Tom, as he grabbed my giggling daughter, Muriel, around the waist. I probably smiled and shook my head, thinking that those two had more love and comfort in the marriage bed than all the rest of us put together. As I held out my goblet again to be refilled, a lump formed in my throat at this bitter sweet memory.

All those taking part in the pageant understood that this was the King's day. His precious royal seed had placed a new prince in the cradle and he reigned supreme...in every part of his kingdom, including the Westminster lists. Fine fighters like Charles Brandon, every inch the King's equal (and even his) superior, and Muriel's Tom certainly understood that.

<<Only Edmund kept the crowd in horrified thrall as he knocked the proud young Tudor to the ground more times than I can bear to recall>>

All the others from that day went on to rise further in the royal graces and to fight other jousts alongside him.

But not Edmund.

ℒ

'I haven't seen you since your recent appointment, Thomas,' said Agnes in a far more polite tone than my eldest deserved. 'Please accept my good wishes.'

Thomas glanced at me as if to say the only praise that counted for anything was from me, not my wife.

His voice when he replied to Agnes was gruff. 'Thank you, Mother. Stepping into Edward's shoes wasn't an easy task, especially with the King in a high temper at the mistakes made at Brest.'

<<*How dare this arrogant snatcher of child brides, and misery giver, insult the memory of his saintly brother. Edward was worth ten of him*>>

'Steady on, Tom,' said his brother, probably remembering all the times his lost big brother had protected him against the blows being rained down on his head, as well as the vicious kicks to any part of his body that happened to be exposed to the Howard son and heir. 'Isn't it a little premature to be laying the blame at Ned's door when he isn't here to defend himself? In truth, you haven't exactly pleased the King yourself so far in your role as Lord High Admiral.'

Thomas had an expression on his face as venomous as any snake I'd ever encountered. He didn't dare raise a fist or a foot in front of the ladies which was probably why Edmund was being so bold. My youngest son by Lizzie wasn't exactly noted for either his tact or his ability to read a situation. But I was pleased to see him standing up to Thomas, his tormentor since birth.

'How is it working alongside Richard Fox?' I asked, my barb not as obvious a slight as Edmund's clumsy effort…but a slight nonetheless. I was pointing out that the commission of Lord High Admiral hadn't been awarded alone as it was in Edward's case, but under the supervision of the old Bishop of Winchester and Keeper of the Privy Seal.'

'I have Edward to thank for that.' Thomas's mouth shut tight with all the force of a trap snaring a rabbit.

<<But not this rabbit>>

'I'll have you remember that your brother gave his life for his country. And I, as a father, have had to endure the news that divers fished his body out of the sea, embalmed it and—'

'Then cut out his heart and sent it to Admiral Prégent!' exclaimed Edmund, shaking his head.

There was a sharp intake of breath at the daring mention of this most heinous of acts. Fiery words bubbled up in the back of my throat but were too tardy to take form. Agnes put a comforting hand on my arm and offered to take William from me but the little one was having none of it.

Suddenly, from the other end of the table, Lizzie piped up: 'I heard that one of Ned's whistles was sent to the French Queen, Anne of Brittany, and his armour to her daughter, Princess Claude. I was very sorrowful to hear this, Father. Your son was a great man. And always very kind to me.'

I admired her for having the courage to get involved in a Howard family quarrel, and hoped it boded well for her future as wife to my churlish heir. Edward had been her saviour and, with him gone, poor Lizzie was on her own, apart from the limited help Agnes and I could give whenever we saw her. She was staring at Thomas as if daring him to admonish her. But he didn't.

Instead he said: 'In answer to your question, Father. Fox and I tolerate each other, let's put it like that.'

<<As I do you, son. As I do you>>

꧜

'At least we have our good memories of Ned,' said Agnes, trying to restore cheer around the table. 'He was generous in life and generous in death.'

'Yes,' said Thomas stiffly, as if he'd rather remove his tongue than say something positive about his younger brother, 'it seems that the Queen was pleased with his silver gilt and ivory loving cup—'

'Yes, she was,' finished Agnes. 'And what wonderful inscriptions were written inside. "*Drink thy wine with joy*", "*Fear God*" and "*Be sober*".'

'Only one of which he really believed,' I managed, thinking of our last joyous drink in that Portsmouth tavern.

'Strange that he gave the care of his two bastard sons to the King and Brandon,' said Thomas. 'And not to you, Father.'

<<Will he never stop with his needling?>>

'Have no fear, Thomas,' I tossed back at him as if his spiteful comment were a slice of good beef past its best, 'your bastard nephews will do well for themselves in the world. I am glad your brother sired sons before he left this world. I don't doubt that there are more we don't know about.'

Stung by my words, reminding him that he hadn't produced so much as a living child yet, Thomas glared at Lizzie; bringing more of my son's wrath on the poor girl's head hadn't been my intention at all. The arrow had hit the wrong target.

'It must have been hard for you, Tom, when the King and Wolsey refused to see you two weeks ago,' said Edmund, changing the subject.

<<Now that, son, is what I call hitting the heart!>>

I entered the fray to show Thomas that I, too, had been displeased to hear that a second Howard brother had failed in his task. 'Perhaps it wasn't the best idea to tell Tom Wolsey that your men would...now, how did you put it? "*Prefer to end their days in purgatory than return to battle*"'

Thomas gave a thin sneer. 'Since when did *Snake* recover his rightful name?'

Agnes turned to him. 'Tom Wolsey has shown kindness to your father, Thomas.'

'Though he didn't show you much, Tom, did he?' laughed Edmund.

'It wasn't my fault,' blustered Thomas as he used to as a young boy when he was caught red-handed in some misdemeanour around Ashwellthorpe Manor. Harassing a servant, hurting his siblings, being cruel to an animal. 'How could I be blamed for the wind blowing in a south-westerly direction, keeping my ships in Plymouth, not in Southampton where they were supposed to be?'

'My lord husband paid for fresh supplies to be sent to Southampton,' said Lizzie, again showing her mettle. 'Out of his own purse.'

'Very wise too,' said Agnes. She looked down the table at Lizzie. 'My dear, you're proving a real credit to Thomas. Now all we need to do is find a wife for Edmund—'

'Please do!' interrupted my third Howard son. 'I still have my sights set on Joyce Culpepper.'

'If you ever catch her for a wife, Edmund,' said Thomas, 'you'll have to change her name to Jocasta. Joyce is far too plain for a Howard wife.'

Edmund made a snorting noise and waved his hands in a mocking gesture. 'Oh, pardon me for daring to breathe the same air as you, brother. We can't all match the mighty Thomas Howard who wed first a King's daughter, then stole one fathered by a Duke.'

'Edmund,' scolded Agnes, 'enough of such incendiary talk.'

'I don't even know why you're sniffing around after the Culpepper widow,' said Thomas, a gloating expression on his face, knowing that (thanks to the law of *primogeniture*) he alone was going to inherit the Howard riches. 'She's hardly a wealthy heiress. More like spoiled goods. How many brats would she be turning up with from her marriage to Ralph Legh? Four…five?'

'As the saying goes, Thomas,' I grumbled, '"*There's more to marriage than four bare legs in a bed.*" Edmund has assured me that Joyce Culpepper will one day bring him a portion of her father's inheritance. Sir Richard Culpeper, Sheriff of Kent. It'll bring a decent enough amount for a Howard son.'

Thomas was about to open his mouth, no doubt to pour more icy water on his brother's marriage plans (as a revenge for all the ribbing he'd received today) when the door to the great hall opened and a messenger ran its length, seeking out the head of the household with his eyes. When he reached me, he gave a stiff bow and held out a letter, bearing a seal I knew only too well.

After thanking the messenger and signalling to my steward to take him to the kitchens, feed him and reward him, I broke open the red seal, peeling apart the familiar words: '*Dominus michi adutor*'. I glanced at the signature with the final flourish of the last letter at the bottom of the page, and began to read the words in the flowing handwriting I knew so well.

Thrusting little William into Agnes's surprised arms, I brought my fist down hard on the table. '*What*! Not go to France. How dare he!'

Startled by my roar, William began to wail and Agnes swiftly summoned Peggy from where she was sitting at the back of the hall.

'Hurry. Take him back to the nursery.'

I could feel the blood rushing to my face and my hands beginning to tremble. Rage like I'd never experienced was bubbling up to the surface.

'My lord,' said Agnes. 'Whatever is it? Who's the letter from?'

'*Snake*!' I shouted. 'That hell-hated, shard-borne creature is behind this.'

'Behind what?' asked Agnes with infinite patience.

'I see Thomas Wolsey didn't hold onto his name for very long,' smirked Thomas.

'Did you know about this,' I said, turning on him in fury.

'About what, Father? You haven't told us yet what's in the letter. So how can I answer that?'

I wasn't sure I could get the words out. 'I-I'm being sent to guard the Northern Marches.' I took a sharp intake of breath. 'Instead of going to cover the House of Howard in glory in France. Packed off like little William to the nursery.'

Agnes placed her hand over mine. 'My dear, don't you think it's because the King values your great experienc—'

I pulled my hand away; I was finding it difficult enough to form sentences, let alone receive wifely comfort. 'It's a shot across the bow for the Howards, letting us know we've been left out in the cold. No glory for me on the battlefield. My final chance to prove myself as a soldier. Sent up the Great North Road to keep the Scots in order. As if I want anything to do with that ungrateful rabble.'

'But you and King James struck up such a friendship when we all went up to Scotland for his marriage to Margaret,' said Agnes. 'And he wrote to the King that Edward's life and talents had been wasted on a futile war.'

'Hardly the time to bring that up, Mother,' said Thomas, his brown eyes mean and cold.

I stood up. 'I must prepare to go to Greenwich at once. To see the King myself.'

'Is that wise, Father?' asked Edmund.

I turned to face him. 'A Howard never gives up easily. Perhaps you would do well to learn that lesson.'

'I will. And I promise you that I'll do you proud over in France.'

I couldn't help myself. '*You*? You're not going anywhere, but with me. Up north. It's in the letter. Your chance to represent the Howards turned to dust the day you threw King Henry into it.'

And with that, I stalked to the end of the dais, stepped down and took off in the direction of the kitchens, in search of my steward.

<<*By the Mass! The day a Howard gives up will be the one when England ceases to exist*>>

NICOLAS

Chapter Thirty-Five

Friday, June 3rd, 1513. Ardres Castle.

He could already hear the raised voices before Tristan and his father stepped out into the sunlit courtyard. The quarrel had been raging for the last few days, with the same accusations and angry comments flying back and forth in the manner of venom-tipped arrows released from a bow. Across from him, Gilles, who was in the process of polishing his sword, raised his eyes heavenwards.

Monsieur Guy was marching several paces ahead, the strain of all his responsibilities and dealing with his errant son showing on his tired pale face. 'Tristan,' he called over his shoulder, his patience clearly stretched more tightly than a string from that same bow, 'you will accompany your mother to Cornwall, and that's an end to it. You will sail on your Uncle William's ship, *"The Morvoren"*, on Thursday morning.'

'Over my dead body!' his son cried, not even waiting the length of a breath, and not showing any of the respect due to the Governor of Picardy, thought Nicolas. 'I'd rather spend my final moments entangled on the sea bed than be dragged off to England like a small boy who hasn't been breeched.'

Nicolas had had enough. He turned to look at Tristan. 'Then stop acting like one, As for ending up in a watery grave at the bottom of the sea, isn't that exactly what happened to the English Admiral in April? Count yourself lucky to be hale and strong, strolling around this courtyard, and not dead without even your heart within your body. I'm sure Sir Edward Howard would agree with me if he were here now.' A look of intense rage mingled with another emotion that Nicolas couldn't quite gauge appeared on Tristan's face. 'You're not fit to lick Edward Howard's boots!' he spat. 'Let alone speak his name. I challenge you to take up your sword.'

'*Mon Dieu*, Tristan! Enough of this shrill-gorged mammering!' snapped Monsieur Guy. 'You never even met the man, apart from watching him once in the lists at Westminster. And having a few words with his father. There are more useful tasks for you to do than attempting to fight your brother.'

'He's not my br—'

'*Le diable m'emporte*! All three of you boys are equal in my eyes. The only reason I haven't invited Nicolas to address me as '*Père*' is out of respect for his own dead one.'

Hearing this, Nicolas was aware of a pleasing warmth enveloping him. <<*Pardi! If you only you knew what a miserable brute my blood father really was, you wouldn't show him one iota of respect*>>

'Now, Tristan,' said Monsieur Guy, 'try and act your age for once. You're fifteen years of age, not five. Your mother has informed me that we are to have guests joining us to dine today. Ah, here they are.'

Nicolas turned to greet Dame Grace but the words died on his lips when he saw who was riding through the arch into the courtyard: Robert de Sapincourt. Followed by his divine wife, Ysabeau. Mounted on a grey palfrey, she was a vision in red and gold. From the corner of his eye, he noticed Tristan immediately straightening up, wiping the sullen expression from his face and pushing some stray blonde locks out of the green eyes that no longer had the appearance of a storm-tossed sea, but rather the calm, sun-dappled waters of a ship that had just docked safely in the harbour over at Calais. To Nicolas's annoyance, Tristan rushed over to help her down from her horse and was rewarded by a smile that was as bright as a summer's day.

Monsieur Guy was clearly pleased to see his friend. Once the two horses had been led away by the Ardres grooms, he beckoned to him. 'Come, Robert, you and I have a lot to discuss before we eat. Grace, why don't you and Ysabeau take a walk around the gardens. Tristan, Nicolas, you can escort them.'

Dame Grace smiled at Ysabeau. 'That's an excellent idea. Nicolas will be happy to oblige, I'm sure.'

'*Certainement.*'

Even though Nicolas had long since abandoned all plans to woo the luscious beauty standing in front of him (and to some extent had lost interest in her), when she was offered to him on a platter, it would be churlish to refuse. Besides, the expression on Tristan's face was priceless: fury and horror in his eyes at the idea of his greatest rival walking off with his prize. But before he had chance to protest, Dame Grace tugged at his arm. 'Come, Tristan, there's something I want to discuss with you.'

And with that, she walked on ahead with her thwarted son, disappearing through the arch and leaving Nicolas (a wolf by his given nickname) quite alone with the most delicious lamb that had ever entered his lair.

'They're headed in the direction of the lake,' he said, feeling his interest in Ysabeau returning with every step they took. Her delicate floral perfume filled the air between them, and it was an effort to avert his eyes from the deliberately bared skin (rising and falling so provocatively) above the square-necked bodice of red and gold brocade. She was exquisite: worthy of a place in any of the paintings that hung in either Ardres Castle, or in his childhood home at Crépy-de-Valois. He glanced at her small hand that was resting daintily on his forearm and it took all his self-control not to grab it, whirl her round, lower his mouth to hers and—

'Your brother is a fine singer, Monsieur Nicolas. Are you equally talented?'

He'd forgotten how dulcet *her* voice was, rolling her 'r's in a particular way that sent a shot of desire coursing through his veins, straight to his groin. When she said his name in that seductive tone, he could well imagine her lying on the pillow next to him in his bedchamber, her hair the colour of warmed honey, luxuriously fanned around her like a halo in a religious painting. 'In truth, Tristan has me bested with his gift for music.'

<<*Be generous. Be modest. And then show no mercy!*>> He lowered his voice, hoping she'd pick up on its amorous intent. 'My own accomplishments lie in other… areas.'

Ysabeau glanced up at him through thick lashes, an innocent expression in her cornflower blue eyes. '*Ah oui?*'

Yes, she could be an angel fallen from the heavens above. Although there was a wealth of possibility in that one tiny exclamation, Nicolas wondered what was going on behind her pretty face. <<*Diantre! You're not half as innocent as you make out, my fine lady. I am sure you run rings around that greybeard of a husband of yours. Beggaring him into the bargain*>>

Ysabeau chattered on, asking him mostly questions about Tristan to which he answered with due civility while weighing up his intended prey. With the eye of a master tailor, he took in every inch of her staggeringly expensive gown with its close-fitting bodice clinging to her every curve, and voluminous skirts (every extra inch stripping a few more *sous* from the besotted Robert de Sapincourt's rapidly dwindling treasure chest). *Par le ventre de Dieu!* How long before the little minx robbed him of his entire fortune? The gown had sleeves that narrowed at the wrists, her slender fingers showing off several sparkling rings, including a ruby one that matched the fine necklace, resting very temptingly on that same area of satiny skin against which he was longing to brush the tips of his fingers. With a nod to the latest fashion seen at the court in Paris (or so he'd heard the ladies at the Castle saying), she was wearing a circlet of pearls and rubies in her hair in place of a cap. Nicolas could still remember Sapincourt's first wife, Denise, a small thin woman (with a face reminiscent of a shrew sniffing out food in a pantry) who bore no resemblance whatsoever to the intoxicating Ysabeau.

'Will Tristan be accompanying you to war?'

'*Mais non*, he's far too young for that.'

<<*Confine him back to the schoolroom where he belongs*>>

'So he'll be staying here?'

'*Non.* He's due to sail for England next Thursday with Dame Grace.'

Ysabeau's mouth settled into something that was half-way to a pout. It certainly made her pink lips look ripe for kissing. 'So I'll be all alone when Robert goes off to fight. No one to protect me.' She looked up at Nicolas again, and this time there was mirth and something of a challenge in her eyes which rather gave the lie to the idea of a helpless maiden in need of a strong protector.

The prospect of Tristan remaining in Ardres Castle to protect Ysabeau was most unappealing. In fact, stronger measures were required to turn her thoughts away from the scurvy-valiant bench-whistler; Nicolas wasn't sure how much longer he could hold out against her incessant questioning. He was beginning to feel like a man burdened with the task of warming the bed sheets until his rival arrived. The wretch in question and Dame Grace had rounded a corner leading to the lake a while ago, so now was the time to act. Seeing another question about to tumble from those perfect lips, no doubt about Tristan's preferred dish, animal, colour, piece of music, dance, or even day of the week; how long he'd be gone for (<<*'ever' would be my preference*>>); or worse still, whether or not he had a sweetheart, he placed the tip of his shoe on the train of

Ysabeau's dress. He only intended for her to stumble a little to give him the chance to put one hand under her arm and steady her to her feet again.

<<*Act the chivalrous hero on the outside. But—*>> To Nicolas's surprise, Ysabeau went flying, giving him no alternative but to lunge forward and grab her around the waist, jerking her back to face him. This action brought unbearable temptation in the form of her lips parted in shock, a mere few inches away from his own. Finding herself in his arms, to all intents and purposes in a romantic embrace, there was finally a spark of interest in Ysabeau's startled blue eyes.

'*Nicolas*! Is everything all right?'

He was so caught up in his moment of triumph that he hadn't heard the twigs crackling underfoot.

Roughly pushing Ysabeau away from him (in not at all chivalric fashion) as if his hands were burning (which they were) Nicolas straightened his doublet and turned to face Dame Grace. She had a concerned look on her face - unlike Tristan who had a murderous one on his.

'What a relief your son was nearby, Dame Grace,' said Ysabeau, showing great presence of mind as she fanned away her blushes with her hands. 'I tripped on a stone and lost my balance. Thankfully, Monsieur Nicolas managed to save me.'

'I am so pleased, *ma chérie*,' said Dame Grace, all smiles. 'Nicolas is known for his good deeds.'

'You were indeed fortunate, Dame Ysabeau,' added Tristan, narrowing his green eyes. They were his mother's eyes…except that hers resembled a stretch of sunlit water, and his an odious, scale-covered snake. He shook his head, as if in apology. 'Nicolas can be so clumsy at times. But *Dieu Merci*, for your sake, not on this day.'

'We should be getting back,' said Dame Grace who perhaps sensed the growing discord. 'The men will be waiting for us.'

۵

When they arrived at the Castle, they made their way to the great hall where Monsieur Guy and Robert de Sapincourt were obviously discussing the war that was almost upon them.

'Ah, *mon trésor*,' said Monsieur Guy, holding out one hand to his wife. 'Come and join us. Tristan, I think I have some news that will please you.'

'*Père?*'

'Robert here has convinced me that it is a good idea for you to stay behind and help run the Castle. He's right. You're of an age where you should have some responsibility.'

'What say you to it, Nicolas?' asked Ysabeau's husband, seemingly completely oblivious to the fact that both young men facing him were intent on making him a cuckold. One…if he remained, one…before he left. 'Do you agree that your brother should stay behind?'

Nicolas was almost unbearably torn. If Tristan was left at Ardres Castle, with both Ysabeau's husband *and* he himself off to war, it would give Tristan ample opportunity to get his greedy hands on his prize. On the other hand, wasn't that exactly what had just taken place? In reverse. To great effect. Nicolas had heard her intake of breath as he held her to him, seen that same flash of unmistakable desire in her eyes he'd seen many times before in others. Let Tristan try and snatch her back now. It would be an uphill task.

He hesitated for a few moments in order for his answer to appear well-considered. And when he spoke, his voice was slow and measured. 'I think Tristan has matured since that reckless outing to Cap Gris-Nez with Jean de Lorraine. And deserves a chance.'

<<*Be noble. Be fair. As if you're in the court of King Arthur, and you're one of the knights seated at the round table. Yet damn with faint praise*>> He

didn't say that the 'chance' Tristan deserved was an attempt to win over Robert's fair Ysabeau; it was enough that he'd drawn everyone's attention to Tristan's recent foolhardiness and made Monsieur Guy question his decision. Although he wouldn't be able to back down now.

'In that case,' Monsieur Guy said, a satisfying frown appearing on his brow, 'on Sunday, Nicolas, you will take Dame Grace as far as Calais. To Gilbert Talbot's house. In preparation for her journey over the Narrow Sea to Plymouth. And you, Tristan,' he said, but with no smile and with far less conviction than a few moments before, 'will remain at the Castle and learn how to guard it in our absence.'

WOLSEY

Chapter Thirty-Six

Monday, June 6th, 1513. Palace of Placentia, Greenwich.

He's here!'

From the window overlooking the Thames, Wolsey could see the distinctive figure of Thomas Howard, Earl of Surrey, placing his feet on the bottom stone, damp from the sparkling water of the river lapping gently against it. Walking next to him, perhaps in case he needed help, was one of the sturdy wherrymen Wolsey had often seen in the Earl's company.

In the chamber behind him, the King and Charles Brandon were behaving like over-excited schoolboys about to embark on their latest bout of mischief. Six years apart in age but similar in height and build, they were jumping in front of each other, shoving and grabbing anything that came to hand: doublet, shirt, neck, hair - gales of laughter accompanying each fitful movement.

'No, you go in front!' a ruddy-cheeked Henry was roaring, reclaiming the silken material of his crimson doublet from his best friend's grasp.

'No, you!'

'You! I'm not facing him first.'

Their behaviour was becoming ever more boisterous. Whatever would Thomas Howard think if he walked in at this very moment?

'Gentlemen, a little decorum please. Unlike me, neither of you are in the firing line.'

This set them off again, picking up imaginary guns and running around the chamber, ducking and diving, pretending to aim it at the other. And then dropping to the floor before leaping up again.

Wolsey sighed. Let them have their boyish games; he was the one who would surely bear the brunt of the Howard wrath. Suddenly Charles stopped in imaginary mid-aim. 'Hal, Tom here is right. Old Thomas is going to think being packed off to the godforsaken northern border is all Tom's idea. That doesn't seem fair.'

Henry put his head to one side. 'Life isn't fair, Charles. But I agree with you.' He thought for a moment. 'If it's true that Tom will get the blame anyway, why don't we have a little fun at the know-all Earl of Surrey's expense.'

Wolsey frowned. 'Surely he's been through enough recently with Edward's death.'

A haunted expression of grief, tinged with guilt, briefly clouded the King of England's face before vanishing again, leaving defiance in its stead. 'If Ned were here with us,' he said, 'he'd be egging us on, wouldn't he, Charles?'

'He would. No one enjoyed a good prank more than him.'

'The Earl might also be aggrieved that Edmund isn't going to France,' said Wolsey.

The King's blue eyes narrowed. 'He can be aggrieved all he wishes. I can hardly believe the great Ned Howard was older brother to such an unappealing individual. Thomas Howard shouldn't kick up too much of a fuss. After all, Thomas the Younger instantly attired himself in his dead brother's uniform. How it must have rankled with him that he wasn't my first choice.'

'He hasn't so far shown himself fit to wear Ned's uniform.' said Charles. 'The complete opposite, in fact. I don't blame either of you for not giving him the chance to explain himself last month when he rushed up to London. If anything, he's an insult to our Ned's memory. Whining about not being able to make his men follow him, or put out of harbour in Plymouth. Shameful.'

All the good humour had left Henry's face. 'He's on his very last warning. There are plenty who would be queuing up for the position of Lord High Admiral of England. Now then, back to our plan.'

Dreading the answer to his question, Wolsey was resigned. 'What did you have in mind, Your Majesty?'

'I know Thomas feels that you're vying with him for the royal favour so why don't we go a little further?'

'I like the sound of that,' said Charles, as opposed to Wolsey who didn't. 'Pray proceed, Hal.'

'W-e-l-l,' said Henry, drawing out the word, 'we all know what a stickler for good manners Thomas is. So why don't we shake him up a little.'

'It's sounding better and better,' laughed Charles.

Worse and *worse*, inwardly groaned Wolsey but said nothing. He would save up his exasperation for when he saw Joannie later.

'When he arrives, Tom,' said Henry, 'I want you to address me as "Hal".'

Charles burst out laughing and slapped his thigh. 'Excellent! I can't wait to see his face.'

Wolsey was appalled. '"*Hal*", Your Majesty? Oh, I don't think I could do that. It wouldn't be correct.'

'Nonsense!' cried the Clown King. 'Of course you can. Thomas blames you already so we will merely be outraging him a little more. Wait and see, it'll be fun, I promise yo—'

A loud knock at the door sent Charles and Henry flying to opposite sides of the room: their roles as innocent bystanders as convincing as two actors about to take part in a street play. They stared meaningfully at Wolsey, urging him - as lead actor - to take his place at the front of the stage. Knowing he had no choice but to obey, he took a deep breath.

'Enter.'

The large oak door opened and Thomas Howard walked in, dressed almost entirely in deepest black, using that most expensive of dyes, as befitted a man of his wealth and position. His collar of the Order of the Garter, decorated with knots and Tudor roses, added to the dramatic effect. Black suited him. For a man in his seventieth year, he was a true phenomenon. The fitted crimson doublet showed there wasn't an ounce of surplus flesh anywhere; his pale face was startlingly youthful and still handsome. Intelligence shone out of the dark brown eyes (no longer swollen and reddened by the ravages of grief), and his long Howard nose lent him an apposite degree of haughtiness. Everything about him was in keeping with a respected soldier and statesman. Unlike his eldest son, Thomas, who in Wolsey's opinion, was a most disagreeable specimen. That one had cruel thin lips and an insufferable manner. Thomas the Elder, on the other hand, had a pair of well-formed lips that wouldn't look out of place on a pretty maid. Wolsey was pleased to see him composed and in control again, unlike at their last meeting at Framlingham. Thomas was obviously weighing up the situation in the manner of a general surveying the battlefield before him. One thing was clear as he approached Henry: he'd hoped for a private audience. But was trying not to let it show.

'Your Majesty,' he said, bowing low and making a fleeting grimace that Wolsey knew was from his knees grumbling that even into their eighth decade, and after many a spell in combat - or even in the Tower - they'd not yet been put out of active service. And were not about to be...at least not at any time in the foreseeable future.

275

'Charles, Tom,' he said, giving Wolsey a quick glance that spoke volumes. Wolsey could almost hear the accusatory words being hurled across the chamber:

What are you doing here, *Snake*? Haven't you caused me enough trouble?

'Thomas,' said Henry, 'so glad that you could make it. Tom told me that you were on your way.'

'I have come to discuss my appointment, Your Majesty. To see how I can best be of use to you.'

Very clever, thought Wolsey. Avoiding a confrontation but stating his position and disapproval of his assignment.

'I thought you'd made it plain,' said Henry, turning to Wolsey, 'that Thomas's great talents are needed on the northern border to protect England against the Stewart traitor. I was in no doubt of your position when I sought your advice about how to defend my kingdom against the hell-hated Scots.'

That's right, thought Wolsey, throw me to the lions. In this case: the four fierce ones to be found on the Howard shield.

Behind Thomas's back, Henry raised his eyebrows at Wolsey, letting him know this was his cue to join the play.

In for a penny, in for a pound, decided Wolsey. Please a king, vex an earl. 'I most certainly did, Hal,' he said, noticing the Earl's mouth tighten. 'My letter to Thomas was filled to the edge of the page with the highest praise indeed.'

If Henry and Charles hoped to see a reaction to Wolsey's use of the diminutive form of the King's name, they would have needed to be very quick. A startled look briefly crossed the Earl's face but hard on its tail was one of gratitude and acceptance. Not for nothing, thought Wolsey, had Thomas Howard weathered six reigns, served four monarchs, and remained at the very forefront of the Tudor court while holding office under two Henries. There was no indication that he wouldn't play a winning hand this time. He certainly wouldn't be mentioning either of his remaining older sons, or the younger ones, for that matter.

'Praise, well-deserved, Thomas,' said Charles, jumping in to back up his royal companion.

If Thomas was aggrieved that his exceptional skills as a leader were not needed in Northern France but in Northern England, he made no outward show of it. 'I shall do my duty and Your Grace shall find me diligent.' He bowed his head a little. 'To fulfil your will shall be my gladness.'

❧

'I am most pleased to hear that,' said Henry, no longer playing his part of powerless bystander but his true one of final decision maker. 'I have every confidence that you will make my fen-sucked brother-in-law pay for any digression.'

'Well said, Hal' said Wolsey, finding it wasn't so difficult after all to address the twenty-one-year-old king thus.

For the first time, true anger flashed across Thomas's face, the anger he felt inside at being excluded. Or perhaps it was having to tolerate the dizzying rise of Wolsey who now dared to address the King as 'Hal'. Fortunately, Thomas was able to direct his ire to a different target, namely James Stewart, a man with whom (unlike Wolsey) he'd once struck up a great rapport. He held up a fist and shook it in a northward direction at the imaginary Scottish King seated on his throne of thistles. 'Sorry may I see him ere I die. He that is the cause of my abiding behind in England. If ever he and I shall meet, I shall do everything I humanly can to make him sorry he was born.'

'Strong words,' said Charles, 'exactly what we need.'

Thomas turned an inscrutable stare on Charles. Hard to read, decided Wolsey. Was he offended to be congratulated by the son of a man who'd given his life on Bosworth Field, on the opposite side from the Howards who supported the Yorkist Richard to the last.

'Thank you, Charles, I hope I can live up to them.'

'I don't know about you three,' said Henry, now tiring of their little charade and eager to move on to new distractions, 'but I'm starving. Time for dinner.'

As they made their way out of the chamber, Henry and Charles were ahead, swaying a little from side to side, jostling each other as they collapsed with laughter at some joke, no doubt at someone else's expense. Wolsey caught Thomas Howard by the elbow. 'Thomas,' he said in a low voice, 'As you are aware, His "*Majesty*" loves to play games.'

The Earl looked at him, understanding and even a touch of wry humour in his dark eyes. Of course there was! He'd lived too long on this earth to be fooled by two young men in their twenties. The identity of the real ruler of the waves of the Narrow Sea was clear to both of them. Not Wolsey. But the same ruler that was about to take the warring English over to do battle in France. Leaving Thomas Howard and his out-of-favour son, Edmund, very firmly behind.

Thomas gave a small shrug; there was no hostility to be found in his expression, only weary acceptance. 'That may be so, Tom. But has it occurred to you that in your eagerness for advancement you might have caught a tiger by the tail? The foolish games of today are ones that will turn deadly tomorrow. I've already lost a beloved son and son-in-law to this accursed war. Unfortunately, there's no going back now.'

NICOLAS
Chapter Thirty-Seven

The same day. The Old Staple Inn, Calais.

So far no one had mentioned the imminent war. Perhaps they all wanted an hour or two's respite from it, thought Nicolas. Or were being cautious because of an enemy in their midst. Namely himself.

'This is excellent wine, Sir Gilbert,' he said. 'And the roast venison is cooked to perfection.'

Their host looked pleased. 'Thank you. I'll pass on your kind words to our cook.' He leant over and helped himself to a large helping of the porridge dish that Nicolas knew was so popular in England. 'I'm partial to the Frumenty myself. I always ask the cook to add more saffron and almonds than usual. As for the wine, we're drinking an excellent Bordeaux. Newly delivered.'

Nicolas liked Gilbert Talbot; the two of them had played many an animated game of chess. He was an intelligent, thoughtful man who'd had a long and distinguished career. His support for the first Henry Tudor on Bosworth Field had guaranteed him royal favour for life, according to Dame Grace. Nicolas knew that the post of Deputy Governor of Calais was an important one, requiring the skills of a soldier, administrator, diplomat, and benevolent host. Not to mention the tricky task of negotiating with representatives of other countries.

Dame Grace was talking to the Deputy Governor's wife. 'I've been enjoying your quince jam, Audrey. You know what a *penchant* I have for it.'

'Indeed I do. I intend to give you several pots to take over to William.'

'And a hogshead of claret, as well as a couple of hunting dogs I promised him,' added her husband.

'Thank you. He'll be delighted.'

'You can tell him Gilbert and I are still enjoying the Saint Buryan's mead he sent over last autumn,' said Lady Audrey. She smiled at Nicolas. 'Do you like mead? I know it isn't to everyone's taste.'

'I do, Lady Audrey. Thanks to Dame Grace, I've become very well acquainted with everything Cornish.'

'Well, if you spent time under our roof, you'd be fortunate enough to sample products from all over England and Wales. Not only Cornwall. On occasion, we even receive cloth from the Pale of Dublin.'

Through the large windows which looked out onto vast, well-cared-for gardens, came the distant call of a peacock, probably looking for its mate, Nicolas guessed. It was clear the Gilberts led a very comfortable existence: the hub of the outlying castles of Guînes and Hammes, in both power and influence. Expensive carpets, hangings and cushions gave what the Gilberts called 'The Dining Chamber' a welcoming air, as did the Flemish tapestry upon the wall. The footstools, covered in cloth of crimson satin to match the velvet on the chairs, suggested a husband and wife who valued their comforts.

Audrey Gilbert, like her husband, in her early sixties, had a kindly face and was clearly contented in her role as wife to the Deputy Governor of Calais, one in which she seemed in her element. It was obvious that she took full advantage of every available benefit. The embroidered tablecloth had very likely been purchased in the Low Countries, or even given as a present. Nicolas knew that gifts were regularly sent back and forth to England from this last remaining outpost in France. They were intended to curry favour with various members of the extravagant Tudor court, but most of all with the King and Queen. Venison, boars' heads, baked crane, sturgeon, storks, salmon, partridges, puffins, to name but a few, all made their way across the Narrow

Sea to be placed into eager hands. Fresh quails from Calais or nearby Flanders were another popular item, shipped alive until they reached Dover. Dame Grace had often mentioned how fond the English King was of dotterels which were first taken to his vast gardens in Greenwich to fly free, before ending up on a pewter plate in front of him in the great hall.

    <<Le Roi Henri certainly knows how to enjoy himself>>

Fish travelled in barrels in both directions; lamprey pies arrived in Calais, baked according to a recipe from the Cotswolds, as described by Dame Grace; every variety of hawk, and red and white spaniels, were shipped from France, passing English greyhounds and mastiffs going the opposite way.

'A few months ago, Gilbert sent some hawks to a friend,' Lady Audrey was saying, waving her hands around in the air to illustrate her story, 'but they escaped. And before that, another bird was eaten by a cat in Billingsgate.'

'Don't forget the seal I sent Thomas Howard to give him some good cheer last month,' said her husband. 'After the death of his son. I had to pay sixpence a day to keep it alive in Wapping before it was delivered to his castle in East Anglia.'

'The Narrow Sea both unites and separates us,' observed Nicolas, thinking of all the English and French ships of war reportedly filling up the waters. 'Never more so than now.'

Lady Audrey nodded her head in agreement. 'What a pity that John isn't with us at the moment, Nicolas. I know what great friends the two of you are.'

Nicolas liked their only son who was a few years older. 'We are.'

''Tis a shame he's busier now that he's married and has children of his own.'

Sir Gilbert beamed around the table. 'Nicolas will soon understand how that feels when he's wed to Robine de Croisic.'

'May that day (<<*never*>>) come soon,' said Nicolas, forcing himself to be polite, making his jaw muscles ache with the effort. Only Dame Grace understood how he felt about the grim day that was inching ever nearer: one that would swallow him up and never release him again.

'I always marvel at how well you speak English, Nicolas,' said Lady Audrey. 'If I didn't know any better, I'd take you for a Cornishman.'

Flattered to be associated with Dame Grace...if not her son, Nicolas returned her smile. 'I had a teacher *par excellence*, Your Ladyship.'

'My wife is right,' said Sir Gilbert. 'Shame Guy never followed Nicolas's lead, Grace.'

Dame Grace made an apologetic noise. 'Guy speaks Italian because of his first wife, and by the time I arrived in France he had so much daily responsibility, I think learning our difficult tongue was one task too many.'

'I understand,' said Lady Audrey. 'But for you, Nicolas, it meant you could converse freely, not only with our John, but with Tristan. That must have been a blessing for the pair of you.'

This time Nicolas did give Dame Grace a sideways glance, not surprised to see her looking amused at the very notion.

'It was,' he replied, hoping he at least sounded sincere. After all, he was half-speaking the truth.

<<*It's always given me the greatest of pleasure to be able to understand every word that trips off Tristan's qualling tongue*>>

Sir Gilbert was looking thoughtful. 'Grace, I have to admit I was surprised to see Nicolas with you last night, and not Tristan. Ten days ago, Guy seemed most emphatic that he would be travelling over the Narrow Sea with you.'

Dame Grace gave a small shrug. 'It wasn't my wish, but Robert de Sapincourt persuaded Guy that Tristan would benefit from staying behind.'

'Oh, Robert de Sapincourt!' exclaimed Lady Audrey. 'That man should keep more of an eye on what is taking place inside his own home before he hands out advice to others. I've heard some hair-raising tales about that little flibbertigibbet he took to wife. My poor friend, Denise, must be turning in her grave at how the old fool is behaving.'

Ignoring his wife's comment (probably because he, too, was smitten with the fair Ysabeau, thought Nicolas, and would be equally tempted), Sir Gilbert gave a nervous cough. 'Unfortunately, when the inevitable happens and war breaks out between France and England, they will be more than ever two separate countries. And I won't be able to ride over to Ardres to keep an eye on Tristan.'

'Don't worry, Gilbert,' said Dame Grace. 'Guy and I have every confidence in our steward. Tristan only *thinks* he's going to be in charge.'

'Bernard Guillart? Yes, yes,' said Sir Gilbert. 'A very capable fellow. You couldn't leave anyone better in charge.'

'I'm not sure Tristan realizes that,' said Nicolas, adopting a concerned brotherly tone but secretly revelling in seeing Tristan lose his status of temporary Lord of the Castle. Unlike Tristan, *he'd* never been demoted in such a humiliating manner when he was 'left in charge'; at least he'd been considered second-in-command to the Castle steward. He had every intention of letting Tristan know what had been said about him. That would put a speedy halt to his recent boasts to Nicolas that he would soon be the most powerful person in Picardy.

Seated at a table with an Englishman and two Englishwomen, Nicolas was again conscious of being a fish out of water. In normal times, there was a constant flow of communication and goods between Picardy and Calais: between the Deputy Governor's house and Ardres Castle. But these were no longer normal times.

'It seems strange,' he said now, 'that all of a sudden, friends have become foes.'

Lady Audrey shook her head. 'More's the pity, Nicolas, that is only too true. Let's just pray it won't be for long.'

આ

'There *is* one foe who is your friend, Nicolas,' said Sir Gilbert, lifting his napkin to dab at his mouth, signalling to a servant to remove the plates in preparation for the next course. 'But is no friend of ours.'

Lady Audrey playfully tapped Sir Gilbert on the arm. 'My husband so enjoys riddles.'

Nicolas was confused. Who could possibly be his friend and not theirs? It couldn't be Tristan; with him, it was the other way round.

Sir Gilbert's brown eyes were full of mirth. 'Can you guess, Grace?'

She shook her head. 'I'm afraid not.'

'Why, the King of Scotland, of course. The moment the English leave their country unguarded, James Stewart will be up to all kinds of tricks on that northern border, near Berwick. I heard that his advisors tried to persuade King Henry not to lead his army but to remain in England.'

'But I'm sure he was having none of it,' sighed Dame Grace. 'He seems as stubborn as a mule. Like so many other young men of his age.'

Nicolas felt her green eyes resting on him as she said this. Meanwhile, he was thinking about Sir Gilbert's riddle. The Auld Alliance between France and Scotland had been in existence for over two hundred years in order to curb unwanted invasions from England.

'You have no need to look disquieted, Nicolas,' said Sir Gilbert. 'You're very much our friend. Not a foe. But with pure French blood flowing through your veins, you, too, are part of that alliance.'

'Unlike Tristan who has both English and French flowing through his,' said Lady Audrey. 'So he may choose whether to be friend of foe.'

<<Definitely foe!>>

'Gilbert had word from England that one of his oldest friends is being sent up to guard the border,' she went on.

Sir Gilbert picked up his goblet of wine. 'Yes, the Earl of Surrey has been put in charge of the defence.'

'Thomas Howard,' said his wife, manoeuvring a piece of strawberry tart onto her silver spoon. 'The man to whom Gilbert sent the seal. Are you acquainted with the Howards, Grace, my dear?'

'I might have met them once or twice. But I can't be sure.'

'Knowing Thomas as I do,' said Lady Audrey, rolling her eyes, 'I can imagine his displeasure at missing out on a war on French soil.'

'What she means,' grinned her husband, 'is that Thomas is probably marching around Framlingham at this very moment, or his London house in Lambeth, cursing and shaking his fist at the unfairness of it all. Complaining that Dame Fortune has dealt him a heavy blow.'

'Especially after the recent deaths of his son and daughter,' said Lady Audrey. 'You heard about Sir Edward's death, Grace, coming so fast after poor Muriel Howard went. We heard she starved herself to death out of love for Tom Knyvett.'

'Yes. Yes, I did.'

Nicolas thought Dame Grace sounded a little distracted; she hadn't touched her strawberry tart which he knew was one of her favourites. No wonder Sir Gilbert and his wife were not exactly lacking in padding if they ate like this on a daily basis, he reflected as he bit into one of the season's early strawberries, savouring its sweetness. *<<It must be trying for Dame Grace to live in a foreign land, knowing that her country of birth has declared war on her adopted home. And so disappointing to have produced a son who is one third English, one third French, and one third demon>>*

'Damned shame about Edward!' exclaimed Sir Gilbert, holding out a particularly fine piece of Venetian glassware for more claret. 'With time and experience, he would have made a fine admiral. He possessed that rare quality of being able to win people over. I haven't seen that too many times in my life. And now that surly older brother of his has been falsely rewarded, in my opinion.'

'I recall Tristan coming back from England a few years ago, talking incessantly about Edward Howard,' said Nicolas. *<<Until it made my ears bleed>>* 'I think he met him at a tournament.'

Sir Gilbert and Lady Audrey looked at Dame Grace. 'Tristan has never met Edward Howard,' she said a little stiffly.

'That does surprise me,' said Nicolas. 'He always spoke so warmly about him.' *<<How typical of the roguish hugger-mugger to invent a friendship with a man he's never even met. No wonder Dame Grace looks so discomfited>>*

'It's a pity Tristan didn't meet Edward Howard,' said Sir Gilbert. 'I think they would have had a lot in common.' He sighed. 'But there it is. Dame Fortune intended Edward to end his short life at the bottom of the sea. And there's nothing any of us could have done to prevent it. All I can do is help my boyhood friend. It makes me wish Thomas were coming here. So I could help him with the grief.'

'He's too old to come over here,' said Lady Audrey. 'He's even older than you, Gilbert.'

'Thank you for those words of support, my dear,' Sir Gilbert replied, but with affection in his voice. 'I very much doubt whether Thomas would agree with you though. He's a proud man who's never let the years stand in his way.'

His wife pulled out a handkerchief and dabbed at her eye. 'I am just glad that they managed to recover the admiral's whistle belonging to Edward, and send it to Thomas. Forgive me, Nicolas, but what the French Admiral did to Edward after his death lacks any kind of humanity. I could hardly bear to listen to the gory details.'

Nicolas, too, had been shocked by the news that Admiral Prégent wanted to keep his rival's heart. 'I agree, Lady Audrey,' he said. 'It did seem unnecessarily savage.'

'Come, come, my dear,' said Sir Gilbert. 'It is hardly Nicolas's fault if the French Admiral chose to behave in such an unchristian fashion. Nicolas might be a Frenchman through and through, but not all Frenchmen are the same. War is a cruel, often shameful business, with no place for womanish tears. Thankfully, that is why we go to battle and you do not. All we can do now is pray that Edward's soul is at rest and hope his father finds some peace.'

NICOLAS
Chapter Thirty-Eight

Nicolas was curious about the evil Scottish King, intent on wreaking such havoc on the border between England and Scotland. 'What do you know of King James, Sir Gilbert? Have you met him?'

Sir Gilbert winked at him. 'Your "*ally*", you mean. No, I haven't had the pleasure. I've heard both good and bad reports of him. Depending on whom you talk to. He impressed the Earl of Surrey when he had dealings with him about ten years ago. And trust me, Thomas isn't easily impressed. I recall him telling me he had the greatest respect for the King of the Scots. The rapport they struck up back then is probably why James wrote to King Henry, telling him that Edward had died a needless death in a war without purpose.'

'I thought the Scottish were supposed to be wild and uncouth,' said Nicolas. 'No better than robbers on a darkened road.'

'That may be true for many of them,' said Sir Gilbert, 'but not their King. He's a very learned man, speaks several languages, is an outstanding sportsman and devout. He is musical, interested in architecture and medicine, can mend a broken bone as well as any surgeon—'

'Next thing you'll be telling us this saint is adept at needlework,' laughed Lady Audrey.

Her husband smiled at her. 'He has a keen sense of humour. And a small army of servants he treats very well. Can never keep still for a moment. Likes his horses and dogs and, in particular, his hawks.'

Nicolas's ears pricked up at this. 'He can't be so bad if he likes his hawks.'

Sir Gilbert laughed. 'I'd forgotten how much you enjoy the sport. They say the Stewart King spends a great deal on them every year. But that's not all. He's been known to spend seventy pounds in one evening on a single game of cards. When he's not dancing or playing music, that is. He likes chess, beautiful objects—'

'And the ladies,' interrupted his wife again. 'They say women are attracted to him and fight for his attentions. And he doesn't resist. I've heard he's very handsome.'

'I must say such a man doesn't exactly sound like our foe,' said Dame Grace. 'Guy says that our English King has pushed him into a corner and that King James wants peace...not war.'

There was a knock on the door and a servant came in bearing some letters on a silver tray.

ℒ

'Thank you, Peter,' said Sir Gilbert, picking them up and laying them on the table. He started to sift through them. 'Ah, here's the letter I've been expecting. From Thomas.'

'The Earl of Surrey repeating our imagined conversation, no doubt,' said Lady Audrey, 'with plenty of exclamation marks.'

Sir Gilbert looked up. 'There's something here for you, Grace,' he said, handing her a small package.

'For me?' Dame Grace sounded surprised. 'I wasn't expecting anything.'

'The sender forgot to use their personal seal,' said Sir Gilbert.

'It's probably from William,' she said, slipping it into her pocket. 'He always worries about me until I reach the safety of Zennor.'

'What a tender brother you have,' said Lady Audrey. 'Has he always been that way?'

'Yes. Ever since we were small children. But even more so after our mother died. I know he has my best interests at heart.' She smiled. 'Though sometimes it's as if he thinks we're both still living in Zennor Castle.'

'We saw William's daughter very briefly when she landed in Calais,' said Sir Gilbert. 'On her way to the court of Margaret of Austria. What a pretty girl she is.'

'Yes, she is. Unfortunately, you didn't meet her, did you, Nicolas,' said Dame Grace. 'Nor her friend.'

'No, I didn't,' he said.

'A strange time for two young girls to be gadding about the place if you ask me, said Sir Gilbert. 'But I suppose Tom Bullen is eager to place his daughter at a foreign court where she can help the family.'

'Yes,' said Dame Grace. 'William and Alys were most unhappy about it. But it seems Tom Bullen is a determined man and brooks no resistance.' She turned to Nicolas. 'You should be getting back soon if you are to reach Ardres before dark. I was wondering whether you'd like to come down to the quayside with me before you go.'

'Aren't you afraid I'll see too much and report back to the other side?' teased Nicolas.

Dame Grace looked serious. 'No, I am not. I would trust you with my very life.'

'In that case, I would be delighted to accompany you. Sir Gilbert, Lady Audrey, will you be joining us?'

Sir Gilbert held up his hands in protest. 'Oh, no, my boy. After a delicious meal, young legs need to stretch and old ones to rest. But please go and enjoy yourselves.'

Nicolas had been to Calais harbour many a time and always enjoyed seeing what was going on along the quay. In times of peace, there would be passengers either leaving or arriving; merchants haggling for the best deal; and various tradesmen rushing up and down, on their way to carry out repairs. Amongst them, eager sailors with a new spring in their step would be smiling at the prospect of a visit to the local brothel. He and Gilles had often covered their smirks as a brightly painted woman or two, displaying their enticing wares, gave them a conspiratorial wink or knowing smile as they flounced past.

"*Two sous for my time, mon beau gentilhomme,*" one of them had said to Nicolas last time they were here. "*You look as though you'd know how to please a lady,*" she grinned, boldly holding out her hand. Today, however, there were no worldly demoiselles to be seen and it was quite clear that a war was on the horizon. For the sake of Dame Grace, Nicolas tried not to look at the bustling scene, and unusually large number of ships in the harbour, with the eyes of an enemy but as a casual observer. He was at the very heart of the English Pale of Calais: one hundred and twenty miles of territory, including the town of Boulogne which lay twelve miles away, in a south-westerly direction.

'Let us take a seat here,' said Dame Grace, pointing to a low stone wall. 'We can sit in the sun for a while. I miss the sea and always relish every opportunity to be near it.'

Nicolas was only too happy to oblige; he found the salty tang of the sea air refreshing. 'You must miss Zennor Castle,' he said, following her lead by continuing to speak English. The French tongue was not exactly popular in Calais right now.

'Indeed, I do. Sometimes when I awake during the night, I imagine myself back in my bedchamber listening to the sounds of the sea, and the waves crashing against the rocks below. Then I remember where I am, and can hear nothing but silence outside.'

There was a wistful look on her face, as if she were remembering a lost life and trying to recover it. 'What about you, Nicolas. Do you have any happy memories of your childhood?'

He hesitated, but then remembered that Dame Grace was the one person in the world who knew him better than anyone. 'Perhaps that time I've told you about when a carpenter carved out some tournament figures for me. That day was probably the happiest I ever knew. Even if I had no one my own age with whom I could play.'

'You poor boy. It pierces my heart that you had to endure such misery. Guy and I have tried hard to show you a different kind of family life.'

Worried that she might think him ungrateful, Nicolas was at pains to set her right. 'You have. I've never been so happy since I moved to Ardres Castle. But you were asking me about my life before.'

'I was. And I don't understand how your parents can have been so neglectful. I would have been the proudest mother on earth to have you as a son.'

A searing stab of jealousy shot through Nicolas at the thought of all the affection she'd lavished on Tristan before he arrived at the Castle. 'I wish you'd been my mother.'

She reached out and took his hand. 'Although I'm too young to be your mother, to all intents and purposes, that is what I am to you. And I know Monsieur Guy feels the same.' She let out a sigh. 'In many ways he is more comfortable with you than with his own son. He and Tristan are so different.'

'They certainly argue a lot,' said Nicolas, trying to be diplomatic and biting back the harsh words that came so easily where the younger Ardres son was concerned.

'Monsieur Guy finds Tristan too...too rebellious. And can't understand why he can't be more like Gilles...or you.'

'What do you think, Dame Grace?'

She smiled and shook her head. 'I would never try and break Tristan's spirit. It's bad enough that he has no choice but to go into the Church. Sadly, I am powerless to prevent that but I can give him plenty of freedom while he is still young.'

'Tristan's very lucky to have you. So am I.'

Dame Grace adjusted the skirts of her gown; from his time reading to the ladies of the Castle in the bower, Nicolas knew the colour of the satin was Lady Blush and Pease-Porridge-Tawny. He couldn't help wondering how it would look on Ysabea—

'Nicolas, I know that you are approaching your marriage to Robine de Croisic with a sense of dread. Indeed, I understand your feelings only too well. You are not alone in that.'

Surprised to hear that Dame Grace might once have felt the same, Nicolas tried to remember what he knew about her marriage to Monsieur Guy. It had been one arranged by the two families, and blessed by the English King, that much he knew. But it had never before occurred to him that she might have been unhappy entering into it. Certainly not as wretched as he felt, knowing there was no way out of marriage to the sickly little heiress from Brittany to whom he'd so reluctantly pledged his troth.

Dame Grace was watching him closely. 'Yes, Nicolas, there was a time when I felt exactly the same way as you. I was desperate not to leave all that was familiar to me - all that I loved the best in this world.'

'But you had no choice either?'

'No. I had no choice either. I arrived in France with the heaviest heart imaginable. Hoping against hope there might still be a way out of this marriage to a stranger who didn't even speak the same language as me.'

'I'm sure Monsieur Guy was kind to you though.'

'Oh, yes. Very. And I was careful never to let him know the true extent of my sense of loss. For a long time, I still had hope that somehow matters would unravel, and I would miraculously find myself back at Zennor. But then Tristan came along and I—'

Her voice trailed off and Nicolas filled in the final words himself: *gave up*.

'Did things get better quickly?' he asked.

She smiled at him. 'Yes, they did. I look back now at my feelings as those of a young girl pining for what she wanted most in the world but couldn't have. Eventually I managed to shake myself out of my silliness. After all, I had two little boys in my life. And then when you entered our lives: a third. I was being selfish and ungrateful. In that way, happiness stole up on me before I realized it, and one day I was suddenly content. It didn't even hurt to visit Cornwall. Gradually, everything from my past started to resemble a sweet fragmented dream I'd once had.'

A sudden gust of wind forced her to smooth down her skirts again. As she did, she pulled out a small yellow package from her pocket.

'Oh, William's letter. I'd quite forgotten about it.'

'I wonder how they produce such an eye-catching colour,' remarked Nicolas, admiring the cloth while thinking about a possible future gift for Ysabeau to match her hair.

'There was a dyer who used to live just outside Pendeen when I was growing up in Zennor. He would create this shade by dyeing the wool with onions, cow parsley, nettles, and the bark of an oak tree.'

'Truly a magician of colour.'

'He was. He could create blue and purple by using the fruit of the sorrel tree; or grey, by using the bark of an alder tree, as well as yellow iris.' Tugging at the cloth, she began to open it.

Nicolas couldn't see what was inside, only that it was some kind of jewellery, maybe a pendant or a necklace. It was long and silver, encrusted with jewels: clearly an expensive item. There was a letter, too, which she unrolled. She suddenly let out a small gasp and turned extremely pale. Closing her eyes and tilting her head backwards, she let the letter slip from her grasp. Worried that it might blow away in the breeze, Nicolas bent down to retrieve it. It wasn't really a letter, just a couple of sentences scrawled on a piece of parchment in neat handwriting:

'*I am returning to you what I once took from you. Please forgive me.*'

Nicolas didn't know what to make of it, but whatever was inside the package had clearly upset Dame Grace.

'Dame Fortune is playing fiendish games with me,' she gasped, staring straight ahead at the sea. More to herself than him, he decided. 'Mocking me and punishing me for my hasty words.'

Nicolas didn't say anything as he could see she was trying to control her emotions. Undoubtedly for his sake. If she'd been alone, he guessed she would have allowed the tears to flow. At last she turned to him, her face still chalk white and her green eyes blazing.

'Please don't mention this when you get back to Ardres, Nicolas. It's something from my past that I wasn't expecting. Nothing for you to worry about. What's done is done.'

 e

They walked back to the Old Staple Inn in silence. Fortunately, Dame Grace recovered quickly from her shock and was able to behave normally in front of the Gilberts. Later, as he said his goodbyes to the husband and wife and was about to mount his horse, Dame Grace pulled him into an embrace. Holding him tight, she murmured into his ear: 'Remember, not a word to anyone about the package. Now, don't fight with Tristan if you can possibly help it.' Pulling back and pinching his cheek, she smiled at him. 'And don't go chasing after any women who are wed!'

As he galloped back across the fields in the south-easterly direction of Ardres, Nicolas thought about the mysterious gift and letter Dame Grace had received. But then he put them from his mind. Another face had emerged there: that of a man with long flowing hair, dark intelligent eyes, and a strange lilting accent: the enigmatic King of Scotland, seated on his throne in that wildest of lands, across the waters of the North Sea. Nicolas's ally.

<<If Tristan was able to have his Admiral, then I am entitled to my King>>

HOUSE OF STEWART
Chapter Thirty-Nine

The same day. Holyrood Palace, Edinburgh.

Ye have the verra patience of a saint, James. I woulda lost mine with Harry of England long afore this.'

James shrugged at Sir William Cumyng, his most senior herald, and trusted Lord Lyon, King-of-Arms, who was seated on a chair with a green velvet cushion James had purchased from Lombardy. They were in his inner chamber in the South Tower: a place of both privacy and opulence. Scarlet hangings, lined with Breton cloth and bordered with black velvet, adorned the walls, while a canopy of state covered in cloth of gold stood beside a cupboard containing silver and gilt plate. Turkey carpets ensured the royal feet were never chilled, cushions littered around the chamber guaranteed his comfort, and two tapestries on opposite walls satisfied his artistic leanings: one depicting exotic beasts surrounded by a border of pretty flowers and foliage, bought from an Edinburgh merchant; and the other: a stirring scene with Hercules, one of James's heroes - a historical figure, both valiant and cultured - in the centre. The summer sun was streaming through expensive panes of coloured glass, creating a mollifying rainbow effect. Curtains of green serge, a fabric that combined cloth of wool with silk, framed the windows. James, who'd been involved in even the smallest decision concerning the furnishings, was more than content with the end result.

<<*A chamber indeed worthy of the King of Scotland*>>

'And so would I have lost my patience with Harry,' was James's eventual reply to his friend and advisor. 'I am no' a saint as you well ken. And had I not been wed to his sister, matters woulda been verra different. But for the sake of

God and family, I have tried my best to be a friend to my Tudor brother-in-law and no' his foe.'

'I woulda run him through with my dirk!' exclaimed Alexander, moving away from the window. 'And turned to the new pope for help to rid myself of his sister.'

James laughed. 'Then thankfully it is I who is king and no' ye.' He wagged a finger at his son in mock reproof. 'And as the Archbishop of Saint Andrews, it is hardly seemly to talk of regicide. Or putting aside my queen, no matter what ill-will ye bear her.'

His son's cheeks turned bright red. 'I dinna care. She's never shown a dram of kindness to any of your royal bastards. And her brother is a fork-tongued gomeral. No' braw, wise and fair like ye. I would spit on the ground beneath that one's feet!' he cried (doing just that), yet fight for ye 'til my dying breath.'

On the other side of the outraged Alexander, William winked at James. 'Alexander, your father speaks the truth. I'm sure both your former tutors, the humanist, Desiderius Erasmus, who taught ye rhetoric and Greek; and the royal secretary, Patrick Paniter, would be dismayed to hear such words coming out of your royal mouth.'

Alexander stuck out his chest in defiance. 'Then let them be dismayed. Speaking as the Lord Chancellor of Scotland, my father needs my help and I'm giving it to him.'

James was verra proud of this second bastard son of his - whom the entire world thought was his first. Now that Patrick Hepburn, second Earl of Boswell, was dead, there was no one else except his sweet Janet who knew of his older boy's existence. He stared at his handsome son, dark-haired and dark-eyed, no' even twenty, so passionate, so clever, so accomplished. In some ways, he felt he'd betrayed the memory of his first love and her son by finding comfort so quickly in the arms of Marion Boyd. But he woulda gone mad without a new woman, and now he wouldna exchange Alexander for the world. Two years younger than the son his Madeleine had borne him, whom she named Nicolas (although his adoptive parents might well have changed the wee bairn's name), Alexander had been educated in Padua and Siena. Erasmus had written fondly of how his boy entertained him in the afternoons by playing the lute or recorder. James could see so much of himself in his son…both good and bad. So much passion was commendable but no' if it encroached on common sense, or encouraged rashness.

<<A chip of the same block of wood, for sure>>

''Tis true,' said William, taking a glass of *aqua vitae* that James was holding out to him, 'that Louis of France hasna made a difficult situation easier for us. There ye are trying to avoid war with the young "*gomeral*", as Alexander calls him, in the kingdom below, and all we get from France are polite phrases but nothing we can get our teeth into.'

'Aye, Father,' said Alexander, 'the auld King asked ye to send your best ships, in return for 50,000 francs, so that he could fully equip them with powder and guns. He even promised ye seven galleys and Prégent de Bidoux who saw off Edward Howard so cunningly in April. But is that enough for us?'

James pursed his lips. ''Tis is a good question. With his offer, Louis wanted to give me the verra best chance of invading Harry the moment he took off for France. Using French words, as sweet as honey on a warm bannock, about how he'd help me regain the realm and crown of England - mine by right as the heir of Saint Margaret, Queen of Scotland, and through my Tudor bride, Harry's older sister.'

'It was a stroke of French genius, or so Louis thought,' said William, 'to throw in Richard de la Pole as an added sweetener.'

Alexander snorted. 'Och, but he didna ken then that the English butcher had already ordered the execution of Richard's brother, Edmund. How long did he spend in the English Tower, Father?'

'Seven long years for the sin of being a Yorkist and Harry's great-uncle. It seems Harry did the dirty deed his father never quite managed. Probably out of deference to his Yorkist Queen. Harry's mother.'

'If only your Queen's older brother, Arthur, had survived, we might have had a peaceful King on the throne below,' sighed William. 'Now your best chance is to make a foray into England while the cream of the Tudor soldiers are abroad with their boy general.'

'It doesna help that the new Medici Pope, Leo, has sanctioned the English King's invasion of France,' said Alexander.

'Aye, I have been caught between a rose and a lily for a long while now,' said James, slowly shaking his head from side to side. 'Both of them easy on the eye—'

'Give me a thistle any day!' cried Alexander, 'or a wild sprig of heather.' He held up one hand and put it to his nostrils, as if he were inhaling the distinctive Scottish fragrance of the two plants to be found in abundance on the moorlands, glens and hills.

'If I show too much favour to the English,' James went on, 'I would lose the French—'

'And if ye show too much favour to the French,' said Alexander, 'ye'll have *Gomeral* snapping at your heels. I dinna envy ye.'

James laughed. 'I dinna envy me either. My poor wee ship "*The Great Michael*" is caught in the middle of Harry and Louis, with both of them nagging me for the use of it like a pair of scolds wearing a good man down with their ceaseless demands.'

'But,' said William, draining his glass in one gulp and holding out his hand again, 'ye stood your ground and refused to hand it over to either of them.'

'I did indeed, *mo charaid*,' said James. 'Captive as I was between the Scylla of Yea and the Charybdis of Nay.'

'Ha, Father. Verra apt,' grinned Alexander. 'Most men would be dashed on the rocks if faced with a six-headed monster on one side of a strait, and a whirlpool on the other. But thankfully no' ye.'

'Which leaves me sitting above the strait with the monster and whirlpool...contemplating my next action,' said James.

William downed another small glass of *aqua vitae* in one, as if to give him strength to deal with the problem. 'La Motte, our fine French Ambassador, brings news that Louis is content with our plan to invade England in midsummer, but is holding back his money and guns until we join him in French waters.'

Alexander started pacing the floor. 'And ye wrote to *Gomeral*, Father, offering to join the Kings of France and Aragon, if he would do the same.' He paused. 'But of course he didna.'

James shrugged. 'It probably didna help that I mentioned Edward Howard to him. A Stewart thistle pricking his Tudor conscience. How did I put it again, something like this: "*We think of the loss of your late Admiral who died in honour. The said valiant knight woulda been better off pitting his skills against the enemies of Christ than trying to capture a few French galleys.*"

'Verra droll!' said William. 'Such words must have stung as surely as an entire patch of English nettles.'

'Good,' said Alexander. 'Nothing less than he deserves.'

'They say that Edward Howard left two bastard sons behind,' said William.

James shook his head. 'Poor wee boys. And pity the father. Robbed of the chance to watch his sons grow up.'

<<I ken only too well how heavily that weighs on a man>>

ॐ

'We are still woefully underprepared, James,' pointed out William. 'We have three ships but without enough guns or men. And a fourth with no men at all.'

James threw up his hands. 'I ken, I ken. That's why I've ordered fifty carts to carry guns from Edinburgh to Leith. And put out an order to enlist sailors.'

'I only hope we dinna run out of time,' replied William, still clearly fretting.'

'William,' said Alexander, reproof in his tone, 'we need fighting talk not weak—'

A knock at the door interrupted Alexander and a young messenger rushed in, out of breath and eager to reach James.

'Your Majesty, I was told that it was of the utmost importance and that I should place this letter into your hands, and none other.'

'Who's it from, Father?' asked Alexander, eagerness in his voice, waiting for James to open it.

<<I woulda been eager too at nineteen. Before I had the full weight of kingship placed upon my two shoulders>>

James held up the piece of parchment. 'My spies never let me down. If that brother-in-law of mine knew how well-informed they keep me, I doubt whether he'd sit upon his chamber pot without looking down first.'

William, his cheeks rosy-cheeked from the aqua vitae coursing through his soldier's veins, let out a roar of mirth. 'And?' he asked.

'Patience the pair of you,' smiled James. 'It seems that the auld Earl of Surrey and I are to meet again.'

'Thomas Howard,' said William, wrinkling his brow.

'Aye, the dead Admiral's father, who is now father to the new English Admiral, is to stay behind in England and ensure that he keeps his master's property safe from the wicked Scotsman above.' James began to chuckle. 'I am certain Thomas was less than pleased to be ordered up here instead of crossing the Narrow Sea.'

'Didna ye and he meet once before?' asked Alexander.

'Aye, son, that we did. I still greatly admire him. He might be auld now but he's far from finished. We played chess—'

'But he is no' coming up here to play chess,' William pointed out, glancing over at James's chess set on a walnut table in the corner.

James gave him a rueful smile. 'No, that he is no'. But I bested him once. And I will again.' He rubbed his hands together. 'Such talk has given me an appetite for a game. What say ye, Alexander?'

His son's eyes shone. 'Aye. But I'm no more skilled at chess than the auld Earl. I've never managed to best ye either.'

James turned to William. 'Thank ye for your advice. It is always most welcome.'

⁂

'Father, where's your head today because it's no' on this game. You've never let me take your queen before.'

James glanced down at the beautiful piece made from gleaming chestnut, part of the set he'd ordered from Cremona, in Northern Italy. He smiled at his son. 'There is a first time for everything. Enjoy the moment. It shows ye had a fine teacher.' For some reason, watching his son's head of dark curls bowed in

303

concentration, James found himself thinking of that other boy. The lost one. Alexander's brother. How shameful for Madeleine's sainted memory that he didna even ken if Nicolas (or whatever he was named) could play chess.

<<*Would that he could be here engaged in combat with his younger brother instead of me right now. I'd gladly watch the pair of them the whole day long*>>

As this thought came to him, it was as if a Hogmanay firework had exploded in his head, showering his thoughts with bright embers. He almost jumped out of his chair.

<<*By sweet Saint Marie! Why am I moping like a swain who canna make a hinny his own. I am no lovelorn swain but James, King of Scotland. Once this confounded war is settled, one way or the other, I'll ask Louis of France to help me. He owes me a favour. Even if it means scouring the Kingdom of France from one end to the other, I'll find my son and bring him home where he belongs. I'll be no Edward Howard deprived of his sons. I want my eldest with me, by my sid—*>>

'Checkmate, Father!'

This time, James did leap out of his chair and kiss his second son roundly on both cheeks. '*Mes félicitations*, my son! Ye have my word that ye'll be well rewarded for your success this day.'

<<*Rewarded by the appearance of a brother ye didna ken existed but who'll stand by your side forever and a day*>>

TRISTAN

Chapter Forty

Tuesday, June 7ᵗʰ, 1513. The library, Ardres Castle.

Tristan! Did you even hear what Bernard said to you?'

I came to with a little shake. '*Oui, Père,*' I mumbled. 'He was talking about the drawbridge.' Praying I'd guessed correctly, I pulled an apologetic face at our trusted steward who didn't deserve such ill manners. 'Forgive me, I was miles away.'

<<Wondering what Ysabeau de Sapincourt looks like when she first wakes in the morning. If her eyes are bluer, her lips—>>

'Well, don't be miles away!' growled my father. 'Be here. Right now. So you can find out how best you can be of help to Bernard when we have all gone.'

"*Best be of help?*" The words rankled, just as much as the ones Nicolas had spoken while we broke our fast earlier. Full of his journey to Calais to see Mother off, he'd been more flap-mouthed than usual. Why did he look to *my* mother for succour when he'd had one of his own? True, she was dead and - according to Gilles - had possessed a face like a withered crab-apple, and had not a tender bone in her body. My half-brother managed a fraternal closeness to Nicolas to which I could not…and would never wish to aspire. As sorry a state of affairs as having such a miserable wretch of a mother might have been, it didn't mean he could try and usurp my place by playing the 'saint-without-a-sin, prodigal son' in front of my parents at every opportunity. It also irked me that (thanks to Mother) he was able to change back and forth from French to English (or in his case, Italian, for that matter) as seamlessly as myself.

"*Your mother made me promise we would not fall out,*" he'd said before, immediately after a barbed dig about who would be in charge of Ardres Castle when the war began. "*Strange, despite what you've told me, your mother didn't seem to think you'd be in charge. In fact, she more or less said the same to the Gilberts. And they were surprised to see me and not you in Calais.*"

The implication was clear: I was not fit to be left in charge, and was better suited to clinging to Mother's skirts during a lily-livered voyage of escape across the Narrow Sea to Cornwall. Incensed at the implication, I had every intention of putting Father right this morning.

'Please explain again about the drawbridge, Bernard. You have my full attention,' I said, avoiding Father's glare.

'We were just saying it is imperative, Monsieur Tristan, that the drawbridge must be raised at all times if we think the enemy might be in the vicinity.'

I nodded my head in what I hoped was a sage manner, imagining a shock of white hair on my head and a grave expression on my face, not the usual blithe one permanently fixed on the features of a fifteen-year-old.

<<*Is Ysabeau's skin as smooth as it looks? Are her lips as soft?* >> What about what lay beneath her bodice. I couldn't believe I was actually envying a piece of clothing because it was fortunate enough to rest against her—

I still hadn't forgiven Nicolas for using that cunning ruse with Ysabeau last Friday when Mother dragged me off into the gardens, leaving the two of them alone: a perilous risk. For Ysabeau…and for me. The memory of finding her reclining in his treacherous arms - like some blushing maiden, helpless to resist his brutish ways - still left me feeling queasy. I'd tried to get under his mettle this morning: "*Never fear, Nicolas. The moment the sun has stopped glinting on your brand-new armour as you disappear over the brow of the hill beyond the Castle, I intend to take back what is mine.*"

Trust him to be wily enough to catch my meaning in an instant. He'd given me that demonic smile of his and switched to French. "*I rather think that ship has sailed, mon ami. But by all means, feel free to try and lay siege to what has already surrendered. Please forgive me for changing the vocabulary from the navy to the army. Doubtless reminding you of what you are missing. I know how disappointing it must be for you to be left cleaning out the latrines, or what ever other task Bernard has in store for you."*

The library door opened and, as if some dark magic forces were at work, the source of this vicious taunt strolled in (a smirking popinjay) to the warmest greeting in the world from Father and Bernard. Not from me. But then I felt Father's eyes upon me. In order to avoid any further trouble, from somewhere deep inside I managed the semblance of a grunt: the kind a protesting pig might give on its way to market as it was spurred on by the prodding of a cruel stick. Instantly, Father had disappointment and accusation written on his face that I wasn't showing enough warmth to my 'brother'.

I watched as he bestowed his best smile on Nicolas to make up for what he'd found wanting in me, I supposed. 'Bernard was just going through some final instructions to Tristan here. For the time after you, Gilles and I have left. How was Dame Grace when you left her?'

There was the smallest moment of hesitation on Nicolas's part which I noticed. I couldn't read the expression on his face but it was soon replaced by one I recognized only too well. 'I think she was a little troubled about Tristan, to tell the truth.'

<<*"Truth"? I doubt whether he's ever told it in his entire life*>>

'*"Troubled"* about me?' I forced myself to sound nonplussed, borrowing the shock of white hair once more as if I were an actor opening up a theatrical box of tricks. If it was Nicolas's intent to try and scupper my plans and send me packing across the Narrow Sea, I had to stop him at all costs.

'*Oui*. It seemed as though she would have preferred you as a travelling companion, rather than think of you on the periphery of a war.'

<<*Had he been coached at the underworld court of Satan himself? Spouting such seemingly innocent words coated in venom. "Travelling companion" reduced me to the status of a lady's maid. And "periphery" reminded me that I would never come within a ten-mile radius of anything worth experiencing*>> I felt my mouth go dry.

'*Eh bien*,' said my father, a tad impatiently. 'It's too late to change matters now.'

It didn't take the small silence that followed to know that what he really wanted to say was: And if I could go back now, my decision would be different.

Mon Dieu! How I detested Nicolas. Although I was safe, he'd done everything in his power to spoil things. And had come very close to succeeding.

To my relief, the conversation rapidly moved onto the real business of war, not whether or not I could be trusted to raise the fen-sucked, wooden drawbridge outside the gatehouse. Father and Bernard were quizzing Nicolas about his trip to Calais. For once he seemed unusually unforthcoming, merely saying it'd been far busier than usual. Strange. He was never one to hold back if it meant he was the centre of attention for a little longer. At any rate, it provided me with the chance I'd been waiting for. I'd received a letter from Jean, and hadn't had chance to read it before Father marched me off to see Bernard when he caught sight of me in the courtyard. As I crept towards the door, I caught Nicolas's eye. Was he going to throw me to the lions? There was the merest look of amused malice on his face, then he straightened up and began speaking again: 'Whatever the English are preparing at Calais, we'll be ready for—'

و

Once outside the door of the library, I drew out the piece of parchment and unfurled it, knowing that anything from Jean would restore my flagging spirits. His distinctive slanted writing leapt across the page with all the energy of the youth himself:

May 25th, 1513.   *Bar-Le-Duc, Lorraine*
'*My friend,*

I was so sorry to learn of the sad end of your English Admiral, and can only imagine how sore at heart you felt when you received the news. It is said that the King of Scotland sent a letter of reprimand to the King of England, chastising him for throwing away the life of a good soldier instead of allowing him to take part in a crusade against the Infidel.

Will you be going to Cornwall with your mother or staying in Ardres? Perhaps if you travel across the Narrow Sea, you can jump ship at the other end and join one travelling the other way.'

I smiled at this, thinking of the many times Jean had teased me for being half-French and half-English, choosing my side depending on my mood. I looked down at the letter again:

'*If you are with your mother, then you are in good company because my brother, Antoine, has decided that I should remain here with mine. I offered to accompany him to Paris as a chaplain, but for some reason, he did not think it was a good idea.*

I still think of my time at Ardres, and of our adventure, with great fondness apart from the time when you forced me to act as your idiot brother. It should have been the other way around. If you remain in Ardres, it will leave you free to pursue that alluring young dame to whom you took such a fancy. Especially with no husband to guard her. Though with you around, I think he'd be well-advised to forgo a foray into battle.

Whichever way, write back as soon as you can or, in verity, I will go witless from the tedium. At least you'll be free from the qualling Nicolas for the duration of the war.

Your companion in mischief and mayhem,

Jean, Bishop of Metz '

I grinned at Jean's ridiculously grand title at the end, knowing he'd written it tongue-in-cheek. I glanced back at the library door thinking that his comment about Nicolas couldn't have been more prescient. As for what he wrote about Robert de Sapincourt, even if Ysabeau's gorbellied husband remained, there were more ways than one to reach Rome...or in this case, the paradise that housed one of our nearest neighbours...and the nearest to my heart.

PART FIVE

PREPARE TO CONQUER!

'Now the time is come, That France must veil her lofty-plumed crest, And let her head fall into England's lap.'

Henry IV, Part I. William Shakespeare (1564-1616).

WOLSEY
Chapter Forty-One

June 15th, 1513. Palace of Placentia, Greenwich.

Standing at the window of an upper chamber, he could see the young King alighting from his personal barge with its pennons flapping in the breeze: the red Tudor dragon and haughty golden lions side by side in a splash of vivid colour. Even from this distance, it was easy to see Henry was in high spirits. Dressed in summer's green and gold, with sunlight glinting on his auburn hair, he looked the very embodiment of the season. Joking with his attendants, he had his head thrown back in laughter as he slapped one of them on the back. Long may his good humour last, thought Wolsey, who'd recently been on the receiving end of many an unseasonable downpour.

'It'll either mean our meeting will last a very short time,' he announced to the empty chamber, 'and he'll want to feast and keep company with far younger than me. And I'll be free to get back to Joannie and little Tom. Or matters will take an awkward turn and he'll keep me until the moon in the night sky resembles a segment of an orange.'

It seemed to be his lot to take on the ill humour of others; it was only a fortnight since he'd watched Thomas Howard setting foot on the same wooden landing stage, thwarted in his plans to travel to France and determined to find an easy target for his ire.

Now that the King had defeated the old guard in their desire for peace, the Earl had longed to take part in the same war that Henry was here to discuss. Two warriors: one a fledgling general, the other a seasoned campaigner, both seeking glory on the European stage.

In terms of warfare, a king and his army were worlds apart, sighed Wolsey as the King disappeared from view. Not for young Henry the experience of deprivation: he would never have to drag heavy equipment through the mud but would ride around the countryside on horseback, accompanied by a dozen or so young pages. He'd be clothed in gold, and protected at all times by a group of his most experienced guards who were prepared to sacrifice their very lives if necessary. In other words, his personal danger was minimal but his personal comfort was most definitely maximal. He would never have to eat biscuits infested with weevils, or drink beer as sour as a crab apple. His table would be no less plentiful than at home here in Greenwich (thanks to one tent for his cook, and another for his kitchen); he would not even be expected to forgo a good night's sleep under a hedge, but would close his eyes in his own enormous bed, with its expensive cloth of gold hangings - that had already been transported across the Narrow Sea - more likely than not in a splendid marquee of cloth of gold, quite up to the standards he expected. Or he'd spend the night in his so-called 'house of timber': eight feet in height, with lantern horn windows. To add a touch of realism, the outside of the building had been painted to resemble brickwork—

'Needless to say, Your Majesty,' said Wolsey a short while later, in answer to Henry's question, 'I have personally seen to it that you will have a modicum of privacy…even though it's a wartime situation.'

Henry smiled. 'Very good, Tom. It pleases me that you have been such a help to Charles. Making him Lord High Marshal of my troops was a reflection of my esteem for him. But knowing you've been by his side every step of the way has been a great comfort to both him and me. Now tell me more about this privacy. A king must have privacy. At all times. In my palaces, too.' Henry started to pace the floor, still speaking: 'Especially for those times when his need is greatest.' He turned, letting Wolsey know the direction of his thoughts by placing his two hands in front of him, cleverly conjuring up the delights of an ample female bosom.

Wolsey couldn't even pretend to be disapproving. It was just as well that strait-laced pair, Warham and Fox, were not privy to this conversation. 'I quite understand.'

'How well I can rely upon you. You seem to have thought of everything.'

Wolsey bowed his head slightly as if accepting his monarch's praise. 'In order to ensure your privacy, Your Majesty, the royal camp will be laid out in four distinct parts, separated by wide 'streets' measuring at least thirty paces, stretching from one side to the other.'

The King was enthusiastic. 'It'll be as if one of our very own English towns is going to France to show the French how a proper town should look. And how all their towns will look when we're victorious.'

'Exactly. Within the camp there will be a marketplace and a place of assembly, in case of attack. The central area of the camp will be kept for your use alone, Your Majesty. There will be at least two hundred feet between the guy-ropes of your tents, and those of the nearby ones.'

'It sounds like a small town of tents.'

'You couldn't have put it better. Any visitor arriving at the camp will have to pass first into one tent and then into another larger one. Then into a passage which will eventually lead to more tents partially decorated with gold—'

'Excellent! The man will be struck dumb.'

'Oh, of that, I'm quite certain. Finally, he'll come to the most magnificent of all—'

Henry's blue eyes gleamed. 'Mine, by any chance?'

'Yes, Your Majesty. Yours. A tent of gold from ceiling to floor. I think we can safely say it'll be the envy of Emperor Maximilian's tailor. I've estimated that at least thirty-three florins have been spent on each ell of material.'

'What about inside?' Henry flung himself down onto a day-bed, decorated with red and white Tudor roses. He patted a place next to him. 'Come, Tom. Sit. Sit. Take the weight off your feet. I take it the interior is equally suited to a king.'

Wolsey sat down next to the King. 'I don't think you'll be disappointed with the tapestries of gold, or the exquisitely carved sideboard I personally commissioned from a cabinet maker in Stepney. Drinking cups of solid gold will be displayed: to show all who set eyes upon it what kind of man the English king is—'

ℊ

There was a peal of royal laughter. 'One made of gold, you mean? They'll be calling me "The Golden King" next!'

As was his wont - in typical Tudor fashion - switching from one high emotion to a far lower one in the blink of an eye, a frown suddenly appeared on the King's face. Wolsey's heart sank. He could almost see that sliver of orange in the sky approaching much faster than he'd anticipated. The King's mouth had narrowed to a sulky pout, stripping him of even more of his young years. Leaping up, he drew out an invisible sword from a scabbard and began advancing in an impressively menacing manner up the chamber, thrusting and parrying with a tiresome foe. Wolsey only hoped it wasn't him. After several moves, Henry paused in mid-thrust. 'Don't think I don't know that some think I should stay at home.'

This was a sore point and it was up to Wolsey to smooth the ruffled royal feathers. Both men knew Henry could have appointed a lieutenant to act in his stead and (as a king thus far without heirs) remained at home. However, Henry claimed (with justification, in the eyes of those at court who knew what was good for them) that men fought better if accompanied by their sovereign, acting as general. It was also a factor that if the King were in England, communication would of necessity be painstakingly slow. Having a lieutenant abroad, waiting for urgent instructions was not a desirable state of affairs. No man, not even the King of England and his magnificent army, could avoid being at the mercy of the winds and the currents in the Narrow Sea.

Wolsey knew that flattery was needed in order to avoid an ugly scene. It was as well that there was no one on earth who was better equipped than the King's almoner to dole out lashings of it, as if he were a cook about to plunge his ladle into a pan of spiced custard. 'Your Majesty,' he began, hoping to watch the custard dribble onto a pie of Tudor pride, 'those who say such things don't understand the machinations of war like yourself. After all, you were born to it. There are far more that say you will be the greatest general since your Lancastrian forebear, Henry, took his rightful place on the throne of France.'

Wolsey breathed a huge sigh of relief. His king might be young…but he was not foolish. Or easily pacified if the Tudor blood was up. But, thank goodness, there it was…a royal smile…one that was spreading from ear to ear. Peace had been restored to the precious kingdom within this chamber. And Wolsey, the perspicacious cook, could thankfully return his ladle to its rightful place on the rack in the kitchen of young Henry Tudor.

Being with the mercurial monarch always made Wolsey feel as though he were somehow equally basking in the royal sunshine; after all, he'd played an enormous part in making this campaign happen. He didn't mind the weight of it resting on his broad shoulders; this was a mere trifle to what he felt he could bear in the name of his king and England. If he felt a little weary at the end of a long hard day, there was always Joannie waiting to give him some comfort in their warm tester bed.

'What about discipline?' Henry was asking now. 'It's important that our army sets an example to all the others. I want every single person in Europe to spread tales of its excellence.'

'They will, Your Majesty. Sir Charles and I have it all completely under control.'

'Tom, again…what would I do without you? Now, tell me how you intend to achieve this.'

'All men involved in war, including yourself, know that discipline amongst the men is paramount. The officers have been instructed to lay down various stringent measures to be carried out to the letter. For example, if a man murders another, his punishment is to be bound to his victim and tossed into the sea.'

Hanging onto Wolsey's every word, Henry nodded in agreement.

Getting into his stride, Wolsey frowned. 'If a man cries "*havoc*" too early, he'll face death and his companions be imprisoned.'

Everyone knew that '*havoc*' was the centuries old cry given by the commander-in-chief of an English army, indicating to the men that their time had come to cease fighting and begin looting. The rules governing this were very strict and '*havoc*' could only begin once the enemy was completely vanquished. Then each man could hope to increase his personal wealth by setting upon a defeated population.

'Any disobedience to Your Majesty will be punished by being drawn by cart to a place and then hung and quartered. Disobedience to a lesser officer will still merit death but by the arguably gentler method of merely being hung.'

❧

'All this sounds very promising, Tom. I've heard the Governor of Picardy is much admired for the discipline he maintains over his troops.'

'Guy d'Ardres?'

'Is that his name? Let's hope he doesn't prove too much of an obstacle to our success.'

'Oh, I'm sure that's impossible, Your Majesty.'

'If you say so.'

Henry flung himself down on the day-bed once more. 'In truth, I'm concerned about the Cornish. Can we guarantee their loyalty? We all know Scotland isn't to be trusted. I don't want Cornwall to go the same way.'

'Of course not. I understand your qualms after the troubles of '97. But Thomas Bullen recently introduced me to a boyhood friend of his. One he assures me would sacrifice his life for you in an instant. The two of them have young daughters in the service of Margaret of Austria, in Mechelen. I liked the fellow. Sir Charles has put him in command of the troops from Devon and Cornwall. Strangely enough, he's the brother-in-law of this same Guy d'Ardres.'

The King raised an eyebrow. 'The Governor of Picardy?'

'That's right. It seems he took a liking to one of our Cornishwomen and married her.'

'How interesting. Needless to say, my great-grandam did it in reverse. She was a French Queen who took a liking to a Welshman.'

'That certainly worked out well for all of us, Your Majesty.'

'It did. Well, if this Cornishwoman's brother has the backing of you, Tom Bullen, and Charles Brandon, that's good enough for me. So his family was no friend to the rebels who ended their days either with their heads on spikes at the end of London Bridge or in graves at Blackheath. I was only five at the time, Tom, but I still have grim memories of hiding in the White Tower with my mother that June.'

Wolsey looked sympathetic. 'I am sure you do.'

'The Cornish didn't help themselves a few months later when they supported Perkin Warbeck: the Tournai boy who pretended to be my Uncle Richard. The boy prince murdered by the rogue king, Richard - the bad apple of my Yorkist kin. As usual, my Scottish brother-in-law rushed in to help the traitor. Look at him now. Wed to my sister, but still willing to stab me in the back.'

Wolsey was becoming worried the conversation was heading in the wrong direction again; filling the young King's head with vengeful thoughts was not what he'd intended at all. He wanted Henry to forget about the army of fifteen thousand who'd marched from the Lizard Peninsula to Blackheath, just outside London. They'd been protesting about the old King's heavy taxes to pay for a war against Scotland. Wolsey couldn't help wondering what the Cornish people thought about this latest expedition against France. Or the Cornishwoman, now married to the Governor of Picardy. How did she feel about her husband and brother being at opposite ends of the battlefield?

As luck would have it, he'd had a very good impression of William Tredavoe who seemed highly intelligent, loyal and level-headed: vital qualities in a leader of men. Somehow he had to steer the topic back from stormy seas to much calmer waters. 'Your Majesty, listening to your tales of the past makes me glad we live in far better times. Look at how much you've done to further your father - the King's - excellent legacy, in just three short years. As you yourself said, this new Cornish leader has Sir Thomas Bullen *and* Sir Charles Brandon to vouch for him.'

It was hard to tell whether the King had been pacified. 'And the man's name?'

'William Tredavoe, Your Majesty.'

'I'd like to meet him.'

Wolsey gave a little nod of his head: one that conveyed the unspoken words between them... *Your wish is my command.*

و

'We need to talk about other vices in our army,' said the King, changing the subject. 'Gambling, for example.'

Wolsey kept his expression serious; if he found any irony in the question asked by someone who heartily enjoyed all forms of this particular 'vice', particularly with his Lord High Marshal, he certainly wasn't going to show it. 'Anyone found gambling will have to forfeit any money earned and face imprisonment of eight days. Longer, if discovered a second time. As for being caught with a woman in the camp when this is expressly forbidden, an offender will find himself both in prison and the poorer by a month's wages.'

Henry let out a sigh, always a worrying sign for those around him. But better a sigh than a roar, thought Wolsey.

'All this is excellent,' said the King. 'And I applaud your thoroughness, Tom. But it can't all be doom and gloom for my men.'

Wolsey nodded his head vigorously up and down. 'You anticipated my very next sentence. First I must say, how typical it is of you to think of others, not yourself, Your Majesty.'

'Tom, don't flatter me overmuch or my head will start to swell. Now, let's end on a positive note. Enough of putting my men to death. How can we treat them well?'

'They will be paid their wages in advance, and the English army will be equipped with the best and most up-to-date artillery.'

Henry beamed. 'Good man. Good man. That's what I want to hear. Both of these are guaranteed to make my campaign into France a sure-fire success.' He stood up and stretched his arms above his head again, before vigorously swinging them in the manner of a Catherine Wheel. Wolsey could almost see the Tudor colours of red, green, and white spinning before his eyes. 'And now,' Henry announced, 'I must leave you. I've promised Kate a stroll around the gardens before supper. She says she has something important to tell me.'

'You don't think there's a chance she's with—' The dangerous words, so likely to offend, were out before Wolsey could stop them; rapidly approaching fatherhood must have addled his wits. Fortunately, Henry was smiling happily, and the orange segment seemed to have all but disappeared.

'That's exactly what I'm hoping for. Now don't forget I want to meet that Cornishman.'

And with that, the second Tudor King of England was off...to discover whether or not he'd be leaving a future heir behind. A weary Wolsey mopped the sweat from his brow thinking that, at times, it was far easier to deal with the whims of his infant son than the ever-changing moods of his young master....

WOLSEY

Chapter Forty-Two

A week later.

W hat a marvellous sight, my friends!' exclaimed Henry. 'Looking at this countryside makes me proud to have a goodly number of Kentish born men by my side today.' From his position at the coveted head of the procession alongside a chosen few, Wolsey followed the King's gaze back past the sweet violet and ox-eye daisies, until it came to rest on the heralds, trumpeters, and assorted members of his household, including the six hundred archers of the royal guard in their brand-new green and silver-white liveries.

'And you're a king any man would be proud to have as his general,' cooed Katherine in that unmistakeable Spanish accent of hers. Dressed in a flattering scarlet and gold gown with a matching headdress, she was noticeably glowing today in her role of supportive wife, on the way to Dover to wave off her husband to war,

Always at the ready with a positive word or a comforting touch, the Queen was indeed with child again for the third time. Happily for her, and undoubtedly as a reward for the new Tudor babe in her womb, and a token of his esteem for her, Henry had appointed her Regent and Governess of England, Wales, and Ireland in his absence. Wolsey knew he still had an enormous amount of faith in his clever wife, entrusting her with power over Church elections, and the right to appoint anyone she saw fit, in the interests of the defence of the realm.

Wolsey had been with the King and Queen when she first heard of the plan. *"Every word that leaves your lips will be as if they are from my own,"* Henry told his Queen Consort. The news of Katherine's pregnancy couldn't be more opportune, guaranteed as it was to save her from her husband's wrath. Her father, the treacherous sixty-two-year-old Ferdinand of Aragon, a man who couldn't be trusted to pass a man the salt, let alone act as an honest ally in war, had withdrawn his support, going behind England's back to make a secret agreement with old Louis of France.

The colourful little cavalcade following the narrow lanes of Kent included that most fortunate of men: Charles Brandon, who'd just been created Viscount Lisle. Riding shoulder to shoulder with Henry, in identical green and white costumes (apart from a streak of royal gold for the latter), he looked every inch the Lord High Marshal of England. Just behind, at the Queen's side, sat Henry's younger sister, Mary, in the centre of various ladies of the court, all of them as pleasing as any Tudor roses. Wolsey made a leisurely study of the tall slender princess who - in honour of her brother - was also dressed in green and white, with full sleeves of scarlet and white attached to the square-necked gown that complemented her sister-in-law's outfit. A circlet of pearls adorned her delicate neck and various rings flashed on her fingers. The irony of an English princess wearing an elaborate French hood (a newfangled fashion lately arrived from the palaces of Paris, with its curved horseshoe-shaped front, and fine net of gold tissue at the back to scoop up long locks) to bid her royal brother farewell on his way to war with France, was not lost on Wolsey.

At just seventeen, with a face as fair as any Queen of the May, and with those distinctive, fine Yorkist features: a mane of hair spun from gold and cobalt blue eyes, Mary was England's very own jewel in the crown. As usual, his mind began to work in the manner of a merchant at a market, eyes darting everywhere, from one stall to another, on the lookout for the best bargain. This led to him chewing on his lip as he pondered the question concerning which great match could be made for her. No throwing pearls to swine with this one…that was for sure. She was as valuable a commodity as the ones that adorned her headdress. He would have to have a word with Henry when all this war business was finished. At present, she was leaning forward in her exquisitely caparisoned saddle, calling across to her brother in a sweet, high voice:

'Hal, I almost wish Kate and I were coming with you over the Narrow Sea. Everything will seem so dull at court without all of you.'

In reply, Charles Brandon turned to grin at her even though the question hadn't been directed at him. 'Then who would there be to greet us on our return, Your Grace? It would be a sorry sight to see the quay at Dover quite deserted.'

Wolsey noticed the blush that suffused Mary's cheeks; twice-wed Charles, with his good looks and sportsman physique, was notorious for his charm with the ladies.

'If you and Kate came with us, we'd have no time for war,' chuckled Mary's brother, looking back at his wife and winking at her. 'The pair of you would have your needles out in a thrice to darn our shirts if you saw so much as a stitch undone.'

All the ladies giggled at this comment: every last one of them an ardent follower of this chivalrous band of brothers off to defend their honour. They weren't in the mood to dwell upon the harsh realities of war. At least, not on this glorious summer's morn. That would come later, with tearful goodbyes on the quayside in Dover. Wolsey didn't need to swivel around in his saddle to know that the ripples of mirth at the very front wouldn't have stretched as far as the Howard clan, falling into line close behind. Led by the boot-faced Earl, every mile they covered must be serving as an unwelcome reminder to him that he would be returning to London with the petticoats, not marching onwards with the plates of armour.

◈

Still, he wasn't about to let Thomas Howard spoil his good humour. The air was filled with the sweet scent of honeysuckle entwined in the hedgerow for mile upon fragrant mile, at times, heightened by the tang of wild thyme or sweet rocket. Far above their heads, a family of skylarks was giving voice to a joyous song that seemed to be exclusively for the benefit of the royal party. Meanwhile, just above eye-level, came the low humming of bees as they gently competed with the fluttering army of White Admiral butterflies for pride of place in the wild flowers adorning the hedgerow, like so many garlands hung to honour the valiant warriors on their way to glory.

In their midst, creaking its slow passage through the narrow lanes of the lush Kent countryside, amidst the rolling hills and valleys, flanked on either side by tall banks of greenery, came the royal baggage-train. It was laden with additional supplies to those that had already been shipped across the Narrow Sea to Calais, in readiness for the planned campaign against the French, in neighbouring Picardy. These included a variety of suits of armour, and green and white striped tents to shelter the officers of Henry's gathering army who awaited them on English soil. There were two entire wagons filled with tents, plus one for his enormous tent of cloth of gold, not to mention his very own close-stool: a privilege only enjoyed by five members of the King's retinue. By rights, as an almoner, Wolsey should not have been amongst this number, but he had proved so invaluable in the arrangements that he earned his right to a privacy equal to a king.

❧

When they paused a little further along the route to take some refreshments, Wolsey walked over to Henry, accompanied by two men; one of them was Thomas Bullen, the other a stranger to the King. 'Your Majesty,' said Wolsey, 'may I have the pleasure of presenting Master William Tredavoe, a nobleman from Zennor in Cornwall, and presently Captain of the Royal Battalions of Devon and Cornwall.'

'And my oldest friend,' put in Thomas Bullen, hardly missing a beat.

Wolsey watched as Henry made a thorough appraisal of the man in front of him: fair-haired, pleasing to look at…tall…somewhere in his mid-thirties, with an honest face and wide green eyes that didn't seem to have any thoughts of rebellion in their depths. Heavens be praised, thought Wolsey.

'Others speak highly of you, Master Tredavoe,' the King said, at length. 'I trust it is well-deserved.' There was a definite question in the raised inflection in the final two words.

After giving a small bow, the Cornishman raised his eyes to the King's. 'Your Majesty, it pleases me to hear that. I am eager to prove my worth to you.'

Wolsey went very still, poised for what was coming next: not sure whether Henry would be praising or pouncing. But allowing no time for that to happen, William Tredavoe was speaking again:

'I also want to prove the worth of every last Cornish or Devonshire born man who has joined up to support his king with his very life.'

There was rather an alarming pause where several of those listening - including Wolsey and Thomas Bullen (he was sure of it) - collectively held their breath. The signs did not look good. At first, the crimson rosebud mouth looked as if it was going to tense into an angry thin line, and Wolsey began to regret asking Bullen to seek out the Cornishman. But after several moments, the Tudor lips opened up into a beaming smile, like petals seeking the sun after a storm. 'Verily, Master Tredavoe,' said Henry, leaning forward to put one hand on the Cornishman's right shoulder, 'that took some courage to say to a king.

And I applaud you for it.' He turned to one of his servants. 'Bring an extra goblet so that this good man here can share our flagon of small beer.'

Now that the threatening black clouds had passed overhead and the royal sun come out to play, everyone breathed a sigh of relief. The talk veered away from the dangerous topic of Cornwall, its dubious past and unproven future, to the families they'd all left behind. 'Tom,' said the King, handing Thomas Bullen a small beer in a golden cup, 'you've left two boys behind. But I hear one of your girls has already crossed the Narrow Sea.'

No one was surprised at the King's comment, least of all Wolsey; Henry was widely admired for his phenomenal memory for facts and faces.

'That's right, Your Majesty,' answered Thomas Bullen. 'My Nan and William's Cecily left about six weeks ago. In January, they had the great pleasure of meeting you on a sled on the Thames, of all places.'

Henry looked momentarily nonplussed, and then his face creased into a grin. 'Of course. I remember them now. My lady mother, the late Queen, always used to say that her younger sister, Cecily, was the prettiest of all King Ned of York's daughters. And your girl is a winsome little thing, Master Tredavoe. Your two as well, Tom.'

'Thank you, Your Majesty,' said the newcomer. 'So I've been told.'

The King took a swig of his beer. 'I like the name of Cecily for a daughter.' He smiled at the Cornishman before glancing across at his wife. 'But that will do for later. After the birth of our son.' He set his beer down again. 'I've also heard that your sister crossed the Narrow Sea a long time ago. And what is more, decided to make her home amongst the French.'

Staring across the impressive ramparts to the sea, beyond the admirably thick outer walls of the Castle that followed the lines of an Iron Age hillfort, Henry fancied a half-submerged Neptune was beckoning to him, a golden, three-pronged spear held aloft in his right hand. Calling out to the King of England to come and reclaim what was rightfully his. He turned to his friend. 'It's hardly a hundred years since the English mocked the King of France for being "*le roi des Bourges*".'

Charles raised his goblet in the direction of the Narrow Sea. 'By Saint George! A country reduced to the size of a small town in the centre of the country—'

'Yes. Bourges was all that was left of the mighty kingdom of France. And so it will be once more.'

'The English back in France where they belong. The eighth Henry finishing what the fifth began.'

'I'll drink to that. Back in those times, our territories in Aquitaine and Normandy were secure. In the north-west, rebellious Brittany was mirroring Wales in its bid to be independent. In the south-west, Navarre boasted its own king. The Counts of Toulouse had laid claim to lands south of the Massif Central.'

'What about Provence, in the south-east? A place in the sun.' Charles gave him a friendly nudge with his elbow. 'Perfect for lovers, or so I'm told.'

Henry tilted his goblet, as if attempting to catch the rays of sunlight bouncing off the stone wall next to the nearest tapestry. 'Then you and I need to travel there one day and set our blood alight with the fierce heat. In keeping with your description, Provence was behaving like a fickle lover, alternating between Anjou and Savoy.'

'And what role did the Church play in all this? I'm sure she wasn't exactly retiring.'

'She wasn't. The Church managed to get her greedy hands on Avignon.'

331

'Have we included all of France? Or should I say: "England's rightful inheritance"?'

'There's the House of Savoy. It had possession of territory in the east, stretching from the Alps down to the river Rhone.'

'Ah, there's one more. Burgundy.'

'My dear Charles, as always, I was saving the best for last. North of Savoy, lay the lands of the most dazzling European potentate of them all. The Duke of Burgundy—'

'Whose memory in history will dim compared to yours. The Dukes of Burgundy will be remembered as a noble line with no discernible face amongst the lot of them. But there will only be one King Henry VIII of England.'

Henry raised his goblet heavenwards once more. 'Amen to that!'

The next day.

Stepping out onto the ramparts, Henry beamed at the small crowd in front of him. It was a mixture of his own followers, castle workers (as fiercely loyal to their King as any of his three million subjects beyond) and town dwellers from the four hundred or so houses that crouched beneath the Castle. They'd all gathered to give their monarch a fitting send-off. He took note of the brightly-dressed foreign dignitaries dotted amongst his own people, and was pleased they were witnessing such overwhelming support. Besides, today was his twenty-second birthday and he had every cause to celebrate.

'We have money in our coffers,' Henry announced whilst allowing himself an easy, unfeigned smile in his role of fledgling general, and thrusting out the forty-inch chest that had already been admired by the obliging Venetian

Ambassador. 'God is on our side and, by Jove, we'll show the lot of them we're equal to any Agincourt!'

At this, a general cheer went up, several hats were thrown into the air, and cries of 'God save King Harry!' abounded. The King looked at the expectant faces about him; they were his subjects and were depending upon him to lead them into glory. In the crowd, he caught sight of Thomas Bullen, next to that Cornish friend of his.

A man upon whom he was now certain he could rely.

Henry had to bite his lip to prevent a laugh escaping when he saw Thomas Howard's scowling face next to that insipid bull's pizzle of a son of his. Edmund. A sorry stockfish if ever he saw one.

Suddenly he clenched his fists, the smile died on his lips, and he narrowed his eyes to become once more the two icy blue flints reflected back at him in the mirror when he'd been practising his lines before. He could feel his pale skin - an annoying Tudor family trait, but quite useful now - flushing deep red. If it was the last thing he did, he would prove to the whole world that Harry of England was capable of following in the footsteps of the great victor of Agincourt. Let no man say that his forefather (who sacrificed his health to become the undisputed ruler of England and France) had fought in vain.

Judging by the expression of dismay on many of the faces of the onlookers on the ramparts of Dover Castle who'd noticed his frown, he could tell they feared they'd somehow offended him. But then he caught the eye of his Kate, and thought of the son she was carefully carrying in her womb, or so she'd promised him (giving him her word there would be no more foolish expeditions until the day their boy entered the world). Her expression was a gratifying blend of adoration, gratitude that he'd allowed her to witness this, and respect for him as a soon-to-be conquering general of an army. He could feel the colour fading from his cheeks as rapidly as it had appeared, and he could afford to be all smiles again. He bowed to his cherished queen and blew her a loving kiss which brought forth a roar of approval from the crowd. This pleased him greatly.

After all, why should he be seen to lose his good humour? Hadn't he been preparing for this moment for as long as he could remember? He and his advisors had taken every possible precaution against rebellion in his absence. That was why a surly Thomas Howard was remaining in England (*"to bend poor Kate's ear"*, as Charles had put it yesterday): to deflect the very real threat from Margaret's despicable Scottish husband. Edmund de la Pole was dead. In the calamitous event of Henry not returning from France, there must be no chance of the Yorkist being rescued from the Tower and placed on the throne.

"I could do nothing to prevent his execution," Henry told Charles at the time...as if someone higher than himself had issued the order.

"Of course you couldn't, Hal," soothed Charles in that way he had of pouring a healing unguent upon an open wound. 'His fate was sealed when Louis of France recognized that exiled brother of his as Richard, King of England.'

If Edmund's death did anything to tarnish Henry's golden image, it was not commented upon; he knew he was still the people's prince: their dazzling monarch who made them proud to be English. His subjects began to cheer again and it was all he could do not to thrust both arms into the air to encourage them to continue...and never stop.

ℒ

After the crowd of well-wishers had finally dispersed, Henry strolled over to the far corner of the ramparts. Being near to the sea always filled him with a tremendous feeling of peace and well-being. He gazed out beyond the flotilla of a goodly number of his three hundred brightly painted ships, described by one of his officers as: *"a fleet worthy of Neptune himself"*. Obviously, it had been impossible to despatch between thirty and forty thousand of his men across the Narrow Sea at one sailing; this was being accomplished in stages, beginning back on the sixth day of June. It was a fleet led by seafarers who made it their business to make a meticulous study of the stars, wind, clouds and sun, not to mention an examination of the water itself. Whilst watching his ships bobbing up and down on the waves, their pennants flapping in the breeze, Henry filled his lungs with the bracing sea air and flung out his arms wide, as if in welcome.

He became aware of another who'd come to stand by his side: his trusted advisor, Tom Wolsey. The very man who'd acted as his eyes and ears for most of the campaign planning. After exchanging a friendly greeting, the two of them gazed ahead at the calm waters, a mere twenty-five fathoms in depth. Only twenty-one miles away lay the English stronghold of Calais, guarded in times of peace by around eight hundred trusted men, with regular inspections of the walls which began with the tolling of the great Flemish bell every evening. It was said that the security measures against the French at Calais were no less strict than the ones taken by the Castle of St. Peter in Rhodes, against the Turks. Henry was aware that the town, so like one of his own, with its own mayor and council, was readying itself for his arrival.

'When you leave the ship you'll be led across Paradise, Your Majesty,' said Wolsey in that rich, deep voice of his that always reminded Henry of warmed molasses. 'That's the garden separating the harbour and the town. Then you'll pass through the Lantern Gate, on your way to the church of St. Nicholas where you'll hear mass and a Te Deum.'

Henry had often noticed how his and Tom's thoughts merged so closely - as in a mirror image of Chancery Lane and Fleet Street in the country's capital - that they almost had no need of words. He hadn't quite worked out how it came to be but there was a touch of wizardry about their association.

'And sustenance, Tom? I hope we'll have plenty of that.'

'In abundance. You and your party will repair to the lavish Staple Inn for refreshments. This will act as your headquarters while you're in Calais.'

Henry could hardly wait. The very thought of all this lying ahead of him almost took his breath away with excitement as he continued to stare out to sea.

He did not look back....

VALENTINE
Chapter Forty-Four

July 12th, 1513. La Colombe.

Don't go, Papa! Please don't go.' Valentine was clinging to her father's legs, trying to stop him mounting his horse.

He signalled for one of the servants to take his horse's bridle then knelt down alongside her. Valentine knew from his worried expression that her eyes must be red and swollen from crying, and her cheeks tear-streaked and dirty.

'I-I don't see w-why you have to go,' she stammered in between sobs. 'We need you here. If you stay, I'll dance for you and Maman all day long to make you both smile again.'

Using his thumb, her father tenderly wiped away a tear that was sliding down her chin. 'That sounds *charmant, mon enfant*. And you have no idea how much I'd rather watch you dance. But I have no choice. A Roman general once said: "*Si tu veux la paix, prépare la guerre.*" Our King needs me much more than you do today. Because—'

'Because the King of England is evil!'

'Hush now, Valentine. You mustn't upset yourself so. I will be back before you know it…in time to welcome your little brother to the world.'

Valentine gave a wail and flung her arms around her father's neck. 'But that's not for ages and ages. Maman said not until the harvest is finished.'

337

Nearby, the horses were starting to grow restless under the weight of all the supplies loaded into the saddlebags. Valentine saw her father glance up at a lattice window where they could see her mother and Grandmère Symonne staring forlornly down at them in the courtyard. Gently he prised Valentine's arms from his neck.

'*Chérie,* I have to leave now. Send me off with a smile, there's a good girl. And promise me faithfully that whatever happens, you'll take care of your mother and your little sisters. When I come back, you and I will take the greyhounds and go hunting again.' He held out his hands to her. 'Come. You may ride with us as far as the entrance.'

As he set her down at the end of the long drive, Valentine tried her hardest to find a farewell smile from somewhere although, by now, she was weeping so hard that the tears were blinding her. Fighting back his own emotion, her grim-faced father finally turned away. While he and his men paused to have some last words before they trotted through the archway out of La Colombe, Valentine raced across into Grandmère Symonne's garden from where she knew she would have a better view of their departure. A few minutes later, she stood there - her hands clasped together very tightly - watching the little company leave.

In spite of her distress, she couldn't help noticing a single red rose growing straight and tall right in front of her.

It was very beautiful…there was no denying that.

And extremely fragrant.

But it had also come to symbolize everything Valentine hated about England. Almost hoping the thorns would prick her fingers to replace the pain in her heart, she snatched it up in a rage and dashed it to the ground, taking a grim satisfaction in watching the petals scatter in all directions. Seeing it lying there, crumpled and destroyed, made her feel slightly better - even though she hoped Grandmère Symonne wouldn't notice she'd harmed one of her precious roses.

Valentine remained in the same position long after the small party had disappeared over the hill, her eyes fixed on the horizon.

She did not look back....

Chapter Forty-Five

21ˢᵗ July, 1513.

P on my honour, I could hear the cheers from here. They were loud enough to stir a dead man in his shroud,' said Robert, pushing his oar against the side of the landing stage in Westminster to take me down river.

As usual, when it was just the two of us, we were using one of his smaller boats to afford us the maximum of privacy. And to ensure we weren't summarily packed off to the Tower for any treasonous talk during our journey.

Robert looked at me. 'You'll be glad the Queen's speech was well-received. It's sure to be reported over in France.'

'I am. She told the captains to be prepared to defend England, and that God smiles down on those who protect their own.'

'She's right about that.'

'We must hope and pray that it is so. The cheers you heard were probably when she said that no other nation can equal the English for courage.'

Robert laughed. 'Not bad coming from a Spanish princess.'

'A Spanish princess, mayhap, but now an English queen accepted by the people, and clearly so in thrall of her husband she would probably like nothing better than to rush before him, scattering red and white Tudor rose petals in his path.'

'Even with his roving eye?'

'I know from Edward that his occasional dalliances cause her great pain. And wound her excessive pride as an infanta of Castile and Aragon. Knowing he strays from her bed to that of a woman not of royal blood. But don't forget, Robert, that he rescued her from a pitiful state of neglect and downright poverty. Marrying her almost as soon as the last breath had left his father's body. Raising her up to the clear blue skies above, decking her out in jewels and planting a crown of gold, sapphires and pearls upon her head. What woman wouldn't want to scatter rose petals for a man that does that for her?'

'Now all she has to do is provide him with an heir. Let's hope for her sake this one is a boy, and stronger than the one that came before. The King isn't known for his patience.'

I nodded. ''Tis true. Four years is a long time to wait. Especially at their age.'

'Don't forget she's five years older than him which is no small matter. I heard she barely ate during those long years spent at *Goose*'s court. Preferring to pray for many a long hour in a chapel so cold she was chilled to the bone, and her knees rubbed raw.'

'I always marvel at how you gather so many facts, my friend. Out here on the river, it's almost as if part of you is inside at the court.'

Robert smiled and touched his nose. 'You're right. What takes place at these Tudor courts of ours spills out onto the Thames to such an extent that I often feel as though I'm there in person.'

'Luckily for me.'

'In good earnest, Thomas. Luckily for you.'

'I am still aggrieved at being left behind in England, like some feeble greybeard discharged from his duties for want of success.'

Robert rested on his oars for a moment, giving easy control to the (presently) peaceful Thames, his boon companion for so many years, through storms and sunshine. 'Thomas Howard, I couldn't think of a description that sounds less like you. A man who has lately single-handedly recruited five hundred men from his own household and tenants. And proudly presented them today to Thomas Lovell, Treasurer of the Household. God's Crown! You're the most important man in Katherine's council.'

'You mean, more useful than William Warham, Archbishop and Chancellor, who wastes his time trading insults with the holier-than-thou Bishop of Winchester.'

'Richard Fox should know better.'

'They both should.'

'Katherine recognizes your worth. I heard how grateful she was for your kindness to her on the way back from Dover.'

I rolled my eyes. 'How in the name of Sweet Mary, Mother of Jesu, do you know that?'

'From María de Salinas, or should I say, Baroness Willoughby de Eresby, Katherine's favourite lady-in-waiting. She was our first passenger the morning after you returned.'

'It's all very well that Katherine values me. But it's the King's ear I'm in danger of losing by being so far from his side. I'm a soldier by trade and heart, and it's a disgrace not to be part of the flower of all the nobility accompanying him to France.'

'Who's he taken in your place that so vexes you?'

'Thomas Grey, to name but one. Especially after that disgraceful hogwash of a campaign in Northern Spain last year. And Thomas Darcy. Who's taken valuable men from Northumberland when I might have need of them.'

'I can see your point. Such choices are a mark of Henry's inexperience.'

'And arrogance.' I swallowed hard. 'When Edward was still alive, he was a Howard proudly representing our family: whether in the King's chamber, at the tilt, or at the helm of one of his ships. At all times, I was able to reach Henry through him.'

'You still have Thomas and Ed—'

'Don't even mention that last one's name to me. As for my eldest, so far, all he's done is anger Henry and prove to the whole world he's no match for his younger brother.'

'Give him time, Thomas. He's all you have. We both know Edward was too rash at the end.'

I could feel my shoulders sagging. 'A mistake he paid for with his life.'

'Things can change overnight, you know that. A battle at sea or on land can turn with the speed of a coin landing on the opposite side to which a man expects. Robbing him of his last groat; sending him to the Tower; rewarding him with riches beyond his wildest dreams...or—' There was a sudden catch in his voice. 'Snatching away his very life.'

I slowly nodded my head and closed my eyes.

Robert's voice was infinitely gentle. 'Don't despair, my friend. It doesn't become you. It's unworthy of the man I've known practically my whole life. Since I was old enough to sit upon this bench. Remember, you'll always be Edward's "*phoenix*".'

'I still miss him, you know, Robert. I've lost other boys...and my beautiful girl, of course. But there was no one quite like Edward. He was my golden child.'

Robert turned to me with a look of sympathy on his face. 'I know you still miss him. So do all of us. Henry, too. Perhaps one of the reasons he didn't want you to go to France was because it would be a reminder of his failure to help Edward more with supplies.'

'I doubt whether that's the case. Far more likely he didn't want an old soldier like me, with a wealth of experience under his belt, telling an overeager stripling like him what to do. *Snake* will act as his perfect foil: aiding him - but acting as though every decision comes from Henry, not him.'

'And you think you wouldn't have been quite as politic?'

I stared at him and we suddenly both burst out laughing. It was such a relief to find comfort in mirth that we ended up bent double, holding our sides. Wiping tears from my eyes, I was the first to speak. 'Unquestionably not. Anyway, let's hope the headstrong Tudor pup doesn't end up getting himself killed. With no heir, it would be a sorry state of affairs indeed.'

'Indeed 'twould. James of Scotland would fly down to London on a winged horse as if his very life depended upon it, seeking what he'd claim was his through his Tudor wife.'

I shuddered. 'Let's away from such dark thoughts. It's bad enough hearing from my spies what the Stewart King is planning.'

'What's that?'

'He's been studying the tactics of the Swiss mercenaries and Imperial *Landsknechte*, hoping to emulate the way they use tight rows of soldiers bearing pikes.'

'But surely the Scots won't be able to learn such a complicated procedure in a matter of weeks.'

'My spies tell me that wily old Louis of France is sending a group of captains to teach them.'

Robert paused as he thought about this. 'Well, just as Rome wasn't built in a day, so a Swiss mercenary wasn't prepared for battle in one either. Nor a canny Scotsman. You, Thomas Howard, Earl of Surrey, have taken seventy years to reach this point.'

I cupped my irksome knees in my hands. 'Don't remind me. I'm hoping my joints aren't going to trouble me unduly, and I won't need to be placed in a cart only fit for urchins and livestock. Rattled around like a rat in a trap.'

'Just as well we're on the Thames, away from prying eyes and ears. And not on dry land. That isn't exactly fighting talk.'

❦

I threw up my hands. 'I can't help it. I keep thinking about Edward and how he now knows what I did.'

'What you *did*?' Looking bemused, Robert reached up and scratched his head as if it would help him find the answer. I watched as the expression on his face changed. 'Oh, you're talking about the Cornish girl?'

'Yes. I sometimes awaken in the night, unable to get the thought out of my mind that I deprived him of his fair share of happiness. Robbed him of his son.'

'You did what you had to. Edward will understand that now. Besides, you sent Grace Tredavoe his Admiral's whistle. And apologized to her.'

'Even that was half-arsed. I couldn't sign my name in case my letter fell into the wrong hands. I sent it to Gilbert Talbot in Calais, knowing it would find its way to her. She probably loathes me more than before. And sees me as a lily-livered varlet, not fit to be Edward's father.'

Robert let out a sigh as he picked up the oars again. 'It all happened a long time ago. How old is the boy now?'

'Sixteen in the autumn.' I smiled at the memory of the young boy in the garden, bating the dark-haired French lad who'd shown such promise as a future soldier. And restraint as the man he would become. 'As much of a rascal as his father ever was, from what I saw of him. God's Nightgown! I'd give anything to see Edward and Tristan together. Father and son. Affectionate and fiercely loyal Howard men. As they should be....as they should *have been*,' I corrected myself, feeling tears pricking at my eyelids in the manner of a hundred miniature swords.

'Thomas, you're going to bring madness upon yourself if you continue in this way.'

The weather-beaten wherryman seated in front of me, my friend for so many years, like his father before him, was suddenly looking very stern. 'Cuds me! You need to gather your wits about you by tomorrow before you leave for Doncaster. If not, James Stewart of Scotland will have your guts for garters! Mark my word 'pon it.'

There was something in his tone that roused me from my pitiful stupor, unworthy of a lowly lamplighter in the streets of London, let alone an earl about to lead an army north. I shook myself with all the vigour of one of my more adventurous hunting dogs after an unauthorized leap into a river. 'Rest assured,' I said, 'I don't intend for any king of Scotland to *"have my guts for garters"*. Let you and I heed the words of Queen Katherine today and believe that God is smiling down on those who defend their own.' I quickly crossed myself...as did Robert.

His face was as serious as I'd ever seen it. 'Never forget. I'm with you in spirit all the way.'

HOUSE OF STEWART

Chapter Forty-Six

26th July, 1513. Holyrood Palace, Edinburgh.

'Och, William, there will always be naysayers like Elphinstone who will try and shout down any murmurs of war in the Council.'

James's good friend and faithful Lord Lyon, King-of-Arms, nodded his head in agreement. 'Verra true. And as Bishop of Aberdeen, Elphinstone had no choice but to plead for peace. He is but a follower of the stiff-necked new Pope in Rome who chastises ye for wanting to make war on your so-called brother in England. And willna reverse the threat of excommunication issued by his predecessor.'

'Aye, damned Medici spawn! And William Elphinstone is a mammering auld fool of eighty-two who doesna grasp that this new English king is no' like his father before him.'

'That he is no'. He's a warmongering young hothead.'

'My Maggie's wee brother has the throne of France in his sights, and leaves me no choice but to join with auld Louis in battle on land and sea.'

'There's no surprise in that. The English were expecting ye last summer.'

'I had to wait until Louis drew out a bigger purse. And agreed to put his hand in it. Now with any luck, we'll have help from the Danes; my cousin, Charles, Duke of Gueldres; and Hugh O'Donnell of Ulster.'

'It pains me to say this but we canna pin all our hopes on any of those three to stand alongside us. No' when Harry of England has Maximilian and his daughter, Margaret, on his side. A Holy Roman Emperor and an Archduchess of the Burgundian Netherlands.'

James let out a sigh. 'I ken. 'Twas a great pity that my Uncle Hans died this past February. We canna rely on Danish ships now as we did before. And

O'Donnell is more interested in what we can do for him in Ulster than he for us.'

'Then there are the men who didna want to sign up. Ye ken from William, Lord Livingstone, that there is no great interest amongst his tenants in joining a Scottish fleet that is looking to the auld King of France for its supplies.'

'I canna blame them, William. In their place, if I were young again, I, too, would want to cross the border and fill my knapsack with swag from Northumberland. And no' sign up for forty days' service at sea that might bring me nothing at best. Death at worst.'

'We should be pleased that the Scottish fleet sailed out into the Forth yesterday, under the command of your cousin, James. Some say no' but I agree with ye that the Earl of Arran is well up to the task.'

James made a clucking noise with his tongue. 'There are those who dinna think James is up to much, I'll give ye that, But he has many a year's experience beneath his belted plaid. I'll be following tomorrow on "*The Michael*".'

'As far as the Isle of May?'

'Aye.' James walked over to a small oak table and picked up a golden coin. 'I wanted to show ye this.'

William took it from James and placed it in the palm of his hand where it gleamed brightly. 'I can see it's a match for the English rose noble.' He turned it over and grinned. 'Verra fitting. Saint Michael smiting the dragon, back-to-back with "*The Michael*", bearing the arms of Scotland. "*Salvator in hoc signo vicisti.*"'

'"Saviour, by this sign, hast Thou conquered." It's intended as a wee nudge to my warring brother-in-law that I am his heir, supported by the two Michaels on the coin, each showing that I have divine support.'

'Who has divine support?' said James's queen, a pleasing sight in crimson and gold, as she swept into the chamber unannounced.

❧

James could tell she was in a good mood; their lovemaking at dawn had lasted way beyond the breaking of the fast. He could still see traces of their passion on her swollen lips and noticed a livid mark on her neck he didna remember putting there. He'd teased her that her womanly wiles would be the death of him.

"*Hush, my lord, don't even let such words pass your lips,*" she'd scolded, drawing his hand back down to her heavy breasts, reddened from the onslaught of his caresses. He could see the places where his teeth had nipped her skin in his eagerness to pleasure her. "*Especially after a new life might even now be beginning in my womb.*"

Delighted and further aroused by her words, James brushed his fingers down past her soft belly and gently splayed them across her broad pelvis. He was suddenly seized by overwhelming possessiveness and a fierce love for his Maggie. "*Och, hinny, ye have truly created a sea of forgetfulness for the two of us. One that will always draw me back to ye.*"

"*More than your other women?*"

He put a finger to her lips. "*There are no other women. And if there were, they are no more.*"

"*If it's a boy, I want to call him Alexander.*"

James saw a stubborn look appear on her face and her lips pucker in determination. He knew the reason for her request: to push the first Alexander, his beloved bastard son, back into the shadows where he belonged. Overweening Tudor pride was a terrifying sight to behold but at this verra moment, it pleased and excited him to do battle with it. He pulled her on top of him and skilfully pushed her upright, steadying her fleshy hips with his hands. "*Ye have my word that ye can call him whatever name ye wish, my Queen.*

That's it," he coaxed her, *"arch your back and show me once more how a true queen rides her king to victo—"*

'The King was just telling me,' said William, interrupting this lustful train of thoughts, 'that his new coin will show the world that God is on his side.'

'And not on my brother's, you mean,' said Maggie.

'I didna mean to offend ye,' began William but she stopped him with a small wave of her hand.

'No offence taken, William. My brother deserves everything that is coming his way. *He* has forced Scotland into war. Not the other way around.' She crossed herself. 'Against my wishes, for sure. But he doesn't care about that. He's long favoured our younger sister over me.'

James picked up her hand and kissed it, amused that he could still detect a faint musky scent from their lovemaking. He almost felt like dismissing William so he could take his pleasure of her again right now. His fiery Stewart blood hadna yet cooled in his veins, and all this talk of war was turning it into molten gold once more. It would be a most welcome way of doubly ensuring another prince arrived to take his place in the royal nursery. 'Princess Mary couldna hold a candle to the bright flame of the Queen of Scotland,' he said, holding up her hand as if in triumph. 'My fine English wife.'

Maggie batted away his compliment, tugging back her plump, bejewelled hand. But he could tell from her blushes she was pleased. She turned to William. 'I've told my lord that he has no place going off to war when we only have one small boy running around in the nursery, and no infant boy in the cradle.'

'Your brother doesna even have that,' retorted James, glancing over at the daybed over in the corner, and thinking again of all the things he wanted to do to his spirited queen. 'And even though your sister-in-law is reportedly with child again, she is no' hale and hearty like ye.' He narrowed his eyes and gave her a meaningful look, intending for her to want to be alone with him again as much as he wished it.

Dimples danced in Maggie's cheeks and her blue eyes were sparkling. Och, aye. He knew she could feel the blood thrumming throughout her body too, her womb beckoning him back home where he belonged. She arched an eyebrow. 'James, are you suggesting I'm stout?'

'Ye, stout, my flame-haired beauty? She who is the verra image of Sandro Botticelli's Venus. No, no' stout, merely a mother. Something Harry's bride may never be.'

'I hear you're leaving for France tomorrow, William,' said Maggie, changing the subject.

James smiled at her burning cheeks, reflecting her inner struggle to behave in a regal fashion. In the end, her Beaufort grandam's strait-laced upbringing won out, forcing Maggie to restore some decorum in the presence of the Lord Lyon, King-of-Arms.

'Aye, Your Grace. To deliver a letter to your brother in Thérouanne. Your husband has just dictated it to me.'

'Is that so? I'd like to hear it if I may,' said Maggie, settling into a chair.

William looked over at James who gave him a brief nod. 'With pleasure,' he said to his Queen, picking up the piece of parchment and beginning to read:

'*Brother,*

It is with a heavy heart that I am writing this letter to ye. We are bound to one another through close family bonds, and a shared border of our kingdoms. God is watching over the two of us and wishes us to live in peace with one another.

However, I canna ignore your actions that intend such harm to my French brother, Louis, with whom I am also bound through the Auld Alliance. I am asking ye now, brother to brother, to desist from further invasion and utter destruction of our brother and cousin, the Most Christian King, to whom we are bounden and obliged for mutual defence, the one of the other, like as ye and your confederates be obliged for mutual invasions and actual war. We are informing ye that we will take part in defence of our brother. And we will do what thing we trust may cause ye to desist from pursuit of him. Please take heed of my words for all our sakes.

Your own loving brother, and devoted husband of your royal Tudor and Stewart sister, Margaret,

James, King of Scotland.'

None of them stirred for a long moment so powerful were the words that James had dictated, and William read with such dignity. The air in the room fair crackled with the aftermath of this passionate plea for mercy that couldna fail to move most men. But Henry Tudor the Younger wasna most men, thought James.

It was Harry's older sister who broke the silence first, smiling at William as she rose to her feet. She began to clap slowly. '*Bravo*, gentlemen. And James. An excellent effort. One that would have brought down the Senate of Rome in olden days.' She gave a little frown. 'But one I fear that will drive my sheep-biting little brother mad with fury. It will be as if he is the boar and you are the hunters prodding him with your spears. I predict that he will bellow at you that my husband only holds Scotland at his bidding. And that James owes homage to him.'

William was looking grim. 'With respect, Your Grace, your brother doesna fill with me with fear. Quite the opposite, in fact. Forgive me for my soldier's forwardness.' He looked over at James with shining eyes as he knelt down on one knee and bowed his head. 'I only answer to one king, and he is standing right next to us.'

'As do I,' said Maggie. 'You both have my word that I am a true Queen of Scotland, and will remain so until the end of my days.'

James leant down and clapped his friend on the back. 'Excellent man. Hopefully, Henry Tudor the Younger will remember his manners and at least give ye a wee dram for your efforts in delivering my letter.' He winked at William. 'And now if ye'll excuse us, King Henry of England's sister and I have some unfinished business that canna wait....'

TRISTAN

Chapter Forty-Seven

28th July, 1513. Ardres Castle.

The sound of female voices drifted up from the courtyard below my bedchamber. Good. Ysabeau de Sapincourt was here at last. I was glad I'd given instructions for the drawbridge not to be raised again immediately after Bernard's departure, despite our trusty steward's strict instructions to the contrary.

'Nothing to be gained by feeling guilty about that now,' I remarked to the portrait of my mother on the opposite wall. 'By the time Bernard returns, Ysabeau will be long gone and no one any the wiser.' Was it my imagination or was my mother's younger self glaring at me. The green-eyed girl with an almost haunted expression, perched on a rock beneath Zennor Castle, was hardly much older than me. I knew the portrait had been done shortly before her departure to France to marry Father. With her long fair hair whipping around her face and her yellow velvet dress clinging to her slender form, I could almost feel the wind and smell the tang of salt in the Cornish air. There was an air of mystery about her, making me believe she was quite capable of harbouring secrets of her own. I stood up and walked over to the painting, reaching up to remove it while wondering how to cover the unsightly ochre stain on the wall beneath. 'Forgive me, Mother,' I said as I carefully placed her precious image next to an oak chest near the window, 'but you're older now and there are some things you wouldn't wish to witness.'

Bernard had left the Castle - that was the most important part of my plan accomplished. I'd watched him ride through the archway with several men in tow to ensure there were no enemy soldiers lurking in the vicinity.

"You must stay behind this time to guard the Castle," he'd told me. *"No adventures today."*

Well, that wasn't strictly true but he wasn't to know that. A couple of days ago, I'd been with him and a party from the Castle when we helped a French force (hiding in the woods) ambush one of the daily convoys *en route* from Calais to the English camp at Thérouanne. Triumphantly we'd seized one of the wagons.

"Bien joué, Monsieur Tristan," Bernard had praised me, *"you've been of invaluable help to me since your father and brothers left. I will certainly tell him on his return."*

We'd arrived back at the Castle flushed with success, with a welcome supply of: excellent wines; dozens of tins of biscuits; fresh bread of the highest quality; salted stockfish, salmon and herring; the best cuts of meat; tasty slabs of butter, and even several healthy cows. Word had reached us that prior to leaving English shores, King Harry had ordered twenty-five thousand oxen from Lincolnshire and Holland to be slaughtered and salted, all intended for himself and his greatest nobles here in the Pale of Calais and France. Twelve thousand Flemish suits of armour had been delivered and no expense spared on his personal equipment. Over one thousand pounds alone had been spent on eye-catching chains and buttons for the royal personage. It was so great a sum I couldn't even begin to envisage it in my head, let alone think of anyone paying that much in the pursuit of personal vanity. Well, apart from Nicolas, who seemed to spend every last *denier tournois* on similar, but vastly cheaper, decorative items for himself or Machiavelli. As he and the English King were born only weeks apart (or so Mother had told me), I wondered whether perhaps I, too, would one day grow fonder of creature comforts.

"I've never heard such nonsense!" Bernard had exploded the other evening at supper. *"They say Henri d'Angleterre has eleven tents of cloth of gold, and a sideboard displaying golden cups for his wine. I'm sure he hasn't*

even noticed the rain that's been coming down in sheets. Unlike those poor devils who serve him."

Bernard's outrage didn't end there. *"Par le sang de Dieu!"* he breathed, *"'All that glisters is not gold.'"* Disapproving as he was of all the priceless trinkets the English King had acquired for himself and his horses, our steward gave a smile of satisfaction knowing that after our little raid, the enemy would need to be more careful. *"In future, they'll probably look to the Low Countries for some of their victuals."* He held up a purse of coins and let out a bark of laughter. *"But it'll cost them far more to travel a road less hazardous than this one."*

I didn't give a tinker's cuss about the future; all I cared about was presenting the English King's tempting morsels to an alluring young Frenchwoman.

Spies and scouts had been keeping the Castle abreast of all the goings-on over in Calais. King Harry had arrived off the coast of France on the last day of June with a shrill-gorged bang, scaring the occupants of Boulogne half-witless with the noise of trumpets and cannon fire. Turning towards the English stronghold, the ships continued their noisy approach, to be answered in kind by a huge cannon placed at the top of the town walls.

"Sang beuf!" Bernard had exclaimed, pretending to cover his ears in pain, *"they say the cannon fire was so loud it could be heard back in Dover."*

Greeted by my parents' good friend, Sir Gilbert Talbot, King Harry had happily set himself up in the Staple Inn, expecting his every need to be met. The same went for his right-hand man, Thomas Wolsey, who was equally exacting, according to reports. While we held our breath here in Ardres, it seemed that the King was in no hurry to get on with his expedition, instead preferring to tarry with his best friend, Charles Brandon, now Lord High Marshal.

"*Nom de chien!*" grumbled Bernard. "*Keeping us on tenterhooks while he feasts, takes part in tournaments, shows off his skills at the butts, and goes to Saint Mary's Church all decked out in gold. That's what happens when you give a crown to a boy.*"

Or a *castle* to one. Imagining Bernard's reaction to my intended antics this morning didn't bear thinking about. I hadn't believed this day would ever come. After Nicolas's clear success with Ysabeau, it had seemed as if I were now pursuing a lost cause. However, Robert de Sapincourt had played into my hands by leaving his pretty young wife a virtual prisoner in their fine house while he accompanied the other men to war.

"*Locked her up, he has,*" I'd overheard one of the serving maids saying to another. "*Or as good as.*"

"*Ce n'est pas étonnant. The way she carries on,*" had come back the scathing retort. "*I heard he told her it was for her own good. But we all know it was for the good of a man old enough to be her father.*"

I hadn't heard how the conversation ended as words were replaced by bawdy laughter and various snorts of mirth.

The moment I knew Bernard would be away for the day, I sent my faithful valet, Armand Legrand, with a letter for Ysabeau, full of flattery and a disingenuous offer of friendship in the absence of her husband. How easily Ysabeau had capitulated. It was to be hoped that the town of Thérouanne would hold out for longer against the English besiegers.

"*Like feeding pain perdue to a baby,*" Armand said on his return, a huge grin spreading over his face. "*She seems very eager, Monsieur Tristan. She took no persuading at all and said that with her husband away, she missed a man's protection and would be delighted to accept.*"

'*She's probably lonely,*' I replied, not wanting to expose myself to a servant as an unchivalrous rogue. Even if the description was well-deserved.

Armand winked at me and managed to smother a laugh even though amusement was dancing in his brown eyes. I really ought to demand more respect from him, I told myself, as I tossed him a coin for his pains.

❧

Looking around the bedchamber now, I fervently wished it had some of the splendour of the great hall. There, wax candles were fixed to brackets on either side of the fireplace, and in a metal candelabra hung from a beam above. It was operated by a structure of pulleys which adjusted the height according to taste. Sumptuous wall hangings on the richly panelled walls, a glorious painted ceiling above, and a blazing fire in the huge fireplace during the winter months, topped by a mural of a fierce-looking black and golden eagle: all of these completed a picture of wealth beyond a common man's wildest dreams.

Here, Father had insisted that my bedchamber should reflect something of the future calling of its owner. In accordance with his wishes, it was plainly furnished and a special corner had been created with its own tiny altar in case I was overcome by a sudden urge to pray. Hastily I reached up to the wall and took down the wooden crucifix, as well as Mother's New Year's gift to me: ebony rosary beads made of wood, coral, silver and crystal. At this rate, the walls would be bare. I lifted a cloak from a peg by the door with the intention of placing it over the portrait of the Virgin Mary. What she didn't see couldn't hurt her, I reasoned.

None of this was my fault. If I'd been allowed to go off to war with the others, I wouldn't be thinking of dallying with Ysabeau de Sapincourt. I recalled how wretched I'd felt standing on the Castle battlements watching Father, Gilles, Nicolas, and an ever increasing throng of servants and men from the surrounding area, including Ysabeau's old husband, Robert, retreating into the distance, *en route* for an enormous adventure.

From which I'd been roundly excluded…as if I were already the churchman and they the soldiers.

∾

'A young man has to compensate by finding his pleasure elsewhere,' I said to the very sympathetic thin air surrounding me that would have nodded in agreement had it been possible. Unlike Father. With his prosaic outlook on the world, he'd never understand anything like that. Sometimes I doubted whether he'd ever been fifteen.

Was my imagination playing tricks again, or was the Virgin Mary scowling at me as I swept my cloak over her serene features? Turning around, I picked up another miniature statue of the Virgin and popped it into the large oak chest by the door.

'I've already got rid of one mother. I don't need a second…or even a third, thank you very much,' I said aloud again, my thoughts racing ahead to my meeting with Ysabeau. It must have been the maids outside that I'd heard before, as how long could it take for a healthy young woman to find her way up the stairs to my bedchamber? It was not as if those divinely supple limbs of hers were exactly crippled with arthritis.

So where on earth was Armand? He'd promised to bring Ysabeau back again before the clock struck eleven. His initial trip had been so successful because I instructed him to lead his horse stealthily out of the courtyard past the keep, keeping close to the walls, not jumping into the saddle until he was quite certain he wouldn't be seen by any of the Castle workers, particularly Bernard. There had been no more fires in the area since those churches a couple of weeks ago, and I had no fears for Ysabeau's safety as Armand led her back to the Castle again.

This was just as well considering the scraggy Armand would be as much use in an encounter with enemy soldiers as a lamb coming face to face with a pack of wolves. His *nom de famille* might be '*Legrand*' (undoubtedly after an ancestor possessing far more height and girth) but he was anything but. Not that he lacked cunning or courage, that was for sure. A cheerful village boy - about the same age as me, and with the same propensity for getting into all kinds of mischief - he'd been Mother's choice because he spoke fluent English thanks to his Cornish mother who'd been a dairymaid with the Paradise family over at Calais before her marriage. It seemed she'd met her future husband while he was on an errand there for Father. Armand's father had been waylaid by the temptations of nine-pins and dice in the gardens belonging to the Paradise family. Armand's mother had happened to be passing on a task for her mistress when she spotted the handsome young Frenchman, in the middle of a noisy game of nine-pins.

"*And there it was, 'le coup de foudre'. 'Love at first sight'. It sometimes happens between a man and a woman,*" Mother had once told me. "*If Dame Fortune is smiling upon you.*" However, the moment she'd said it, I saw a shadow pass over her face as if she realized this was an emotion her own son would never have the chance to experience. Or she herself. For how could anyone love a cold fish like Father? Let alone be struck by a bolt of lightning. Dealing with him was more akin to having an icy pail of water tipped over you. For a fleeting moment, the image of a dark-haired English admiral came into my head but sadly I pushed it away. Sir Edward Howard, the hero of my imaginings, and probably the object of desire of a hundred females, was no more. And dwelling on his death left me with an emptiness in my heart I didn't quite understand - or know how to vanquish.

Mother always insisted Armand and I speak English to one another, and it had been like that ever since. What pleased her even more was that Armand's mother was originally from St Ives in Cornwall so she spoke Cornish too; I knew that hearing the soft Cornish burr around her made Mother feel less homesick. Once, Father had started to question Armand's suitability as a servant, but one look at Mother's crestfallen face halted him in mid-complaint.

"*Don't make me regret defending the pair of you*," she'd whispered, giving me one of those shrewd looks I knew so well. I'd lost count of the number of times she saved my bacon in a similar way. That was the only good thing about Father: he could deny my mother nothing; indeed, he often teased her he would gladly walk to the ends of the earth to please her. In Armand's case, it must be said that Father's judgement had been correct. With his black curls, impish face and cocksure manner, my valet could easily have strolled out of La Matte, a disreputable *quartier* of Paris known for its thieves.

Looking at the now completely disguised altar, and the invitingly colourful counterpane I'd stolen from my parents' bedchamber to drape over my bed in readiness for Ysabeau's visit, I felt totally prepared. One of the maids had been in earlier to put Mother's best Holland sheets on my bed, the fury with which she yanked back the crimson velvet bed hangings reminding me that she'd been my first conquest after the New Year's encounter with the Comtesse. Ah, that couldn't be helped now. As a finishing touch, I adorned the bed with a few of the fresh rose petals I'd collected from Mother's garden. Forget the fires around Ardres, I fully intended to light one of my own in this very room before the hour was out.

Walking over to the narrow window, I gazed down into the courtyard, a practised smile of welcome already on my face. To my disappointment, it was deserted. But just then, I heard heavy footsteps coming up the stairs and approaching my room. My heart beating as fast as horses' hooves on dry earth, I half-expected to hear Ysabeau's lilting laugh as she crept along the corridor behind Armand: a pair of scurvy-valiant rogues up to no good in the dead of night. Instead, my knotty-pated servant began hammering on my door as if intent on waking Hades' three-headed black dog, Cerberus, from his slumber at the gates of hell. At this rate, he'd bring half the Castle running to my door. Extremely vexed, I grabbed the iron ring of the heavy oak door, wondering how I could give him a piece of my mind while bestowing a charming smile on the fair Ysabeau. Part wooer, part assailant.

'Arm—' I stopped short, my voice dying in my mouth. Armand Legrand was indeed standing on the threshold of my bedchamber, but a wild-eyed version of his usual jaunty self. To my horror, he was as pale as a ghost, and worse still, he was cowering behind the broad shoulders of…Bernard Guillart.

TRISTAN

Chapter Forty-Eight

Having known Bernard my entire life, I'd forgotten how intimidating our family steward must appear to strangers meeting him for the first time. Not for nothing was he renowned in the area for his outstanding wrestling skills, even at forty. His broad chest was a perfect image of one of the wooden barrels of ale kept below the kitchens in the buttery. Those arms looked as though they could lift a man straight out of his saddle as if he were a feather, or batter down a castle door with no assistance. With his piercing blue eyes, hooked nose, and wavy black hair streaked with grey, today he reminded me of a pet eagle that hadn't quite been tamed.

I swallowed hard, knowing I couldn't let Bernard into a bedchamber that was decorated as gaily as any *bordel* in the Beaubourg Quartier of Paris. I might as well have had a red lantern swinging above the door. I'm not sure how I managed it but I miraculously shrank myself into the shape of the letter L on a piece of parchment, and ended up on the outside of my chamber. Before firmly closing the door behind me.

'Monsieur Tristan! What is the meaning of this?' Bernard thundered. 'I leave you in charge and come back to find—' His voice trailed off into an exasperated splutter as he threw his big hands into the air in a gesture of frustration. If his intention was to intimidate me, he had succeeded as well as any captain in charge of an infantry.

Behind Bernard's back, Armand was pulling frantic faces at me and making a sign of a cutthroat, drawing one finger across his neck. What in the name of God's Blessed Mother was wrong with him? If he'd turned blue and fallen at my feet gasping for breath, I wouldn't have been surprised. In the meantime, I knew I had no choice but to own up to what I'd done.

363

'I apologize about Dame de Sapincourt,' I began, the words catching in my throat. I was hoping Bernard would take it man to man, understanding that a young man had urgent needs to be met.

Bernard frowned, his black eyebrows shooting together like a pair of outraged caterpillars. 'So you saw her too.' The caterpillars were quivering. 'What do you have to apologize for?'

To his side, a cross-eyed Armand had turned an interesting shade of *amarante*, the exact shade of one of Mother's dresses.

Taken aback, I wasn't sure how to reply. 'I was, er, I mean—'

'*Bon Dieu!*' bellowed Bernard, not giving me chance to finish my faltering, tickle-brained explanation; I could see he was far too angry for that. 'Without meaning to show disrespect to Robert de Sapincourt, a decent honourable man, I found that simpering baggage of a wife of his loitering outside the Castle gates, as if she were on the way to market to buy some ribbons for her hair, and not in great danger in a time of war.'

I thanked the heavens for Bernard's impatience, not giving me chance to hang, draw and quarter myself with a rash confession. Was it possible that I'd escaped exposure? 'Was she alone?' I squeaked, fear raising my voice by several octaves. Armand crossed himself and placed his hands together. Then he closed his eyes as if offering up a prayer that his muddy-mettled master finally understood what he'd been trying to tell him.

'Yes, she was!' Bernard boomed with as much force as one of the cannons over at Calais welcoming King Harry of England. 'Apart from an equally dizzy-eyed maid. I don't mind admitting that I gave her a piece of my mind, telling her that *no one* was safe wandering around these parts, let alone a noblewoman.'

'What did she say?' The squeak seemed to be here to stay.

'She said she'd come to visit your mother. Even though she's been gone these past few weeks. But what else can you expect of a simpering demoiselle whose head is filled with fripperies and festivities. Poor Robert. He should never have we—'

He was about to continue, but then he suddenly broke off as if he were seeing me for the first time. I could almost see rage beginning to churn once more in his veins, as if it were cream being poured into a pail by one of the dairymaids.

વ

'As for you, Monsieur Tristan.'

This time I was cunning enough to pause and plaster what I hoped was a bewildered expression on my face. '*Moi?*'

'*Oui, toi!* You have no need to apologize for the behaviour of one of your parents' friends. Admittedly, I was horn-mad that I had to waste my time escorting her home. But when I returned back to find the drawbri—'

'Up,' I said rather too quickly. There was nothing for it. I had to lie.

'*Non*, Monsieur Tristan!'

I nearly jumped out of my skin at the force of his reply. The French and English armies must have heard his ferocious roar in their respective camps all the way over at Thérouanne. He began to breathe heavily in a fair imitation of a dragon. Except without the vapour escaping from his nostrils.

'Not up. *Down*! It was lying as flat as a *crêpe* in a skillet.'

I'd never seen a man's eyes bulge like this. Making an effort to make my jaw go slack, I hoped my open mouth was convincing. 'Oh, *Mort de Dieu*! How could that have happened?'

'I was told you'd given explicit instructions for it not to be raised.' His eyes - an azure shade as blue as the background against which the three golden fleur-de-lys of France rested - were ice-cold…his voice deadly.

I tried not to wither beneath his basilisk stare. 'But that's impossible,' I gasped, thinking I should have bribed that flap-mouthed old Guillaume at the gate house with some of the English loot. He was probably still aggrieved after an incident in March when, as a beef-witted prank, Jean and I convinced him English marauders were on their way to attack the Castle. I recalled how our tale nearly gave him an apoplexy, and how angrily he'd shaken his fist at us when he discovered the truth. "*I'll remember this, Monsieur Tristan,*" he'd said in a most threatening manner. Well, his day of sweet revenge had just arrived. And I was about to pay the price.

'I would never have said that,' I protested in a voice that didn't even sound convincing to me, let alone to the one-man battering ram standing over me.

The caterpillars shivered with indignation. 'That's what I told Guillaume but he was adamant. He said he'd stake his very life on it. I've never known him to be wrong about anything before.'

How could I worm my way out of this? But I knew I had to try. I couldn't claim that Guillaume must have been in his cups as I'd never seen anything more intoxicating than the weakest of small beer pass his lips. Or that he was losing his wits as, even at sixty, they seemed to be growing sharper with each fresh chime of the clock in the courtyard. All of a sudden, I clasped my right hand to my forehead as if the answer lay within. 'You know what, Bernard, there's a small chance Guillaume might be right.'

Could a man's eyes pop out of their sockets? And what would I do if they did?

'Wha-at are you talking about?' His voice was so soft now I had to strain to catch the words. Is this what a mouse in the pantry felt like when backed into a corner by one of the kitchen cats?

'Sometimes, when I'm distracted I say the exact opposite to what I m-mean,' stammered the mouse. '*C'est vrai*, I might have said "*down*" when I meant "*up*".' This time the squeak seemed very fitting. And even to me, my excuse sounded as lame as a thief caught with his hand in a collection box, protesting that he was taking it to distribute to the poor.

Bernard didn't speak for a moment and seemed to be considering my words. His cheeks were dragon's blood red and he seemed to have doubled in size - or had fear and guilt made me shrink? Eventually he spoke, his voice as flat as the drawbridge that had welcomed him home: 'Then, Monsieur Tristan, it's just as well you're going into the Church, and not the army. There's an enormous difference between telling someone to light a candle at an altar and ordering them to light a burning taper at the mouth of a cannon.'

I inwardly groaned, knowing I'd just undone all the good work of the past weeks. And scattered my reputation to the four winds above the Castle.

In front of me, Bernard suddenly let out an enormous sneeze and his eyes began to water. '*Pardieu!*' he roared, wiping tears from his eyes. 'It smells like a rose garden up here, or a whore's boudoir.' In the wake of this somewhat colourful language, I watched his head spin around to Armand, faster than the Castle weathervane in a gale. 'Go and give instructions to the maids not to cut so many roses from Madame La Comtesse's garden tomorrow.' With that, he nodded a cold farewell to me, and made an impatient gesture to Armand to follow him.

All hope now gone, I watched their retreating backs as they reached the end of the corridor: Bernard's broad one, wide enough to fill the doorway of a gaol cell in Le Grand Châtelet in Paris, with shoulders hunched in fury; while slightly behind him was Armand's reed-thin one, on his way to 'obey' Bernard's curt order. I knew he'd probably hide in an alcove until he could hot-foot it back to me. Wearily I reached out for the iron ring to my chamber. The black lion holding the ring in its jaw normally gave me a cheery welcome, but at this moment it was looking as deflated as I felt. Like a groom who has waited in vain for his bride to appear and is left with a table laden with exotic fare he has no desire to sample. With a heavy heart, I slowly began to dismantle all my preparations.

I'd failed miserably as a lover…and would never have the chance to know how it felt to be a soldier.

'God's Bones! That was a close one, Monsieur Tristan. Even for you.'

Armand was brushing leaves from his brown jerkin and dust from his hair. 'I had to climb through the window of your parents' bedchamber and down the ivy to stop old Guillart spotting me. He's certainly got it in for you. Wouldn't stop muttering to himself about the Church as we walked along the corridor.'

'All right. All right. You don't need to kick a man when he's already in the gutter. How did you manage to avoid him seeing you with Dame Ysabeau?'

'My mother always says I'm like a cat with nine lives. And she doesn't want to be around for the ninth. I heard a commotion at the entrance and dived into the nearest bush. I felt guilty leaving Dame Ysabeau to fend for herself, but she didn't let Bernard frighten her.'

'Well, I'm sure she won't speak to me again.'

Armand gave a sly smile. 'Perhaps not. But her maid will to me. A dainty little morsel called Joachine. She took me down to the kitchens while her mistress was getting ready.'

I might be peeved that Armand's day had been more successful than mine, but couldn't say anything knowing he'd risked instant dismissal, as well as his neck, to help me. Nobody could have a more loyal servant.

'I picked up some tasty morsels in the kitchen, and not merely the kind you eat,' continued Armand, aware of my abject misery. 'There's news of the Emperor.'

Now he had my interest. Maximilian, the Holy Roman Emperor, might not be far behind Guillaume in age, but whereas the latter only had his gatehouse as his empire, the former ruled over Germany, Switzerland, Burgundy and the Netherlands, and had Charlemagne as his illustrious ancestor. 'What have you heard?'

'That he's on his way, and has even offered to fight for the English under the banner of Saint George. As a lowly pikeman.'

I was amazed. 'That can't be true.'

Armand put one hand on his heart. 'I tell you no lie. He says he's going to wear a tunic bearing the red cross of Saint George.'

I thought about it for a moment. 'Father says the Emperor has got Henry of England in his pocket, and is using the King's heavy purse to pay for his own pursuits.'

Armand nodded. 'That's what I've heard too. But Henry's so rich thanks to his dead father I doubt whether he cares.'

I thought of what would happen to me when Father returned to be regaled with tales of my latest wayward behaviour. 'Lucky him.'

'They say Henry prances around in a gold tunic decorated with jewels, and wears a dazzling red cap adorned with as many feathers on the rim as his tailor could find room for. And that fourteen young boys dressed in gold and scarlet, with horses all in silver, accompany him everywhere he goes.'

I laughed at the image. 'What a sight! I'd love to meet him. My cousin, Cecy, seemed to like him.'

'He has it in his mind to be a conquering hero. And so he should be with those heavy guns of his, the ones nicknamed "The Twelve Apostles". They were saying in the kitchens that it took twenty-four Flanders mares to pull them,

369

and that thirty-two tons of gunpowder will be needed each day for Henry's entire arsenal of weapons.'

I let out a low whistle. 'I wouldn't want to be a Frenchman on the receiving end of that. Better to be English, eh, Armand? On that day, at least.'

Armand grinned at me; the two of us had often discussed how strange it was having one parent from England and one from France. "*Like having one foot in the Narrow Sea and the other in La Manche,*" he'd once joked, referring to the name the French gave the channel of water that separated our two countries. 'The sleeve' they called it.

'Some might say you and I have the best of both worlds, Monsieur Tristan,' he said now. 'We can decide which army we want to support. If you had a choice right this minute, which one would you join?'

I considered his question, unsure of my response. After all, both of us had family and friends risking their lives for the sake of France…even the clapper-clawed Nicolas. 'That's a hard one,' I replied. 'But if I were a gambler, not just an idle card player, I'd say King Henry has the smallest advantage.'

'If you're right, then he deserves the name the Sapincourt servants gave him. "*Le roi d'or*".'

'"The golden king".' I repeated, thinking of how I'd also heard that Henry had nearly a thousand attendants, including a single lutenist to entertain him with sweet music during the campaign. 'It suits him well.'

'But we mustn't forget that King Louis has the experience that comes with age.'

'And lacks the impetuosity of youth,' I said ruefully, my mind on what had just happened to me.

Armand gave me a broad wink. 'That can get you into all kinds of mischief.'

My best-laid plans in tatters, I couldn't rid myself of the picture in my head: a pair of accusing blue eyes turned away from me, and a pair of pink lips frozen in a pout for eternity. 'God's Bones! You speak the truth.'

'It seems we're no nearer to knowing whether King Henry will beat King Louis…and all our kinsmen here in France.'

I lifted my hands as if in prayer and looked heavenwards. 'My friend, nobody knows the answer to that one. Apart from God and Dame Fortune. All we can do now is wait.'

๛

Armand cocked his head to one side. 'Or not.'

I stared at him, wondering what was coming next.

'Your father, Monsieur le Comte, might have ordered us to stay here. And from now on, old Bernard will be watching us both like a hawk—'

I made a noise of impatience. 'I hardly need reminding of our hopeless predicament. Your point being?'

My valet thrust out his chest (going bright-red with the effort) as if it were every inch a match for the cast-iron barrel of a chest belonging to Bernard Guillart. Then he brushed a few more stray leaves from his jerkin. 'My point being,' he said, 'is that the bodies of men may be kept in captivity.'

I had no idea what Armand was talking about as he tapped the side of his nose. 'God's Blood, Arman—

'But not their minds.' Reaching into the air with an extravagant gesture, he retrieved an invisible sword which he proceeded to use with so much skill that I ended up applauding him.

'*Bravo*!'

He twirled his sword a few more times and then did an impressive lunge, every bit as good as the ones Nicolas practised at least a dozen times a day in the Castle courtyard. '*Aux armes*!' he cried. '*Au nom de Dieu. Du Roi Louis. Et de la France.*'

Following his lead, I reached up and plucked an invisible version of *Excalibur* from somewhere above my head, loosening and tightening my grip on the longsword to adjust to the weight of Guillaume Gouffier's gift. I could almost hear it swishing through the air as I turned in the direction of Calais. 'To arms!' I mimicked in my best soldier's voice, the recent squeak quite vanished, to be replaced by something far deeper and more suited to a sword-wielding member of the English army. 'In the name of God. King Henry. And England.'

I paused, closing my eyes tightly. There was fire in my belly and my heart was swelling with pride. All of a sudden, I could feel myself elsewhere. Floating somewhere above the foam-tipped, green waves of the Narrow Sea, not far from the coast of France. Able to picture this enchanted, sunlit scene with every fibre of my being, I filled my lungs with the bracing salt air. 'To arms,' I repeated, satisfied to hear my voice restored to its full state of manliness just in time to deliver my next words with the aplomb they deserved: 'In the name of the great Sir Edward Howard! Long may he live on the lips of every true-born Englishman and Englishwoman....'

Author's note

Welcome back to the House of the Red Duke! For more antics at the candlelit courts of Europe.

Book One included four maps and several recipes, plus an extensive glossary at the back. There is another one at the back of this book for all the new words and expressions. There's also a *Who's Who* of characters, each one showing their age on January 1st, 1513.

Instead of the recipes, I hope I've managed to give a different flavour of the period in Book Two. In their place are a few letters and pieces of dialogue, using actual words spoken or written by real people in the sixteenth century…intermingled with those from my own imagining.

Whenever possible, I used the original words from the time, changing them only when necessary, yet still retaining the meaning. When I re-read them, knowing they were authentic (not my fictional version), I found it thrilling. Almost as if I'd conjured up benevolent, slumbering spirits, breathing life into them once more.

If you enjoy *Beware the Lizard Lurking*, I'd be very grateful if you could leave a review on Amazon, Goodreads, Facebook etc; Or kindly spread the word. Your support makes an enormous difference to any writer's success.

On that note, I'd like to thank all the people who gave me such encouragement for Book One. And the extraordinary group of writers, and others I've had the pleasure to meet on Twitter and Facebook. A huge thank you, also, to those readers who expressed their pleasure in glowing terms - either in a review, or in a personal message to me. Every single one of those words of praise means so much to me.

Best wishes,
Vivienne Brereton
October 31st, 2020.

GLOSSARY

A

Ah bon?	Is that so?
Aïe!	Ouch!
Allons-y	Let's go.
Amarante	a sixteenth century French dye, amethyst- purple.
Angleterre	England.
Arrête!	Stop it!
Auld	old. After the fourteenth century, it became a distinctly Scottish word.
Avec Plaisir	With pleasure.
Avevo il mio occhio su quello, bastardo!	I had my eye on that one, you bastard!

B

Bannock	a Scottish oatcake.
Base-court	the lower court in a castle.
Bench-whistler	an idler.
Bien joué!	Well done!
Bon Dieu!	Good God!
Bon sang de bon Dieu!	By the blood of Christ!

Braw	brave, splendid, worthy.
Brose	Scottish dish of seasoned boiling milk poured over oatmeal or peasemeal.

C

Cast	throw of a dice; that which is cast.
Candia	Crete.
Ce n'est pas étonnant.	It's not surprising.
Certainement	Of course.
C'est vrai?	Is it true?
C'est vrai, n'est-ce pas?	It's true, isn't it?
Charmant	charming, delightful.
Common-kissing	to kiss in a vulgar manner.
Cuds me	an oath. A cud is literally food that is chewed twice by an animal such as a cow.
Cullionly	mean, base.
Culverin	a sixteenth century cannon.
Cum rara egestione	With a rare performance.

D

Deo gratias Anglia redde pro victoria!	England, give thanks to God for victory!

Diantre!	Heavens!
Dis donc!	Listen!
Dizzy-eyed	cross-eyed, foolish, silly.
Dominus michi adutor	Lord be my helper.
Dotterel	a bird belonging to the plover family.

E

Eh bien, alors	Ah, well.
*Enchanté, mes demoiselle*s	Delighted to meet you, young ladies.

F

Fell	the skin or hide of an animal.
Festered	a wound that has ulcerated.
Filles d'honneur	maids-in-waiting.
Foi de gentilhomme!	Upon my honour as a gentleman!
Forsooth!	Indeed!
Froward	a person who is difficult or contrary.

G

Gomeral	an idiot, a fool.

H

Hélas!	Alas!

Hinny	Scottish term of endearment like 'honey'.
Hoyden	ill-bred, boisterous young woman.
Humanist	one who embraced the revival of the study of classical antiquity. As well as the idea of a virtuous Christian prince upholding peace, and turning away from war.

I

Il m'aime a la folie	He loves me madly.
Il m'aime beaucoup	He loves me a lot.
Il m'aime passionnement	He loves me passionately.
Il m'aime un peu	He loves me a little.

J

Jamais	Never.
Je ne sais pas	I don't know.
Je t'en supplie	I beg you.
Jeopardies	dangers, risks.

L

Landsknechte	German speaking mercenaries.
Lieth	rest horizontally; be in a recumbent horizontal position.

Lord Lyon, King-of-Arms	the most junior of the Great Officers of State in Scotland.
Lurking	to lie hidden.

M

Mais non!	Absolutely not!
Malheureusement	unfortunately.
Merci	Thank you.
Mere	a lake or pond.
Mo charaid	my friend, in Gaelic.
Mon enfant	my child.
Mon trésor	my treasure.
Mordieu!	By the death of our Lord!
Mort de Dieu!	God's Death!
Mumble-news	a gossip or bearer of tales.

N

Nom d'un chien!	Name of a dog!
Nom de famille	surname.
Nom d'un nom!	Name of a name!
Nom d'un petit bonhomme!	Good grief!

P

Palsambleu!	For pity's sake!
Pardi!	By God!
Par le ventre de Dieu!	By God's stomach!
Par le sang de Dieu!	By God's blood!
Pizzle	an old English word for penis.
Plume-plucked	stripped of a source of pride; humbled.
Pouldrons	plate armour that covers the shoulder area.

Q

Que le ciel me garde!	Heaven help me!
Quinsy	a severe throat infection.

R

Rede	advise.
Robustious	strongly assertive or boisterous.

S

Sacristi!	an oath on the Sacred Host.
Saker	a medium-sized cannon.
Sang beuf!	Blood of a cow!
Si Dieu le veut!	If God wills it!
Si tu veux la paix, prépare la guerre	If you want peace, prepare for war.
S'il vous plaît, excusez-moi	Please excuse me.

Stockfish	unsalted fish, especially cod, dried by cold air and wind on wooden racks.

T

Tester bed	a four-poster bed with a canopy above.
Toi	You (familiar form).
Triste	sorrowful, gloomy.
Tu parleras couramment le français	You will speak French fluently.

V

Vas-y!	Off you go!
Ventrebleu	Damn! Zounds!
Ventre Saint-Gris!	By the stomach of Holy Christ!
Verily	in truth.
Verus animi et robore mentis	True magnanimity and strength of mind.
Victuals	food, provisions, nourishment. From Old French, pronounced 'vittles'.

W

Ware	beware.

Y

Younker	a youngster

COMING IN 2022

THE WITCH'S PROPHECY

Find out what happens next....